THE AA GUIDE TO

The Peak District

D0530831

RY

3011813339357 3

About the author

Roly Smith has lived and worked in the Peak District for over 30 years, and was Head of Information Services with the Peak District National Park for 12 years. He was recently described as 'one of Britain's most knowledgeable countryside writers' and has written over 80 books, mainly about the great outdoors and the countryside, including *National Parks of Britain* (2011) , *World Heritage Sites of Britain* (2010), and *Heritage Landscapes* (2011), all for the AA. His book, *A Peak District Anthology* (2012), won a highly commended award in the Outdoor Writers and Photographers Guild's (OWPG) 2013 Awards for Excellence.

Roly is vice-president of the OWPG, having stood down as president in October 2013 after 12 years, and is a member of the British Guild of Travel Writers. He likes nothing more than to be out walking in his beloved Peak District, particularly on the northern moors of Kinder Scout and Bleaklow.

Published by AA Publishing (a trading name of AA Media Limited, whose registered office is Fanum House, Basing View, Basingstoke, Hampshire RG21 4EA; registered number 06112600)

© AA Media Limited 2016
First published 2014
Second edition 2016

Maps contain data from openstreetmap.org
© OpenStreetMap contributors
Ordnance Survey data © Crown copyright and database right 2015

A CIP catalogue record for this book is available from the British Library.

ISBN: 978-0-7495-7764-3
ISBN (SS): 978-0-7495-7635-6

Cartography provided by the Mapping Services Department of AA Publishing.

Printed and bound in Italy by Printer Trento Srl.

A05342

Every effort has been made to trace the copyright holders, and we apologise in advance for any accidental errors. We would be happy to apply the corrections in the following edition of this publication.

The contents of this book are believed correct at the time of printing. Nevertheless, the publishers cannot be held responsible for any errors or omissions or for changes in the details given in this book or for the consequences of any reliance on the information it provides. This does not affect your statutory rights. We have tried to ensure accuracy in this book, but things do change and we would be grateful if readers would advise us of any inaccuracies they may encounter by emailing us at travelguides@theaa.com.

Visit AA Publishing at theAA.com/shop

THE AA GUIDE TO

The Peak District

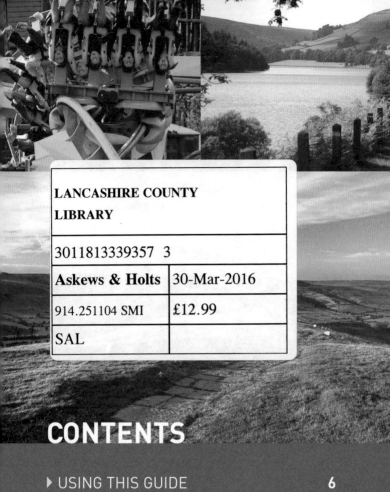

CONTENTS

USING THIS GUIDE

Introduction – has plenty of fascinating background reading, including articles on the landscape and local mythology.

Top attractions – pick out the very best places to visit in the area. You'll spot these later in the A–Z by the flashes of yellow.

Before you go – tells you the things to read, watch, know and pack to get the most from your trip.

Campsites – recommends a number of caravan sites and campsites, which carry the AA's Pennant rating, with the very best receiving the coveted gold Pennant award. Visit theAA.com/self-catering-and-campsites and theAA.com/bed-and-breakfast-and-hotel for more places to stay.

A–Z of The Peak District – lists all the best of the region, with recommended attractions, activities and places to eat or drink. Places Nearby lists more to see and do.

Eat and drink – contains restaurants that carry an AA Rosette rating, which acknowledges the very best in cooking. Pubs have been selected for their great atmosphere and good food. Visit theAA.com/restaurant-and-pub for more food and drink suggestions.

Index – gives you the option to search by theme, grouping the same type of place together, or alphabetically.

Atlas – will help you find your way around, as every main location has a map reference, as will the town plans throughout the book.

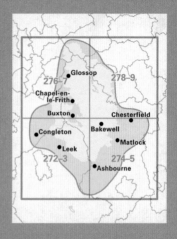

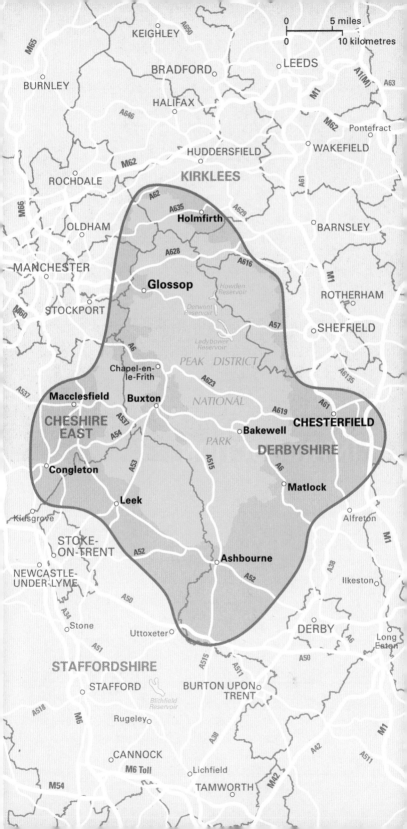

INTRODUCTION

There are really two Peak Districts, each inescapably shaped
by the underlying geology and reflected in the landscape it has
created. Each has its own special characteristics, which could
be said to have imparted almost masculine and feminine
qualities to the outstanding scenery which makes up Britain's
first and most popular national park.

The White Peak
The limestone country of the White Peak in the south and
centre of the district has a soft, feminine feel; a gentle, rolling
limestone plateau split by steep-sided, flower-decked and
often heavily wooded dales and riddled by labyrinthine cave
systems. The evidence of lead mining is everywhere you look.

Arthur Conan Doyle called it 'the hollow country' and
claimed of the area around Castleton: 'Could you strike it with
some gigantic hammer it would boom like a drum, or possibly
cave in altogether and expose some huge subterranean sea.'

Evidence of the shallow, tropical Carboniferous sea which
actually created the limestone, 350 million years ago, can be

found if you look closely at the stones which form the endless miles of pearl-grey drystone walls, criss-crossing the plateau like an intricate spider's web.

Those screw-like formations in the rock are the fossilised remains of the stems of crinoids, a primitive type of sea lily, a creature related to modern starfish and sea urchins, and known locally as Derbyshire screws.

Pretty stone-built villages, often clustered around a village green and mere (pond) dot the plateau above. Here the age-old custom of well dressing, a living and thriving example of folk art, still gives thanks for the precious gift of water on the generally porous limestone. Bronze Age burial mounds top many hills, showing how the ancestors valued these high and lonely places.

The Dark Peak

In vivid counterpoint is the brooding and essentially masculine millstone grit moorland, which takes the contrasting name of the Dark Peak. It encloses the White Peak to the north, west and east like the receding hair round the balding pate of a man's head.

This is altogether sterner country, with miles of forbidding peat moorland stretching as far as the eye can see, and terminated by abrupt, frowning precipices of naked rock, here known by the collective name of 'edges', and topped by weird wind- and frost-eroded tors. Perhaps the most famous of the edges is the 3-mile-long bastion of Stanage Edge, above Hathersage in the Hope Valley. Over 850 rock climbing routes festoon its 60-foot-high face, and it is recognised as one of the birthplaces of British climbing.

Up on the moors, it's possible to experience, as the early 20th-century footpath guide author John Derry did, 'the sadness of great spaces – of the mountains, moors, and seas'. But he added: 'And yet it does one good to get into this upland, age-long solitude, where the primeval world is felt to be a mighty fact, linked on to us.'

After the Enclosure Acts of the 18th and 19th centuries, that freedom to wander at will across this common land was stolen from the people, and the moors became the closely guarded preserve of grouse shooters. The Dark Peak became the centre of the access battles of the 1930s, culminating in the celebrated Mass Trespass on Kinder Scout in April 1932, after which five ramblers were imprisoned for daring to walk on the moors.

It was the catalyst that eventually led not only to the right to roam, encompassed by the Countryside and Rights of Way Act of 2000, but also the creation of Britain's first national park in April 1951.

Fast-flowing rivers like the Derwent and Wye, which rise on the Dark Peak moors, have been fully utilised by humankind over the years. They provided one of the great sources of motive power for the Industrial Revolution, and the world's first water-powered textile mills were constructed at places like Cromford and Cressbrook to take advantage of their seemingly boundless energy.

Over 50 dams and reservoirs have been built in the upper regions of these Dark Peak valleys, most notably in the Upper Derwent, to slake the insatiable thirst of the great industrial cities of the north and Midlands which surround the Peak.

Tucked beneath the scalloped edges of the moors are the landscaped parks and great homes of the aristocracy, the most famous of which are Chatsworth and Haddon, near Bakewell, ducal homes of the Devonshires and Rutlands respectively, and Lyme Park, a sort of blackened

◀ Wards Hill, Edale (previous page) ▶ Sunset on Stanage Edge

version of Chatsworth's Palladian splendour on the outskirts of Stockport.

And then there are the charming small market towns, like Buxton, Bakewell, Chapel-en-le-Frith and Tideswell, still serving the vibrant, living communities of the White and Dark Peak – twin peaks with contrasting yet entirely compatible characters.

TOP ATTRACTIONS

▲ Alton Towers

If you're not the type to enjoy white-knuckle rollercoaster rides, then Alton Towers may not be your cup of Earl Grey. But you'd be wrong if you thought it was all gravity-defying terror and thrills. There's a water park, which is much calmer, and ideal for younger children; and the 19th-century Humphry Repton-style gardens, which offer a more relaxed kind of enjoyment (see page 64).

◄ Chatsworth

Set in 1,000 acres of grounds and gardens, Chatsworth is the Derbyshire seat of the Dukes of Devonshire. It is also a treasure house of art from all over the world; the jewel in the crown of 'Capability' Brown's glorious landscaped parkland (see page 109); and the setting for some amazing interior design. See if you can find all 17 staircases.

◀ The Heights of Abraham

The Heights of Abraham is a hilltop country park with two spectacular show caverns, play areas, exhibitions, the works; the thing that sets this place apart is the trip to the Heights, in cable cars which swing up from Matlock Bath Station to the summit (see page 225).

▶ Lyme Park

Inside 18th-century Lyme Park are remarkable tapestries, the incredibly rare 15th-century Lyme Caxton Missal prayer book, and a marvellous collection of clocks. Outside are 1,300 acres of woodland, moorland and landscaped gardens (see page 206).

◀ Hardwick Hall

Elizabeth, Countess of Shrewsbury, known as 'Bess of Hardwick', enjoyed building great houses; Hardwick Hall was her last and best. It has six towers, huge windows *à la Grand Designs*, and is an all-round classic of architecture, interior design and landscaping (see page 170).

▶ Castleton Visitor Centre & Show Caves

Castleton's caverns – Treak Cliff, Speedwell, Peak and Blue John – offer exciting glimpses into the Peak's underworld (see page 104).

◄ Haddon Hall

Haddon Hall (see page 165) is a bit of a fairy-tale castle. For 300 years it was sunk in ivy-clad slumber, the fashions of the day passing it by, until in the early 20th century the Marquis of Granby began his labours of painstaking restoration. There are even renovated pre-Reformation wall paintings, which really give a clue to the age of the place.

► Poole's Cavern & Buxton Country Park

Poole's Cavern (see page 96) is something of an underground wonderland that makes a lot of 'historic' attractions look like they just came in on the last tide. Parts of the cave have yet to be fully explored – but don't go getting any ideas...

◄ Crich Tramway Village

Crich Tramway Village is a mile-long tramline that includes a re-created Edwardian street, using authentic buildings from around the UK, as well as renovated electric trams. Buy a ticket and you can ride the trams all day (see page 127).

► Pavilion Gardens

The charming Pavilion Gardens covers 23 acres in the centre of Buxton and include lakes, flower beds, shaded walks, play areas, outdoor gyms and a miniature railway (see page 93).

HISTORY OF THE PEAK DISTRICT

Debate still rages about how the Peak – always singular, by the way – got its name. Many visitors are disappointed when they arrive to find no real sharply pointed peaks but merely an abundance of lofty, relatively flat-topped plateaux. Some even come to the White Peak looking in vain for a snowcapped, glacier-draped Alpine mountain.

The answer lies in the name. The area was first known in the Anglo-Saxon Chronicle of 924 as *Peac Lond* – the land of the *peacs*. So the first recorded dwellers in the mid-seventh century Tribal Hidage were the Pecsaetan –the dwellers or settlers of the Peak.

In the Old English of the time, *peac* meant any knoll or hill, and not necessarily the sharply pointed peak of Dr Johnson's dictionary – which gave rise to the confusion.

Of course, the Dark Age Saxons were not the original settlers of this first outpost of upland Britain. To find those, we have to go back several millennia to the frozen tundra of the last Ice Age.

▲ Thor's Cave

Some of the earliest evidence of humankind in the Peak area is found on its far eastern edge in the magnesian limestone caves of Creswell Crags, on the present-day Nottinghamshire border. Neanderthal stone tools dating perhaps from as long as 60,000 years ago have been found in the Creswell Caves, dating from the Late Middle Palaeolithic, or Old Stone Age, at a time when Britain was still joined to the European mainland. Like today's tourists, they were probably only seasonal summer visitors.

The Mesolithic or Middle Stone Age visitors of around 12,000 years ago left an important and lasting legacy, high on the walls of the water-worn caves of the Creswell gorge. Engraved into the walls of some of the caves and on fragments of bone are skilful representations of red deer, horse, bison and birds – the earliest examples of art yet found in Britain.

Many of the Peak District's caves and shelters, such as Thor's Cave and others in the Manifold Valley, were undoubtedly used in the same way, as seasonal hunter-gatherers sought out plentiful game which followed a warming climate and retreating glaciers.

By the time of the first farmers, during the Neolithic period – (c 4500–2000 BC) – forest clearance had started, as is evidenced by the tiny slivers of flint and arrowheads which occasionally turn up in the brown peat of the Dark Peak moors. It is their monuments, such as the henge and stone circle of Arbor Low, set 1,200 feet up on the limestone plateau near Monyash, and the chambered cairns of Five Wells, near Taddington, and Minninglow, near Parwich, which are lasting reminders of those first farmers.

Arbor Low, with its 248 by 272 foot henge (or bank) and circle of about 50 blocks of local limestone, now all lying prostrate on the

▲ Five Wells Chambered Tomb, Taddington

sheep-cropped grass like figures on a clockface, has been dubbed 'the Stonehenge of the North', but it exudes far more atmosphere than its over-interpreted Wiltshire contemporary.

Five Wells, which once contained the skeletal remains of 17 bodies, is the highest Neolithic chambered cairn in the country, and also commands fine views across the White Peak, as does tree-topped Minninglow, just off the High Peak Trail.

The Bronze Age (c 2300–600 BC) saw large-scale stone clearance and field systems being laid out, especially on the Eastern Moors, as agriculture utilised the light sandy soils. Again, we know most about these people from their burial monuments; over 500 of their barrows have been identified throughout the Peak. Although these barrows are commonly found on the high points in the landscape, most of them are known as 'lows'. The word comes from the Old English 'hlaw', which means a low hill or mound. So, for example, you get the paradoxically named Highlow Hall, near Hathersage in the Hope Valley.

Whereas we know quite a lot about how the people of the Bronze Age treated their dead, we still have little idea how the people of the subsequent Iron Age (600 BC – AD 43) did. What they did leave behind was a legacy of magnificent hillforts, such as Mam Tor at the head of the Hope Valley above Castleton; Castle Naze near Chapel-en-le-Frith, and Fin Cop overlooking Monsal Dale. These were most probably shielings, occupied only during the summer months, from which the grazing flocks could be observed – and they still make wonderful viewpoints for the modern visitor.

Recent excavations at the 12-acre hillfort of Fin Cop have revealed that life in the Iron Age was not all peaceful farming.

The skeletal remains of a large number of females and young children, including four newborn infants, were found. They had been killed and flung into the ditch.

So what did the Romans do for the Peak District? Well, they set out much of the road system which is still in use today, such as the A515 Buxton–Ashbourne road and at least part of the modern A57 Snake Road between Bamford and Glossop. The Romans came to the Peak to exploit the readily-accessible veins of lead, which provided much of the Empire with the raw material for its plumbing. Fortlets at Navio, near Brough, and Melandra, near Glossop, protected these interests, and the thermal baths at Buxton provided for their recreational needs.

Apart from leaving us the name of the area, the Saxon *Pecsaetan* left little evidence of their passing, although some of the first towns, such as Bakewell, were set up under Edward the Elder. The outstanding survival from the so-called Dark Ages is the rich collection of early Christian preaching crosses, such as those now found in Bakewell, Hope and Eyam churchyards.

After the Norman Conquest, much of the northern part of the area was set aside as the Royal Forest of the Peak, and hunted over by medieval kings and princes. The name survives in Chapel-en-le-Frith – the chapel in the forest – and at Peak Forest on the slopes of Eldon Hill.

The royal forest was administered from William Peveril's commanding 11th-century castle, which overlooks the planned medieval town of Castleton, at the head of the Hope Valley. The Norman overlords also erected motte-and-bailey castles at Bakewell and Pilsbury, in the valley of the Dove near Hartington.

▶ Peak District timeline

- ▶ *c* **60,000 years ago** – First Neanderthal hunter gatherers visit Peak
- ▶ *c* **12,000 years ago** – Forest clearance starts on Dark Peak moors
- ▶ *c* **4500 to 2000** BC – Neolithic people build Arbor Low henge and Five Wells chambered cairn
- ▶ *c* **2300 to 600** BC – Bronze Age farmers construct around 500 barrows for their dead
- ▶ *c* **600** BC **to** AD **43** – Iron Age hillforts built at Mam Tor, Fin Cop and Castle Naze
- ▶ *c* AD **70 to 410** – Romans mine for lead and build forts at Navio and

Melandra and create a spa at Buxton
- ▶ **410 to 1066** – Flowering of Dark Age sculpture represented by preaching crosses at Bakewell, Hope and Eyam
- ▶ *c* **650** – Tribal Hidage mentions *Pecsaetan* – the dwellers of the Peak
- ▶ **924** – First mention of *Peac Lond* in Anglo-Saxon Chronicle
- ▶ **1066 to 1154** – Motte and bailey castles built at Pilsbury and Bakewell; Henry II builds Peveril Castle, Castleton; Royal Forest of the Peak established
- ▶ **1154 to 1485** – Great Medieval

Many of the fine churches which watch over Peakland villages – such as 'the Cathedral of the Peak' at Tideswell, Bakewell's fine parish church of All Saints, and St Oswald's at Ashbourne – also have Norman foundations.

Great estates developed, too, such as the Vernon's perfectly formed and much-filmed medieval manor house at Haddon on the banks of the Wye, and these slowly developed into the great landowning interests of the Dukes of Devonshire and Rutland, and the Legh family of Lyme Park on the western edge of the Peak. A smaller and more intimate family home can be visited at Eyam Hall, in the Plague village of Eyam, home of the Wright family for over 300 years.

Much of the wealth of these great landowning families was gained from farming and the Peak's extensive mineral resources, particularly lead mining. At its height in the mid-18th century, it has been estimated that there were as many as 10,000 miners engaged in the industry, most doubling as farmers during the summer months. It's also claimed that it was the profits from the incredibly rich copper resources of Ecton Hill Mine, in the Manifold Valley of Staffordshire, which enabled the 5th Duke of Devonshire to develop Buxton as a spa town, notably John Carr's splendid Crescent, a rival to Bath, in the late 18th century.

Undoubtedly the most impressive of the remains of the once-great lead mining industry are the evocative ruins of Magpie Mine, high on the limestone plateau near Sheldon, where mining went on for the best part of 200 years. But there are interesting displays and a replica climbing shaft for the kids at the Peak District Lead Mining Museum in Matlock Bath.

period of church building and setting up of markets in towns such as Bakewell, Tideswell and Ashbourne. First great manor houses built at Haddon and Chatsworth

▸ **1485 to 1603** – Lead mining develops during the Tudor and Stuart periods, and great estates flourish and rebuild their stately homes

▸ **1665 to 1666** – Plague strikes at Eyam and decimates the town's population

▸ **1700 to 1800** – First turnpike roads constructed in the Peak

▸ **1771** – Richard Arkwright constructs his first water-powered cotton mill at Cromford

▸ **1830 to 1890** – First railways come to the Peak: Cromford & High Peak Railway (1830–31); Midland Railway, Derby–Manchester (1860s); Hope Valley line (1890)

▸ **1840 to 1945** – Reservoirs flood Dark Peak valleys: Longdendale (1840–60); Derwent & Howden (1901–16); Ladybower (1935–43); Goyt Valley (1938 and 1967)

▸ **1932** – Mass Trespass on Kinder Scout

▸ **1951** – Peak District National Park established and today receives more than 10 million visitors every year

BACK TO NATURE

The rocks beneath

Imagine you are standing on the edge of a shallow tropical lagoon, a few degrees south of the Equator. As you look down into the clear blue waters, you can see forests of sea lilies on the bottom, gently waving their feathery arms as the tides pull them back and forth, while waves from a deeper sea break constantly over a fringing reef of coral. In the deeper water, a perpetual fine drizzle of the skeletal remains of tiny sea creatures cover the seabed in a thick layer of organic soup.

No, it's not a modern South Pacific atoll like Bikini or Hawaii. Such a scene would have been played out much closer to modern-day Buxton or Hartington during the Carboniferous Period, an unimaginable 350 million years ago: you were witnessing the formation of the earliest limestone rocks of what we now know as the White Peak, the area which makes up the centre and southern core of the Peak District.

Much later, as a result of further shifts in the earth's tectonic plates, an uplift of mountains to the north – the forerunners of today's Scottish Highlands – gave rise to large and powerful rivers flowing south into that shallow sea. They formed huge deltas of fine sand, grit and silt, much like those found on the Mississippi

◀ Orange Tip butterfly ▲ The Manifold Valley

or Nile today. Dictated by the shifting currents, these fine particles spread thickly over the entire seabed, covering the shelly limestone beds in a thick layer of sandstone.

That was the genesis of the gritstone Dark Peak. Aeons of weathering by ice, wind and rain eventually eroded the gritstone cover from the central and southern part of the Peak, thus exposing the limestone, as previously described, like a classic case of MPB – or male pattern baldness.

Ice Age glaciers and their erosive meltwaters put the final polish on the Peak District's geology, carving out the impressive, rock-faced dales of the White Peak, like Dove Dale, Lathkill Dale and the Manifold, and the broader, U-shaped valleys of the Dark Peak, like Edale and Longdendale.

Natural history

Just as the forces of nature created the bedrock of the Peak, it's the rocks beneath which dictate the flora and fauna of the area. As might be expected, the area's wildlife is heavily protected.

Undoubtedly the ecological showplaces of the Peak are the limestone dales of the White Peak. The flagship site is the Derbyshire Dales National Nature Reserve, which covers 845 acres of Lathkill Dale, Monk's Dale, Cressbrook Dale, Long Dale and Hay Dale.

Up to 50 floral species have been identified per square metre of the velvety greensward of Lathkill Dale, including the gaudy spikes of early purple orchids and, in the rocky upper reaches, the rich, purple-flowered Jacob's ladder – a national rarity. The sheep-grazed carpet of turf of the upper dale is rich in many other wildflowers, such as rockrose, bloody cranesbill, bird's foot trefoil, eyebright and thyme. In turn, these flower-rich grasslands support a wide range of invertebrates, including the northern brown argus, green-veined white and orange tip butterflies.

The Lathkill is one of the few rivers in England which flows for its entire length on limestone – thus making it one of the purest and cleanest in the country. Rivers in the Peak are the home of some aquatic rarities, such as the threatened freshwater crayfish – a kind of miniature lobster locally known as a 'crawkie' – and fine brown and rainbow trout.

Where the rivers enter the cool confines of the ash woods – another Peak District speciality – you might be lucky enough to see the iridescent flash of a kingfisher, but more likely the plump, bobbing shape of a dipper, seeming to curtsy to passers-by from a guano-splashed rock in mid-stream.

In areas where lead was once mined, such as around Magpie Mine, near Sheldon, lead-tolerant plants, such as the mountain pansy and spring sandwort (appropriately known as 'leadwort'), thrive where normal plants would die in the poisonous soil.

▼ Spotted Orchid   ▼ River Lathkill

The extensive Dark Peak peat moorlands of Kinder Scout, Bleaklow, Black Hill and the Eastern and Western moors have been described as one of Britain's only true deserts, and 'land at the end of its tether'. While it is undoubtedly true that these high and desolate, over-grazed moorlands cannot compete with the range of wildlife of the White Peak dales, they do still support a surprisingly wide variety of flora and fauna.

Top of the food chain are the dashing birds of prey, like the peregrine falcon, goshawk, hen harrier and hobby. Among the mammals they hunt on the Eastern moors are England's only population of mountain hares. These distinctive animals change their coats to white in winter and are descended from animals reintroduced by the Victorians.

The most characteristic bird of the heather moorland is undoubtedly the red grouse, however, and we have to thank this plump, furry-footed game bird for much of the glorious purple heather of late summer and early autumn. Most of these moors are managed exclusively for the grouse, which are traditionally shot after the 'Glorious Twelfth' of August (the official start of the shooting season).

Other birds which may be encountered on the Dark Peak moors include the golden plover, the curlew and the dotterel. The 'chinking' call of the ring ouzel, or mountain blackbird, may also be heard in the steep-sided, rocky cloughs on the edge of the moors, so look out for them, along with bobbing dippers and grey wagtails.

▼ Mountain hare on Kinder Scout

LORE OF THE LAND

The rocky, often harsh landscape of the Peak District
is the setting for many tales of ghosts, the Devil –
and even mermaids.

The moors themselves are dangerous places where both people
and animals can get lost with ease, like teenager Abraham Lowe
and his sheepdog Bob, who risked their lives to gather up a flock
of sheep trapped in deep snow on Derwent Edge.

Unable to get back home after completing their task, the pair
took shelter under a rock on which Abraham scratched the words
'lost lad'. Sadly, they perished, and despite the efforts of his
widowed mother and her neighbours their bodies remained hidden
through winter's blizzards. Come the spring, a shepherd discovered
them and with due deference built a cairn in their memory, adding

a stone each time he passed by. Today the hill is still named Lost Lad, and walkers still supplement the memorial – though it is doubtful whether many of them know his story. A tale with a slightly happier ending is that of sheepdog Tip, whose elderly master died while tending his flock in the Upper Derwent valley in the harsh winter of 1953 to 54. When his body was eventually discovered 15 weeks later, she was still by his side – weak, but alive. She's commemorated with a memorial by the Derwent Dam.

On a moonlit night near Onecote you might have the misfortune to meet a headless rider astride a white horse – for most, such meetings have proved deadly to the viewer. Local folklore tells of the farmer Joe Bowden, who by some mysterious power was lifted onto the horse behind the rider, and met his untimely end after being flung off again. Rumour had it that the phantom was the ghost of a knight killed in battle (or possibly a pedlar) until the church stepped in and pronounced the headless horseman to be one of four evil spirits expelled from Heaven and condemned to wander the earth for time immemorial. It's said that the horseman was caught and compelled to confess, though this exorcism appears to have been unsuccessful since he rides the moors still.

As well as its pudding, Bakewell is known for the two 'Bakewell witches', executed in Derby in 1608. As the story goes, a Bakewell landlady evicted her lodger after a dispute over rent – but kept his possessions. The enterprising lodger next turned up in London, claiming to have been spirited there by his landlady and her sister against his will. Implausible enough as it sounds, this was apparently a good enough story to be proof of witchcraft, especially once his clothes were found in their home...

Spirit power

Eldon Hole gets its name from Eldon Hill, or 'Elves Hill', the hill on which it is found near Peak Forest, and a place where elves lived hidden in the potholes and caves of the area. When, in the 16th century, a man died, mute, after being lowered into the hole, people took this as a sign that he had met with the devil.

Peak Cavern, nicknamed 'the Devil's Arse' has long been seen as an entrance to the underworld. One winter a swineherd lost a sow and, in desperation, entered the cavern. At the far end of the dark cave he emerged into bright sunlight to see, to his amazement, a field of wheat ready to harvest – along with the sow, with which he returned, full of tales of a sacred place. In later years the cavern's magic became linked with the devil.

The fairies of the Peak District, residents of the 'Perilous Realm', make their presence known by leaving on the ground minute clay pipes. When picked up and put in a pocket by the 'wrong' sort of person they can cause a prickling sensation and then smouldering – before disappearing. When set in incorrect hands, a pipe lit by its finder may produce a sweet smoke that appears packed with people – who then turn on the smoker and fire darts at him until he drops the pipe for the fairies to retrieve.

All was very different for someone like Elijah, whom the fairies deemed to be 'right'. When he smoked the fairy pipe at Nine Stones Close near Elton, he was transported into a beautiful, enchanted world decked with palaces and abundant gardens and full of sweet music. Elijah experienced the magic of the pipe many times at Nine Stones Close until one day he failed to return from his sojourn in the spirit world.

Peakland phantoms

Sharp, clear Peak District air resounds with the horns of long-dead huntsmen and hounds chasing through Bretton Clough, riderless horses galloping towards Hope, and the bark of the Kinder Boggart, a black dog that haunts Edale. When the mists fall on the moors, fear of meeting this 'faeirie dog', the size of a calf and with saucer-large eyes, strikes terror into walkers' hearts. Shuck, a spectral black dog, is said to stalk Sydnope Hill near Matlock and on any dark night you can hear the ghastly howls of the jet black Gabriel Hounds whose coats are smeared with blood and whose fiery eyes pierce the gloom of cloudy nights. Most usually they are heard, not seen, their yelping believed to be omens of death or the voices of evil spirits hunting the souls of the departed.

More than two centuries ago the body of Hannah, a young servant girl, was found under the staircase of a house in Bradwell. Soon afterwards her ghost began appearing, terrifying the owners of the house and then the people of the village. A wizard, Nicholas Hawthorne, was called upon to end this nightmare. Weaving his spell with the help of a chalk circle drawn on the floor, he summoned up Hannah's ghost and ordered her to go to Lumb Mound, to descend into the waters of Bradwell Brook and to turn into a fish for all time. But each year, on Christmas Day, she would become a white ousel and fly to Lumbly Pool, to return by midnight.

◄ Robin Hood's Stride

A farmhouse near Chapel-en-le Frith houses an aged, yellowing human skull. Said to belong to 'Dickie o'Tunstead', legend says he possesses supernatural powers and must not be moved from his home. Make any attempt at a burial, and disaster will strike...

Folk hero

'Feared by the bad, loved by the good', the hero Robin Hood and his men have many Peak District connections. While Robin was in hiding in the tall, dark slit in the rock cleft of Lud's Church near Gradbach, Friar Tuck is believed to have given him communion. (Lud's Church is also claimed to be the scene of the fateful rendezvous of Sir Gawain and the Green Knight, in the 15th-century Arthurian legend.) Legend also relates that at Robin Hood's Stride, near Birchover, the 15 yards that separate the broken gritstone rocks is where, despite the superhuman distance involved, Robin placed one foot at each end of the towering stones.

A boundary stone, Robin Hood's Stoop, on Offerton Moor marks the spot from where Robin is said to have shot an arrow into Hathersage churchyard, some 2,000 yards distant. Northward, up in the crags of Stanage Edge, is Robin Hood's cave, and in the village churchyard at Hathersage is the alleged grave of his faithful lieutenant Little John, who was so affected by the death of his master that he not only predicted that he would die in three days but pointed out the spot where he was to be buried.

Watery tales

Despite their distance from the sea, Peak District meres – that's lakes to most people – are believed to be inhabited by mermaids and to contain water so evil that no animal will drink from them. These fish-tailed women are dangerous to humankind, even if placated by being offered a sprig of rowan, a tree widely planted as protection against witches. At Mermaid's Pool, nestled among the rocks on the western slopes of Kinder Scout, a mermaid bathes every day, but is visible to human eyes only on Easter Eve, when she is said to cause the deaths of young men trying to outswim her. Men have also perished when approaching the mermaid of the bottomless Blake (Black) Mere on the Staffordshire moors, who at midnight puts out a beckoning arm or emerges from the water to comb her tresses and will call out to anyone who sees her.

In a hollow a short walk from the rocky crest of The Roaches are the dark, doom-ladened waters of Doxey Pool. Here lives the hideous slime-covered hag Jenny Greenteeth with – as her name suggests – green teeth and skin. Jenny rises from the water to a height of some 30 feet until her feet touch the water's surface. Children and the elderly beware – she will quickly pull you into the water to drown.

CUSTOMS & TRADITIONS

The hills and dales of the Peak District have harboured many ancient customs and traditions which have survived the centuries, possibly partly because of the remoteness of the district.

Well dressing

Well dressings are thriving, today more than ever before. Originally found only in the limestone villages of the White Peak, they now take place in over 80 towns and villages in and around the Peak District, attracting thousands of visitors.

Throughout May, each village takes it in turn to decorate their wells or springs with these intricate floral mosaics, which often coincide with the village Wakes (or patron saint's) Week. Well dressing is a real community effort, and many villagers from all walks of life are involved in the process of creating the beautiful floral icons which can take up to 400 hours to complete, using only natural, locally found materials.

It's thought that the custom may have originated in pagan times as a thanksgiving for the gift of water on the fast-draining limestone plateau, and the custom was later adopted by Christianity. The first recorded historical examples took place at Tissington in 1758.

Castleton Garland Day

No one can be sure, but the Garland Day held annually at Castleton on or around Oak Apple Day (29 May), is claimed to be a pagan fertility rite, welcoming the renewal of life and the arrival of spring after the long, hard winter.

More matter-of-fact historians claim it commemorates the restoration of Charles II in 1660, and certainly the main participants – the King and Queen – are traditionally dressed in flamboyant Stuart costume.

The King and his Queen tour the narrow village streets on horseback, visiting and imbibing in all the village pubs, in a procession which includes local schoolchildren clad in white and the village brass band. The 3-foot-high wooden garland is covered in wildflowers and encases the King from head to waist, and is eventually hoisted up to the top of the tower of St Edmund's church, where it is left to wither.

Interestingly, the unique Castleton Garland tune which is sung at the event closely resembles that of the Cornish Floral Dance, and is thought to have been brought to Derbyshire by Cornish lead miners.

Bakewell pudding

Most people will have heard of the Bakewell tart, the culinary delicacy which the ancient market town on the River Wye gave to the world. But don't ever make the mistake of calling it by that name if you're in Bakewell.

Here, the sickly sweet, almond-paste and puff pastry pies are always known by

▶ Bakewell pudding

their proper title of Bakewell puddings – and a pudding is exactly what they are.

Made to a closely guarded secret recipe in three shops in the town, they are now exported all over the world – and they bear absolutely no resemblance to the thickly-iced 'Mr Kipling' variety.

The original Bakewell pudding apparently came about in the 1860s, thanks to a mistake by a flustered cook in what is now the Rutland Arms Hotel. She was charged by the owner to make a strawberry tart for some important guests, but, in her panic, failed to stir the egg mix into the pastry as instructed, and poured it over the strawberry jam instead. So what was meant to be a tart turned out to be a pudding.

The accidental delicacy was so well received by the guests that the cook was instructed to continue making them that way – and the Bakewell pudding was born.

Among the shops which claim to have the original recipe is the Old Original Bakewell Pudding Shop in The Square. The original owner, Annie Wilson, claimed to have been one of the guests at the hotel when the cook made her famous mistake, and she wrote down the recipe in a small notebook, which is now kept in a safe.

Rush bearing

Before the days of fitted carpets, the floors of houses, churches and chapels were regularly strewn with rushes as a renewable, fresh-smelling floor covering.

The ancient custom of rush bearing still takes place every August in the tiny 19th-century chapel of St Stephen – otherwise known as the Forest Chapel – in Macclesfield Forest, on the western edge of the Peak. The ceremony is now seen as an act of spiritual renewal, and attracts large numbers of worshippers.

Christmas carols

Christmas carols are an essential part of the festive season, but in the Hope Valley area of the Peak, each village has its own traditional carols which are sung not only in churches but also in the village pubs.

Castleton, Eyam, Foolow and Hathersage all have their own distinctive carols, most of which probably originated from the farmers and lead miners of the valley.

The carols are surprisingly inclusive, the singers readily adopting popular tunes or songs into their repertoire. The current songbook of the Castleton carol singers, for example, includes favourite sacred pieces such as *The Old Rugged Cross* and *Bless this House*, alongside Harry Belafonte's 1955 hit *Scarlet Ribbons*.

The core of each village's repertoire is still the traditional form of carol, which owes its origin to the psalms of the Georgian period.

DAYS OF ORE

The mysterious humps and bumps seen in many flower-filled meadows of the White Peak limestone plateau are evidence of an industry which was an essential part of the Peakland economy for nearly 2,000 years.

More obvious remains of lead mining include the evocative ruins of Magpie Mine, high on the plateau near Sheldon, which is perhaps the most perfectly preserved lead mine in the country, worked on and off for an astonishing 300 years.

The mining of lead ore (properly known as galena) had gone on since the Romans first entered the Peak in the late 70s AD. The area was known to have plentiful supplies of the valuable and easily accessible mineral, which was used extensively throughout the Empire for plumbing and drainage.

▲ Magpie Mine

Pigs (cast ingots) of lead bearing the letters 'LVT' or 'LVTVD' – which are believed to refer to the as yet undiscovered Derbyshire lead mining centre of Lutudarum, have been found as far away as Sussex. Latest thinking places Lutudarum somewhere around Carsington, where a small Roman villa has been excavated.

The Romans constructed forts at Navio, near Brough in the Hope Valley, and Melandra, just outside Glossop, to protect their mining interests; and Roman artefacts associated with lead mining activities have been found throughout the Peak. Certainly the first Roman roads, such as the modern A515 Buxton–Ashbourne road, would have been used for transporting lead.

Although there is no evidence to prove it, the dangerous Odin Mine near Castleton traditionally claims to be the oldest lead mine in the Peak. It is said to have derived its name from being worked at the time of the Viking Danes, whose chief god was Odin.

Seven *plumbariae* or lead works were recorded in the Peak in the Domesday Book of 1086: three at Wirksworth and one each at Ashford, Bakewell, Crich and Matlock. You can see what an Anglo-Saxon lead miner looked like in a tiny carving in Wirksworth church, which shows an apparently kilted miner carrying his pick and the small basket – or 'wisket' – which was used to collect the precious ore.

The laws and customs of the High Peak lead field were laid down as early as 1288, by order of the *Quo Warranto* of Edward I, and they were administered, and indeed are still administered, by a Barmote Court, one of the oldest courts of law in the country.

These ancient Barmote Courts are still held for the Wapentake of Wirksworth annually at the ancient Barmote Court in Wirksworth, with breakfast and dinner for the Steward, Barmaster and 12 jurors at the expense of the Duke of Lancaster – otherwise known as the Queen.

The extensive 'Liberties and Customs of the Lead-Mines within the Wapentake of Wirksworth' were laid down in a rhyming chronicle for ease of memory by the Barmote Steward Edward Manlove, and first published in 1653.

They include this harsh penalty for a thief caught stealing ore for a third time. The chronicle states that the miscreant:

Shall have a knife stuck through his hand to the haft
Into the stowe (the windlass over the shaft), and there till
death shall stand,
Or loose himself by cutting loose his hand.

The language of the miner was as old and as colourful as the industry itself. Terms like 'slickensides' (fluted or polished surfaces in the rock); 'groovers' (men who worked in the mines or 'grooves'); 'kibble' (a large bucket used to raise ore up a shaft); 'stemple' (pieces of wood wedged across a vein and used as a ladder); and 'scrin' (a short vertical mineral vein) were all in common use. Putting a 'nick' in the wooden stowe or windlass of an apparently unworked mine meant that the Barmaster could award the mine to the claimant – perhaps the forerunner of the modern word 'nicking', used for stealing.

The heyday of the Peak's lead mining industry was during the first half of the 18th century, when there were as many as 10,000 miners engaged in the industry. Water was a common problem in Peak District lead mines, and it was at this time that steam engines were first employed to pump water out of the mines. Before that, an extensive system of drainage tunnels, known as soughs – pronounced 'suffs' – were used to 'de-water' the mines. Many were several miles in length, and were major feats of engineering, some taking 50 years or more to complete.

By 1861, the industry was in decline, and the number of miners, many doubling as farmers in summer, had dropped to 2,300.

Even today, it's been estimated that there are as many as 50,000 open or partially concealed lead mine shafts in the White Peak, evidence of centuries of industry by 't'owd man', as the old lead miners are affectionately known.

THE WONDERS OF THE PEAK

The earliest tourists to visit the Peak District often followed a well-trodden Grand Tour, based on the area's so-called 'Seven Wonders'.

The Seven Wonders of the Peak were natural and man-made features, invented by the fertile minds of the earliest writers to echo the fabled Seven Wonders of the Ancient World.

But while the Peak has nothing to compare with the Pyramids of Giza or the Colossus of Rhodes, this pioneer listing was enough to put the Peak on the tourist map. Travellers sought them out on what became a fashionable itinerary, like the Grand Tours taken by the well-heeled to Europe.

The first listing of the legendary Wonders of the Peak appears to have been made by William Camden, the 16th-century antiquarian and historian, in his *Britannia*, a history of Britain published in 1586. Writing in Latin, he in fact described nine 'wonders', but appears to have dismissed all but three as deserving of the name:

◀ Peveril Castle   ▲ Winnats Pass from Mam Tor

Nine things that please us at the Peak we see;
A Cave, a Den, a Hole, the Wonder be;
Lead, Sheep and Pasture, are the useful Three.
Chatsworth, the Castle and the Bath delight,
Much more you see; all little worth the Sight.

The cave was Peak Cavern (then known as the Devil's Arse) at Castleton; the den was Poole's Cavern, home of the medieval outlaw Poole at Buxton; and the hole was the gaping open pothole of Eldon Hole, on the slopes of Eldon Hill near Peak Forest. Chatsworth was then the home of Bess of Hardwick; the Castle was presumably Peveril Castle at Castleton; and the Bath must have been St Ann's Well at Buxton.

The first writer to list the classic Seven Wonders was the Warwickshire-born poet Michael Drayton, in his *Poly-Olbion* (1622). Drayton added Sandi Hill (Mam Tor, the so-called Shivering Mountain); the medieval Royal Forest of the Peak; and the Ebbing and Flowing Well (at Tideswell, or possibly Barmoor Clough).

The first real tourist guidebook to the Peak was written by Thomas Hobbes, the famous philosopher and tutor to the Cavendish children at Chatsworth. His *De Mirabilibus Pecci: Concerning the Wonders of the Peak in Darby-shire* was first published in 1636, and in it he also listed seven 'wonders' which he had visited during a two-day ride. He described how:

Of the High Peak are seven wonders writ,
Two fonts, two caves, one palace, mount and pit.

Hobbes' Wonders were two fountains (St Ann's Well and the Ebbing and Flowing Well, two caves (Poole's Cavern and Peak Cavern), Chatsworth, a mountain (Mam Tor) and a pit (Eldon Hole).

In 1682 the wonders were rewritten in English for the fast-expanding tourist market, by Charles Cotton, impecunious squire of Beresford Hall in Dove Dale, and the co-author, with Izaak Walton, of the anglers' bible, *The Compleat Angler.*

One of the first visitors to tour the Wonders was Edward Browne, later to be doctor to Charles II, who travelled all the way from Norfolk in 1622. He was impressed by this 'strange, mountainous, misty, moorish, rocky wild country' with its 'craggy ascents, the rocky uneveness of the roade, the high peaks and the almost perpendicular descents'.

Later Celia Fiennes, the daughter of a Roundhead colonel and the first in a long line of adventurous members of that Oxfordshire family, rode through the Peak alone and by side saddle with the

▼ The Painted Hall, Chatsworth

object of visiting the Wonders in 1698. She recorded her impressions in the snappily titled *Through England on a Side Saddle in the Time of William and Mary*.

Celia Fiennes was followed 20 years later by Daniel Defoe, the satirical journalist and political commentator, who is probably best known for his novel Robinson Crusoe. His *Tour thro'the Whole Island of Great Britain*, first published in instalments between 1724 and 1726, systematically debunked Hobbes' and Cotton's 'Wonders', concluding that only Eldon Hole and Chatsworth – 'one a wonder of nature, the other of art' – were worthy of the name.

Defoe pours scorn on the Wonders of the Peak District:

Now to have so great a man as Mr Hobbes, and after him Mr Cotton, celebrate the trifles here... as if they were the most exalted wonders of the world: I cannot but, after wondering at their making wonders of them, desire you, my friend, to travel with me through this houling wilderness in your imagination, and you shall soon find all that is wonderful about it.

Defoe was not exactly enamoured of the Peak District and saw little practical use of the landscape. The High Peak was 'a waste and houling wilderness', and '...the most desolate, wild and abandoned country'. The inhabitants, in particular the lead miners, were 'a rude boorish kind of people' and Defoe claimed that their ancient Barmote Court, which attempted to govern their activities, was 'the greatest of all the wonders of the Peak'.

▼ Peak Cavern

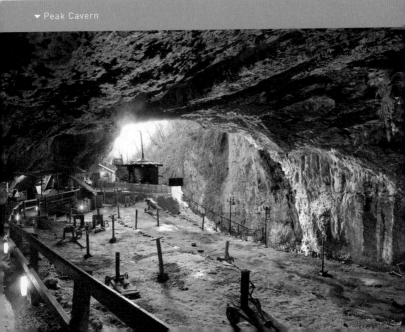

LOCAL SPECIALITIES

ARTISTS

Curiously, the great painters of the Enlightenment seemed to have either ignored or bypassed the scenic wonders of the Peak, on their way to the greater hills of the Lake District and Snowdonia. But there are a number of modern painters who have specialised in Peak District subjects.

▶ The great 'artist of light' **JMW Turner** did a series of pencil sketches on a visit to the Peak in 1831, which were only recently rediscovered. They appear never to have been developed into full-scale paintings.

▶ If there's one modern artist who captures the illusive essence of the Peak, it's **Rex Preston**. Rex was born in Yardley, Birmingham, in 1948, and his family settled in Derbyshire when he was 16. Rex usually paints outdoors on location, and his work accurately captures the changing moods of the Peak District landscape.

▶ **Michael Barnfather** is another accomplished and much-collected Derbyshire-born artist whose favourite subjects include the varied landscapes of the Peak.

▶ Based in Holmfirth, **Ashley Jackson** has become one of the country's best-known watercolourists, thanks largely to his atmospheric paintings of the brooding moorlands of the Dark Peak.

▶ The Peak District is also home to two internationally known wildlife artists. They are **Pollyanna Pickering**, who is based at Oaker, near Matlock, and **Richard Whittlestone**, who works from a studio at Pilsley on the Chatsworth Estate.

LOCAL FOOD

▶ **Bakewell puddings:** Don't confuse the Mr Kipling variety with a true Bakewell pudding. This delicious, almond-paste and puff pastry delicacy, apparently originally made by mistake by a flustered cook, is now exported all over the world by the three bakery shops in the town which claim to have the original secret recipe. One place to try them is at the Old Original Bakewell Pudding Shop in The Square (see page 76).

- **Staffordshire oatcakes** are a type of pancake made from oatmeal, flour and yeast, and cooked on a griddle. It is a local speciality in the Staffordshire moorlands.
- **Derbyshire oatcakes** are similar to Staffordshire oatcakes, but are generally thicker and larger in diameter. Traditional oatcakes could be described as an early form of fast food, like the Cornish pasty. They are often filled with cheese, tomato, onion, bacon, sausage and egg, making a complete meal. They can also be eaten with sweet fillings, such as syrup, jam or banana, although this is frowned upon by traditionalists.
- **Posset cup:** The posset was a traditional Peak District beverage at Christmas time, made from boiled milk or cream, ale, eggs, treacle, ginger, nutmeg and other spices. It was drunk on Christmas Eve from special, multi-handled pots which could be passed round a group. Bradwell lead miners sometimes left a candle burning in the mine on Christmas Eve 'for the old ancient man to have his posset by'. They also left 't'owd man' (the spirit of the old miners) a portion of their dinner.
- **Ashbourne gingerbread:** Ashbourne's answer to Bakewell's puddings is their gingerbread. This sweet, ginger-flavoured biscuit is supposed to have been created by a French prisoner-of-war who made his home in the town after the Napoleonic Wars. It is still made at the Ashbourne Gingerbread Shop in St John Street, Ashbourne.

BEST REAL ALE PUBS

- **The Greyhound Inn, Wardlow** (see page 255). Dating to 1750, this peaceful pub offers fine cask ales.
- **The Maynard, Grindleford** (page 164). Within easy reach of a host of Peak attractions, this old stone inn offers real ales brewed on the Chatsworth Estate.
- **The Old Eyre Arms, Hassop** (see page 173). This creeper-clad inn close to Chatsworth House offers real ales from Peak Ales and Bradfield breweries.
- **The Packhorse Inn, Little Longstone** (see page 230). This cosy little pub serves home-prepared food and real ales from the nearby Thornbridge Brewery.
- **The Quiet Woman, Earl Sterndale** (see page 143). The distinctly non-PC sign outside this traditional pub shows a headless woman. Inside there's a real fire, low beams, pub games and real ales, including those from Leek Brewery.
- **The Swan Inn, Kettleshulme** (see page 212). Timber beams, stone fireplaces and a real fire create a traditional ambience, with a constantly changing list of guest beers.

BEFORE YOU GO

THINGS TO READ

From Thomas Hobbes to Stephen Booth, the Peak District has inspired generations of writers to put pen to paper, describing its many charms, or using its landscapes as a dramatic backdrop for their works of fiction.

▶ **Thomas Hobbes** was one of the first to describe the Wonders of the Peak (see page 34) in his famous poem *De Mirabilibus Pecci*, or *The Wonders of the Peak,* published in 1636.

▶ Staffordshire-born poet **Charles Cotton** regurgitated Hobbes' Wonders in a later work and described fly-fishing on the rivers Dove and Lathkill in *The Compleat Angler* (1653), with his friend **Izaak Walton**.

▶ *Adam Bede*, the first novel written by **George Eliot** (actually Mary Ann Evans), featured Ashbourne as Oakbourne and Wirksworth as Snowfield, while Derbyshire was aptly known as Stonyshire.

▶ **William Wordsworth** visited Matlock, Matlock Bath and Chatsworth, about which he wrote a short sonnet.

▶ Peveril Castle at Castleton was the setting for the opening of **Sir Walter Scott's** melodramatic novel *Peveril of the Peak.*

▶ **Jane Austen** is claimed to have stayed at the Rutland Arms in Bakewell while writing her much-loved and filmed novel, *Pride and Prejudice.* She is thought to have based Pemberley on nearby Chatsworth.

▶ North Lees Hall near Hathersage is believed to have been the inspiration for Thornfield Hall, the home of Mr Rochester in *Jane Eyre* by **Charlotte Brontë**. Charlotte is known to have visited the hall in 1845, two years before *Jane Eyre* was published.

▶ Sherlock Holmes' creator, **Sir Arthur Conan Doyle,** set his spine-chilling short story *The Terror of Blue John Gap* on the numerous caves of the Castleton area.

▶ **Vera Brittain**, mother of politician Shirley Williams, chronicled her tragic experiences while she was living in Buxton during World War I in her best-selling *Testament of Youth*.

▶ Popular children's author **Alison Uttley** was born in Cromford in 1884, and reflected her great love of the Derbyshire countryside in her stories about characters like *Little Grey Rabbit* and *Sam Pig*. Another favourite, *Traveller in Time*, is the story of a 20th-century girl who is transported to the 16th century, becoming involved in the Babington Plot to free Mary, Queen of Scots from the Earl of Shrewsbury's care at Wingfield Manor, near Alfreton.

▶ Another children's author who gained his inspiration from the Peak was **Alan Garner**. Living near Alderley Edge on the western edge of the Peak, Garner is best known for children's fantasy novels such as *The Weirdstone of Brisingamen, Elidor* and *The Owl Service*.

▶ Award-winning children's writer, **Berlie Doherty**, lives in Edale, and many of her books, including *Blue John* and *Jeannie of White Peak Farm*, are set in the Peak.

▶ Multi-award-winning crime novelist **Stephen Booth** sets his popular books – such as *Dancing with the Virgins* and *The Dead Place* – in the Peak District.

▶ **Geraldine Brooks** based her Pulitzer Prize winning novel *Year of Wonders* on the Plague Village of Eyam, which was ravaged by the disease between 1665 and 1666.

THINGS TO WATCH

Local people delight in spotting Peak District scenes in popular TV and film costume dramas. This is because the Peak District has become a favourite location for TV and film producers looking for easily accessible, stunning backdrops for their productions, ranging from *Jane Eyre* to *Last of the Summer Wine* and *The Village*.

▶ The Duke of Rutland's medieval masterpiece **Haddon Hall** is one of the most frequently seen locations, and has served as the backdrop for productions like *The Princess Bride* (1987), *Jane Eyre* (film in 1996, BBC TV series, 2006), *Elizabeth* (1998) and *The Other Boleyn Girl* (2008).

▶ Another much sought-after setting is **Chatsworth**, which featured in *Pride and Prejudice* (2005), *The Duchess* (2008) and the Gothic horror movie *The Wolf Man* (2009).

▶ The imposing Palladian facade of the National Trust's **Lyme Hall** near Disley shot to national fame when actor Colin Firth, playing Mr Darcy, emerged dripping wet from the lake in BBC TV's 1995 drama *Pride and Prejudice*. The Hall's exterior was used as Pemberley.

▶ The stunning gritstone escarpment of **Stanage Edge**, above Hathersage, appeared in *Pride and Prejudice* (2005), *The Other Boleyn Girl* (2008) and *Wuthering Heights* (TV series 2008/9).

▶ Several Peak District villages, including **Crich, Fritchley** and **Longnor,** all starred as the fictional town of Cardale in the popular ITV drama about a doctors' practice, *Peak Practice.*

▶ The famous Dambusters of 617 Squadron used the **Derwent and Howden reservoirs** in the Upper Derwent Valley when training for their epic 1943 raid on the Ruhr dams. The same locations were used in the 1953 film *The Dam Busters*, which starred Michael Redgrave as inventor Barnes Wallis and Richard Todd as Squadron Leader Guy Gibson.

▶ The village of **Hadfield**, near Glossop, doubled as eccentric Royston Vasey in the darkly humorous BBC TV series *The League of Gentlemen* (1999–2002).

▶ Dubbed as the longest-running comedy sitcom in the world, BBC TV's *Last of the Summer Wine* ran for 37 years until 2010, and was set in and around the pretty West Yorkshire market town of

▼ Derwent Reservoir Dam

Holmfirth. You'll come across reminders of the series wherever you go in Holmfirth, from Sid's Café to Nora Batty's famous Wrinkled Stocking Tea Room.

▸ The gritty BBC drama series *The Village*, starring John Simm and Maxine Peake, used **Hayfield**, the village sheltered under the western slopes of Kinder Scout, as its eponymous setting. The 'farm' of the impoverished Middleton family was actually a barn at Highfield Farm in **Edale**.

THINGS TO KNOW

▸ **First and foremost:** The Peak District was the first National Park in Britain, designated in April 1951. It covers 555 square miles – about the size of Greater London. The park receives 10 million visitors every year and an estimated 20 million people live within an hour's drive.

▸ **A special place:** There are nearly 3,000 listed buildings in the National Park, and 35 per cent of it is designated as Sites of Special Scientific Interest (SSSI). It is the only National Park in the UK to hold the prestigious Council of Europe Diploma for Protected Areas.

▸ **No stone unturned:** There are estimated to be 5,440 miles of

▾ Nora Batty's cafe in Holmfirth

drystone walls in the Peak District National Park – roughly equivalent to the distance between London and San Francisco.

▶ **Peakland paradoxes:** Prehistoric burial mounds, or 'lows', are usually found on high points in the Peakland landscape. And there are very few hills which could be described as peaks in the Peak District.

▶ **Rarer than the tiger:** A single patch about 3 feet square, in a secret site under a waterfall in one of the White Peak dales, makes up the entire world population of Derbyshire feather-moss *(Thamnobryum angustifolium)*.

▶ **Bradder Beavers:** The English soldier's tin helmet in World War I was based on the 'Bradder Beaver' – the brimmed lead miners' hat made in Bradwell. Bradwell's other claim to fame (apart from its delicious ice cream) is that Samuel Fox from the village invented the world's first collapsible umbrella – 'the Paragon' – here in 1851.

▶ **Water on demand:** The Peak District has more reservoirs than the Lake District has lakes, and these 50 reservoirs supply the surrounding towns and cities with 450 million litres of water every day.

▶ **Toe to toe:** The World Toe Wrestling Championships are held every July at the Bentley Brook Hotel at Fenny Bentley, on the A515 north of Ashbourne.

▶ **Don't look down!** The recently discovered Titan Cavern near Castleton has the deepest natural shaft in the country – it's a dizzying 464 feet deep.

▶ **Tom Thumb's home?** One-up-one-down Thimble Hall in Fountain Square, Youlgreave, is listed in the Guinness Book of Records as the smallest detached house in the world.

▶ **Beware Triffids!** Two rare plants found on the Dark Peak moors get nourishment from eating insects. The sticky leaves of the round-leaved sundew and the butterwort trap the unfortunate insects and curl up around them. The leaves then secrete digestive enzymes to absorb the insect's juices.

▶ **On the rocks:** Tarmac's Tunstead Quarry in Great Rocks Dale, near Wormhill, is the largest working quarry face in Europe. It is also the largest producer of limestone in the Peak District, with about 5.5 million tonnes extracted annually.

▶ **Jump to it!** Until recently there was a colony of red-necked wallabies living wild near the Roaches, in the Staffordshire moorlands. They escaped from a private zoo during World War II, and bred for a while in the wild.

▶ **Flash money:** The village of Flash south of Buxton is, at 1,519 feet above the sea, claimed to be the highest village in Britain. It also gave its name to counterfeit money, still sometimes called 'flash money', which was once made in the village.

▶ **Rarer than the rainforest:** The blanket peat bogs of the Dark Peak moors are among the rarest and most important wildlife habitats in the world. More than 94 per cent of the UK's peat bogs have been damaged or destroyed – and they are thought to be at greater risk than the tropical rainforest.

▶ **Beware body snatchers:** The Watch House at Higher Bradfield, west of Sheffield, was built next to the churchyard of St Nicholas as a deterrent to body snatchers.

▶ **Not-so-little John:** The churchyard at Hathersage is said to be the last resting place of Robin Hood's loyal lieutenant, Little John. He was a nailor in the village, and returned home after his adventures with the Merrie Men. The 11-foot long grave is now cared for by the Ancient Order of Foresters.

▶ **The foggy, foggy dew:** Dew ponds are a feature of limestone pastures in the White Peak. Because the underlying rock is porous there are no natural ponds, so farmers have created their own, originally lined with imperious clay, but now, more likely, cement. Contrary to common belief and their name, dew ponds are usually filled by rain – and hosepipes – not mists or dew.

▼ Ladybower Reservoir

THINGS TO PACK

The most essential pieces of equipment to take if you really want to get to know the Peak District first hand are waterproofs, walking boots and a good map.

Waterproofs: Like most hilly areas, the Peak suffers its fair share of rainfall – the figures for the higher ground such as Kinder Scout are around 60 inches a year, compared to only 36 inches in the White Peak around Bakewell. So a good waterproof – and breathable fabrics are best – is pretty much essential.

July and August – the peak holiday months – are surprisingly also the wettest months in the Peak District. Paradoxically, the highest temperatures are also usually recorded in July and August. Generally, the driest months are in the spring, May and June in particular.

Boots: With 1,600 miles of footpaths and thousands of acres of free-access open country, the Peak is a walkers' paradise. If you are doing any walking – and why else would you come to the Peak? – you'll also need a good pair of comfortable, waterproof walking boots or shoes. Most of the paths are well maintained and signposted by the National Park authority and Derbyshire County Council, but they can still get very wet and muddy, especially in the moorland areas of the Dark Peak. The peat bogs of the high moors of Kinder Scout, Bleaklow and Black Hill are notorious among walkers, and even the redoubtable Alfred Wainwright once had to be rescued from one by a National Park ranger when he was doing his Pennine Way guide. But many of the most popular routes, such as the Pennine Way and Derwent Edge, are now paved with slabs from disused cotton mills, to prevent ever-widening paths and erosion.

Maps: The other piece of equipment you should take with you, especially when walking in the Peak, is an Ordnance Survey map. The latest 1:25,000, 2½ inch to the mile Explorer Maps to the Dark Peak (OL1) and White Peak (OL24) are highly recommended, because they show access land, footpaths, and even field boundaries.

Good alternatives include the Harveys Maps/British Mountaineering Council's 1:40,000 Dark Peak and White Peak waterproof mountain maps, or Harveys 1:25,000 Dark Peak Superwalker map, which includes the eastern gritstone edges.

If you are doing any serious 'off-piste' walking on the Dark Peak moors, you'll also need a compass and the knowledge of how to use it, and/or a reliable GPS unit. Although the highest Dark Peak moors are only 2,000 feet above the sea, they are on the same latitude as Labrador or Siberia, so they should never be underestimated.

But if you are merely driving around, the OS 1:50,000, 1 inch to the mile Landranger touring map (No. 119) to Buxton and Matlock covers most of the area and is recommended.

BASIC TRAVEL INFORMATION

When winter snows arrive, you'll often hear local people in the Peak talk about 'the Cat' or 'the Snake'. This has nothing to do with the animals, but is just a handy abbreviation for two of the highest, most frequently snowbound and difficult roads which cross the Peak.

The A537 Buxton–Macclesfield road passes the Cat & Fiddle Inn – at 1,690 feet the second highest in the country – at its highest point, so is usually abbreviated simply to 'the Cat'. And the A57 Sheffield–Glossop road likewise passes the front door of The Snake Pass Inn, before crossing the eponymous Snake Pass between Kinder Scout and Bleaklow – only slightly lower than the Cat & Fiddle at 1,680 feet above the sea.

Winter weather and traffic reports on the TV or radio often report that the first cross-Pennine roads to close and the last to reopen during snowstorms are the Cat & Fiddle and the Snake Pass. Because of their high altitude, both catch the worst of the winter storms, and the Snake road is particularly susceptible to overhanging cornices of wind-blown snow in its upper reaches, which sometimes even have to be demolished by explosives.

But generally speaking during the rest of the year, the Peak District is easily accessible for travellers. It's best to avoid Bank Holidays if you are visiting popular towns like Bakewell, Matlock Bath or Buxton, when parking can be a real problem.

Matlock Bath has become particularly popular as a meeting place for the motorcycling fraternity. Most weekends, leather-clad aficionados can be seen admiring each other's gleaming chromium-plated bikes which are neatly lined up along the North and South Parade opposite the River Derwent. In September and October, the Matlock Bath Illuminations feature fireworks, entertainments and lighted boats on the river – and general chaos on the A6, which runs through the town.

Bakewell, the unofficial 'capital' of the Peak, is busy most weekends, and parking is almost always at a premium. This especially applies on a Monday, when the streets of the town are filled with livestock wagons as farmers from all over the Peak bring in their stock to buy and sell at Bakewell Market. This is now held at the modern Agricultural Business Centre on the southern edge of town, but many wagons coming from the north still have to pass through the town to get there. There's also a thriving street market in the Market Square behind the old Market Hall, which on every other day of the week serves as a car park.

Unless you are attending the popular events, Bakewell is also best avoided during the Bakewell Carnival, billed as the biggest and best in Derbyshire, on the first Saturday in July, when the local well dressings also take place; and during the two days of the Bakewell Agricultural Show, held during the first week of August.

RAINY DAY DESTINATIONS

The Peak is blessed with plentiful rainy day destinations, where the kids can be entertained in the dry. Top of the list are probably Castleton's four show caves, and further subterranean delights can be experienced at Poole's Cavern at Buxton, which is even accessible by wheel or pushchair, or the Great Masson Cavern at Matlock Bath.

Younger kids will love Gulliver's Kingdom at Matlock Bath, which is specially designed for families with children aged between two and 13. The wide range of rides and attractions makes Gulliver's Kingdom the best theme park in the Peak. For the more adventurous, a little further afield is the granddaddy of all theme parks and the capital of white-knuckle rides, Alton

Towers in Staffordshire, which also has a water park.

If the kids are more into animals, then a visit to the Chestnut Centre Conservation and Wildlife Park, near Chapel-en-le-Frith, is a must. Among many other indigenous birds and animals, you'll see Europe's largest collection of otters.

Adults and older children will enjoy the Old House Museum at Bakewell, regularly voted one of Britain's best small museums, and Buxton Museum and Art Gallery, which features a Wonders of the Peak time tunnel. The Weston Park Museum in Sheffield (not covered by this guide), contains a collection of archaeological finds from the Peak.

GETTING THERE BY ROAD

The district is effectively bracketed by the motorway system. Coming from the south, the M1 from London to Leeds passes to the east of the district, which can be easily accessed from Junction 28 (Ripley and Matlock) via the A6, or Junction 29 (Chesterfield) via the A619.

To the west, the M6 Junctions 17 or 18 (Congleton) or 19 (Knutsford), give easy access to the western side of the Peak via the A357 Cat & Fiddle or A54 roads. But beware, the Cat & Fiddle road has been officially dubbed as one of the most dangerous in the country, and is much loved by speeding motorcyclists who enjoy the frequent sweeping curves. It can also be subject to low cloud, mist and fog at any time of the year, so take care.

In the north, the busy cross-Pennine A628 through Longdendale is often nose-to-tail with large lorries crossing between Manchester and Sheffield, and is best avoided at peak times. Plans for a new and damaging trans-Pennine motorway through Longdendale have been successfully fought off by the National Park for over 30 years.

At present, the only cross-Pennine motorway linking the A1 (M) and Leeds with Manchester is the desperately overcrowded M62. This gives access to the north of the area via Junction 22 (Oldham). The M60 Manchester orbital gives easy access to Glossop and New Mills via the M67.

There are frequent bus links from the neighbouring towns and cities into the Peak District. The most popular is the frequent Transpeak bus service. Visit highpeakbuses.com to find out more.

GETTING THERE BY RAIL

The Peak District is surprisingly well served by railway routes. To the east, the East Coast main line passes through Derby, Chesterfield and Sheffield, from where there are bus links to the Peak. The local Derwent Valley Line links to the main line at Derby and takes you, via Belper, to Cromford and Matlock Bath to the south of the Peak.

You are likely to share your carriage with booted and rucksack-toting walkers if you take the scenic Hope Valley Line cross-Park service between Stockport and Sheffield. Stopping at New Mills, Edale, Hope, Bamford, Hathersage and Grindleford, it's still known as the Ramblers' Route. On summer weekends, Folk Trains are organised on this line, so the strains of Ewan MacColl's 'Manchester Rambler' will often provide a musical accompaniment on your journey. The Manchester to Buxton local line also stops at Stockport, Disley, Whaley Bridge, New Mills and Chapel-en-le-Frith. For further information on any of these services and to get a timetable visit nationalrail.co.uk.

▼ Dove Dale

FESTIVALS & EVENTS

▶ FEBRUARY

Ashbourne Royal Shrovetide Football
Shrove Tuesday & Ash Wednesday
This day-long boisterous scrimmage through the barricaded streets of Ashbourne, featuring the 'Up'ards' versus the 'Down'ards' (competing teams on either side of the Henmore Brook) who attempt to score a 'goal' at either end of the town. It is thought to be the origin of the game of association football.

▶ APRIL

Peak District Walking Festival
April and May
visitpeakdistrict.com/events
Since the days of the Mass Trespass, the Peak District has always been a hotspot for walkers. The Walking Festival is held in various locations throughout the area and features over 100 events, from guided walks to evening talks.

▶ MAY

Chatsworth International Horse Trials
chatsworth.org/attractions-and-events
Competitors from all over the country and abroad attend this exciting two-day weekend event held in the landscaped parklands of Chatsworth.

The Castleton Garland Ceremony
Oak Apple Day (29 May)
visitcastleton.co.uk
This is an ancient custom which is said to herald the arrival of spring. A Garland 'King' parades through the village on horseback, completely encased in a framework pyramid of flowers, accompanied by his 'Queen'. The procession ends up at the parish church, where the garland is hoisted to the top of the tower.

Well Dressings
welldressing.com
The custom of decorating wells and springs, well dressings, are held through the month across the county. The custom was first recorded in the 18th century in the pretty estate village of Tissington.

▶ JUNE

Buxton Fair
You'll find this fair in the Market Place behind the Town Hall, coinciding with the Buxton Well Dressing and Carnival.

▶ JULY

Buxton Festival, Buxton Fringe and Buxton Literary Festival
buxtonfestival.co.uk,
buxtonfringe.org.uk
These are all held around the same time and centred on the Opera House but including other venues throughout the town.

World Toe Wrestling Championships
bentleybrookinn.co.uk/
toe-wrestling
The slightly more bizarre event is
held at the Bentley Brook Hotel at
Fenny Bentley, on the A515 north
of Ashbourne.

▶ AUGUST

Bakewell Agricultural Show
bakewellshow.org
This two-day show is an
important social event for
the farming community of the
Peak District and a feast of
equestrian, livestock, horticulture
and other events.

Chatsworth Country Fair
chatsworthcountryfair.co.uk
The fair attracts huge crowds,
with country pursuits, cookery,
shopping and crafts. The Ashover
Agricultural Show also takes
place in August.

The English National Sheepdog Trials
englishnationalsheepdogtrials.
org.uk
The top 150 English sheepdogs
and their handlers compete for a
chance to represent England at
the Annual International Trials,
held later in the year.

▶ SEPTEMBER

Longshaw Sheepdog Trials
longshawsheepdog.co.uk
Started in 1848 and said to be the
oldest in the world, the trials take
place at Longshaw Lodge, near
Grindleford, early September.

Matlock Bath Illuminations and Venetian Nights
derbyshiredales.gov.uk
September marks the start of the
illuminations, when the town is
transformed into a fairyland of
dancing riverside lights for about
six weeks.

Wirksworth Festival
wirksworthfestival.co.uk
The two-week festival includes
a contemporary visual arts
programme, as well as new,
classical and timeless music,
innovation combined with
traditional performances and
lots of surprises.

▶ OCTOBER

The Great Peak District Fair
paviliongardens.co.uk/great-
peak-district-fair
The District Fair is held in the
Pavilion Gardens at Buxton, when
locally produced food and drink
from all over the region can be
sampled. It also includes the
Buxton Beer Festival.

The Chesterfield Market Festival
Running from the end of October,
it includes a Continental-style
market and a beer festival,
featuring some of Derbyshire's
finest real ales.

▶ NOVEMBER

Chatsworth Dressed for Christmas
chatsworth.org
Beautiful traditional Christmas
decorations cover the lower floors
of the house, and daily special
events and activities take place in
the house and farmyard.

Castleton's Christmas Lights
visitcastleton.co.uk
Castleton's famous lights are
switched on in mid-November,
and Bakewell's Christmas Lights
follow soon afterwards.

▶ DECEMBER

Santa Specials
peakrail.co.uk
These are run by Peak Rail at
Matlock and various villages hold
carol concerts as the Christmas
season approaches.

CAMPSITES

For more information on these and other campsites, visit theaa.com/self-catering-and-campsites

Carsington Fields Caravan Park ▶▶▶

carsingtoncaravaning.co.uk
Millfields Lane, Nr Carsington Water, Ashbourne, DE6 3JS | 01335 372872
Open Mar–Sep
Carsington Fields is a very well-presented, spacious park with open views and a large fenced pond that attracts plenty of wildlife. The popular tourist attraction of Carsington Water is a short stroll away, with its variety of leisure facilities including fishing, sailing, windsurfing and a children's play area. The park is also a good base for walkers.

Clover Fields Touring Caravan Park ▶▶▶

cloverfieldstouringpark.co.uk
1 Heath View, Harpur Hill, Buxton, SK17 9PU | 01298 78731
Open all year
Clover Fields is a spacious adults-only park, just over a mile from Buxton, with a timber chalet-style toilet block and individual barbecues on each pitch. The site is set out on terraces with extensive views over the countryside. Swathes of natural meadow grasses and flowers cloak the terraces and surrounding fields. There's a small fishing pond and a boules area. The Teapot Café serves a good range of meals.

Greenhills Holiday Park ▶▶▶▶

greenhillsholidaypark.co.uk
Crowhill Lane, Bakewell, DE45 1PX
01629 813052
Open Feb–Nov
Greenhills is a well-established park set in lovely countryside in the Peak District National Park. Lots of pitches enjoy uninterrupted views, and there is easy accessibility to all facilities. A clubhouse, shop and children's playground are popular features.

Grouse & Claret ▶▶▶

marstonsinns.co.uk
Station Road, Rowsley, Matlock,

DE4 2EB | 01629 733233
Open all year
This well-designed, purpose-built park at the rear of an eating house on the A6 between Bakewell and Chatsworth, is adjacent to the New Peak Shopping Village. The park comprises a level grassy area down to the river, and all pitches have hardstandings, electric hook-ups and TV sockets.

Lickpenny Caravan Site ▶▶▶▶

lickpennycaravanpark.co.uk
Lickpenny Lane, Tansley, Matlock, DE4 5GF | 01629 583040
Open all year
Lickpenny apparently means 'a devourer or absorber of money', but the very reasonable prices here aren't likely to cause much in the way of money wastage. This is a picturesque site in the grounds of an old plant nursery with pitches screened by a variety of shrubs and fine views, which are best enjoyed from the upper terraced areas. The bistro/coffee shop is popular with visitors.

Lime Tree Park ▶▶▶▶

limetreeparkbuxton.com
Dukes Drive, Buxton, SK17 9RP
01298 22988 | Open Mar–Oct
Lime Tree Park is an attractive and well-designed site, set on the side of a narrow valley. There's free WiFi and good attention to detail throughout, including the clean toilets and showers. Its backdrop of a magnificent old railway viaduct and views over Buxton and the surrounding hills make this a sought-after destination.

Longnor Wood Holiday Park ▶▶▶▶▶

longnorwood.co.uk
Newtown, Longnor, SK17 0NG
01298 83648 | Open Mar–10 Jan
Enjoying a secluded and peaceful setting, Lognor Wood is a spacious adults-only park, surrounded by beautiful rolling countryside and sheltered by woodland that attracts plenty of wildlife. Expect a warm welcome from the O'Neill family and excellent, well-maintained facilities, including spotless toilets, a putting green, badminton courts, a 4-acre dog walk and dog wash, and super walks from the park gate.

Newhaven Caravan & Camping Park ▶▶▶▶

newhavencaravanpark.co.uk
Newhaven, Nr Buxton, SK17 0DT
01298 84300 | Open Mar–Oct
Newhaven is pleasantly situated in the Peak District National Park, with mature trees screening the three touring areas and good toilet facilities and a large tent field. There's also a restaurant nearby and a children's play area.

VISIT THE MUSEUMS | GET OUTDOORS | EXPLORE BY BIKE | GO BACK IN TIME | TAKE A TRAIN RIDE | MEET THE WILDLIFE
TAKE IN SOME HISTORY | HIT THE BEACH | EAT AND DRINK | GET INDUSTRIAL | VISIT THE GALLERIES | GO CANOEING
TRY HORSE-RIDING | PLACES NEARBY | CATCH A PERFORMANCE | GO ROUND THE GARDENS | TAKE A BOAT TRIP

A–Z of
The Peak District

▶ Alsop en le Dale MAP REF 274 B3

It might seem as if time has passed by the tiny hamlet of Alsop en le Dale, just five miles north of Ashbourne (see page 59). The former station on the Ashbourne–Buxton line which served this quiet, peaceful little hamlet is now a car park on the Tissington Trail (see page 251). The hamlet itself is on a narrow lane east of the main road towards Parwich, just a mile from the wonders of Dove Dale (see page 139).

Alsop en le Dale's church of St Michael is originally of Norman construction, but was substantially rebuilt by the Victorians. The nave retains some Norman features, such as the impressive double zigzag mouldings in the arches, but the west tower is imitation Norman, dating from 1883. An unusual feature is the extraordinary 19th-century square mock-Gothic pulpit, which rather dominates the small church. Opposite is the tall, slender early 17th-century building known as Alsop Hall (private), built in a pre-classical style.

▶ PLACES NEARBY

Alsop is particularly convenient for Dove Dale (see page 139), with the famous Viator's Bridge at Milldale only a mile to the west. This former packhorse bridge is the scene, in Izaak Walton's classic fisherman's tale *The Compleat Angler* (1653), of Viator's complaint to Piscator about the size of the tiny, two-arched bridge: 'Why a mouse can hardly go over it: Tis not two fingers broad.'

▶ Alstonefield MAP REF 273 E3

A candidate for the prettiest village in the Peak, the charmingly unspoilt village of Alstonefield stands two miles from the nearest classified road, at over 900 feet, between the valleys of the Dove and Manifold. It received a charter to hold a weekly market as long ago as 1308 – although don't expect to find one there now, as it had stopped by 1500. The St Peter's church was founded in Norman times, and inside is the box pew of Charles Cotton, Izaak Walton's collaborator in *The Compleat Angler.*

Today Alstonefield is popular with walkers, who love to congregate on the village green under the enormous ash tree, and seek refreshment in the ever-popular The George inn.

EAT AND DRINK

The George
thegeorgeatalstonefield.com
Alstonefield, DE6 2FX
01335 310205

A traditional, family-run pub in the hills above Dove Dale, The George is a firm favourite with walkers. The pub is small, with a bar, a snug and a dining room.

The bar has portraits of locals and historic artefacts, and there is usually a roaring open fire burning in the grate. The dining room and snug have been restored to their original simplicity with lime-plastered walls and traditional farmhouse furniture. Candlelight and fresh flowers add a touch of sophistication and elegance. The owners are passionate about the use of local food and dishes are packed with simply cooked but delicious ingredients. In the summer, the pub's pesticide-free vegetable garden provides the kitchen with fresh vegetables, salad leaves and herbs.

▶ Arbor Low MAP REF 274 B2

Often known as the 'Stonehenge of the North', the stone circle of Arbor Low, standing remote and mysterious at over 1,200 feet on the limestone plateau near Monyash (see page 231), is quieter and less well known than its more famous Wiltshire contemporary, but it is without doubt the most atmospheric and important prehistoric monument in the Peak.

Built in the late Neolithic period around 2500 BC, the monument consists of a circular earthwork or henge with two entrances, an internal ditch and a raised inner platform containing a circle of about 50 prostrate limestone slabs, radiating out from the centre like the figures on a clock. Archaeologists argued for years about whether or not the

▼ Arbor Low Stone Circle

stones were originally upright, like those of every other prehistoric stone circle. Then someone realised that each stone had a matching stump by its side, indicating that they had been pushed over at some time in their 4,000-year history. Of course, the passage of time may have caused them to fall, but, more likely, they were deliberately knocked over.

At the centre of the circle are the larger fallen stones of what is known as the cove. This, the most sacred part of the site, was made up of seven stone slabs and may have been rectangular when they were erect. Part of the mystery of Arbor Low, of course, is that no one knows what rites and ceremonies were conducted here. It is probable that only initiates would have been allowed to enter the sacred cove, their actions concealed from everyone else by the strategic placing of the banks of the henge and the large stone slabs. During excavations in the 18th century, the skeleton of a man was discovered in the cove, lying on its back and surrounded by blocks of stone. The name is a corruption of the Anglo Saxon *Eorthburg hlaw*, which simply means 'earthwork mound'.

Arbor Low has never been short of theories suggesting exactly what purpose it originally served. Some believe it may have been a giant astronomical calculator, a religious centre, a meeting place or perhaps even the focal point of an early market. It is known that by the late Neolithic period, complex trading networks had been built up throughout Britain. Polished axes originating from places as far away as North Wales, the Lake District and Northern Ireland have been discovered in the Peak, and Arbor Low may have been the trading centre for the distribution of goods like these.

Across the fields from the henge lies the Neolithic long barrow of Gib Hill, with a later round barrow built on top of it. The name Gib Hill suggests that it might once have been used for a gibbet, probably in the Middle Ages when it was common to organise executions in such places of local superstition.

In 1848, the pioneer archaeologist and so-called 'King of the Barrow Knights', Thomas Bateman of nearby Middleton by Youlgreave (see page 269), was excavating the Gib Hill barrow when the central 'cist' or burial chamber crashed down on his tunnel, destroying a food vessel and the cremated remains inside. He later removed the cist to his home at Lomberdale Hall, but it has since been returned to its original position.

▶ **PLACES NEARBY**
Parsley Hay Bike Hire Centre
Parsley Hay, SK17 0DG
01298 84493

Cycle hire with easy access to both the High Peak and Tissington Trails. Also offers tandems and wheelchair bikes.

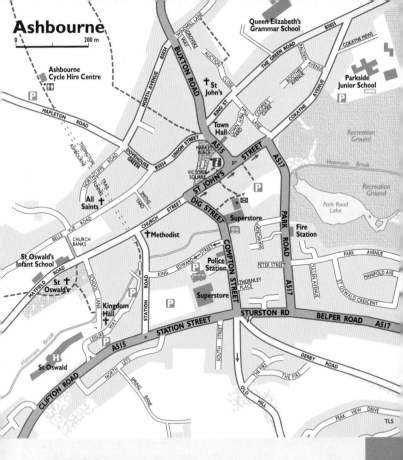

▶ Ashbourne MAP REF 274 B4

Ashbourne is everything that an English market town should be, with an eccentric street plan (made even more confusing by a hectic one-way system), narrow cobbled alleys, a stately parish church, coaching inns, almshouses and a bustling central market place. It needed very little alteration to become 'Oakbourne' in George Eliot's *Adam Bede*, and is probably the best place in the Peak District to shop for antiques – as long as you don't expect too many bargains.

Billing itself as 'The Gateway to Dove Dale', Ashbourne stands at the crossroads of Britain, where the lowland, Midland landscape of fields and hedges gives way to the hills, moors and drystone walls of the uplands of the Pennines.

Your first impression will probably be of St Oswald's parish church, with its elegant, needle-sharp spire, at 215 feet the tallest in Derbyshire, which is set some way apart from the town centre. This means that when you've parked your car, there's a walk of several hundred yards if you want to take a close look at it. It's worth it, though – by doing so, and exploring the Market Place and St John's Street on the way, you'll see the very best of this handsome market town.

Ashbourne's Market Place, opposite the Town Hall, used to be lined with alehouses and, at one time, had its own bullring close to the Wright Memorial, an elaborate piece of Victoriana. It was here that Bonnie Prince Charlie proclaimed his father, James, King of England in 1745, and this is where the famous Royal Shrovetide Football (see page 62), between the 'Upp'ards' and 'Down'ards' used to start.

Behind the Market Place is the Old Vaults pub, which used to be called The Anatomical Horse, with a skeleton for its sign. Down the narrow alley to the left is Victoria Square (once The Butchery and The Shambles) and Tiger Yard, beside a restaurant that used to be The Tiger Inn. The modern Victoria Square is a smart little suntrap, set about with benches.

Ashbourne's side streets and alleys are narrow and interesting; the layout of the old town north of the Henmore Brook dates back to the 11th and 12th centuries, and there are some fascinating nooks and crannies to explore, such as Lovatt's Yard and the House of Confinement – a former lock-up – on Bellevue Street.

However, it is along St John's Street and Church Street that the town's grandest buildings are to be found. Beyond the Clergy's Widows Almshouses are superb mansions and merchants' houses, many now serving as antique shops, culminating in the magnificent stone-gabled Grammar School, founded by Elizabeth I in 1585. And opposite, set behind tall wrought-iron gates and a carpet of daffodils in the spring, stands St Oswald's, perfectly described by George Eliot as 'the finest mere parish church in England'.

▼ Ashbourne

SEE A LOCAL CHURCH
St Oswald's Church
Mayfield Road, DE6 1AN

Claimed to be Derbyshire's finest parish church, and a contender for one of the best churches in England, St Oswald's is splendid both inside and out. The exterior is dominated by a large central tower and tall, thin, elegant spire. Much of the church dates from the 13th century, including the chancel, although the huge east window is later, but contains some medieval glass. There are examples of all the great ages of English church architecture – Early English, Decorated and Perpendicular – throughout the church, especially in the windows.

In the north transept are serried ranks of excellent monuments to the Cockayne, Bradbourne and Boothby families. Among the finest are those to Joan and Edmund Cockayne from 1404, Sir John Cockayne and his wife from 1447, and Sir Humphrey and Lady Bradbourne from 1581.

Also here is the much later memorial, in pure white Carrara marble by Thomas Banks, to Penelope Boothby, who died in 1791 aged just five. The monument shows Penelope as if asleep and is generally considered to be a masterpiece of its kind. Penelope was already celebrated when alive, having been painted by Sir Joshua Reynolds, and Queen Charlotte is said to have broken down in tears when she saw the statue at an exhibition.

VISIT THE FACTORY
Derwent Crystal
derwentcrystal.co.uk
Shawcroft, DE6 1GH
01335 345219

Derwent Crystal of Ashbourne makes lead crystal glassware by traditional, hand-crafted skills, using techniques that have changed little over the last 100 years. The firm was

▼ St Oswald's parish church

established in 1980, and initially obtained its core of skilled craftsmen from Tutbury, a Staffordshire village with a long history in glass making. The Ashbourne plant in Shaw Croft opened in 1985. Hand-made glass has an enormous appeal, and the Ashbourne plant is designed for the customer and tourist to walk around at their leisure and actually watch the beautiful glass being made.

EXPLORE BY BIKE
Ashbourne Cycle Hire Centre
Mappleton Lane, DE6 2AA
01335 343156
Cycle hire with easy access to the flat, traffic-free Tissington Trail.

TAKE OFF
Airways Airsports
airways-airsports.com
Ashbourne, DE6 2ET
01335 344308
This is the place if you fancy a spot of hang-gliding.

WATCH A MATCH
Ashbourne Football
Town centre shop fronts are boarded up and all traffic banned as Ashbourne's rumbustious Royal Shrovetide football game takes over the whole town every Shrove Tuesday and Ash Wednesday. The two teams of local lads, known as the 'Up'ards' and the 'Down'ards' – the Henmore Brook being the dividing line – fight in huge, swaying crowds to score in their opponents'

'goals', which are set three miles apart, originally at the former Sturston and Clifton Mills. A local or national celebrity is usually called upon to start proceedings by throwing the cork-filled ball of decorated leather up into the air on the Shaw Croft.

PLAY A ROUND
Ashbourne Golf Club
ashbournegolfclub.co.uk
Wyaston Road, DE6 1NB
01335 347960 (pro shop)
Open daily all year
With fine views over surrounding countryside, this is one of the oldest courses in Derbyshire and has natural contours and water features.

EAT AND DRINK
Gingerbread Shop
26 St John Street, DE6 1GH
01335 346753
When in Ashbourne, try the delicious gingerbread men made from an original recipe at this cheerful combination of tea room and bakery. The Gingerbread Shop offers remarkable cakes, tarts and, of course, gingerbread men. It is a unique example of a late 15th-century half-timbered building, and has been in continuous use as a bakery since 1805. Four different varieties of tea are served, as well as snacks, sandwiches, cakes and biscuits.

▶ **PLACES NEARBY**
Alton Towers
see highlight panel on page 64

Alton Towers Water Park

altontowers.com

Alton, ST10 4DB

More gentle activities at Alton Towers include the Water Park, which caters especially for children. The Water Park boasts hundreds of fantastic interactive water features, from lazy rivers and crazy cannons to the sensational speed of the Master Blaster water rollercoaster. And if you fancy yourself as a *Baywatch* hero, then try one of the Water Park's lifeguard courses. The park's Caribbean lagoon offers excitement for kids of all ages, and is open all year round.

Mappleton

The roof of the little church of St Mary at Mappleton comes as a bit of a shock in this land of sturdy, stone-built church towers. Dubbed 'Little St Paul's', it is crowned by an octagonal dome with a lantern. The church was built in the 18th century out of stone, but most of the older houses in the rest of this pretty little village are of the red brick of the Midlands, as opposed to the stone of the Peak.

Typical of these is the Clergymen's Widows' Almhouses, just to the west of the church. This handsome five-bay brick house of 1727 has stone dressings and a hipped roof. The centre bay projects and is framed by gigantic rusticated pilasters. The Manor House, overlooking the watermeadows of the River Dove south of the village, is another good 18th-century brick building. Across the Dove in Staffordshire is Okeover Hall, with its splendid deer park and little church at the entrance.

The Jug & Glass Inn

callowhall.co.uk

Mappleton Road, Mappleton
DE6 2AA | 01335 300900

What's not to like about this quintessentially English Victorian country house retreat in 44 acres of woodlands and gardens on the edge of the Peak District National Park, overlooking the Dove Valley and Bentley Brook? Its ivy-festooned walls enfold an old-school set up of antiques, opulent fabrics, fancy plasterwork and oak panels galore, and the vibe in the elegant dining room isn't about to rock that particular boat. The sure-footed kitchen team still does things the old way, smoking and curing meats and fish in-house and doing all of its own baking. The result is country-house cooking in the classic mould.

Wild Park Derbyshire

wildparkderbyshire.com

Middle Wild Park Farm, Brailsford,
DE6 3BN | 01335 360485

Started by husband and wife team Richard and Jenny Else as a paintballing venue 20 years ago, Wild Park Derbyshire is now claimed to be the Midlands' premier paintball, laser tag and quad bike trekking centre.

▶ Alton Towers

altontowers.com
Alton, ST10 4DB | 0871 222 3330 | Open Feb half-term 10–4, last week
Mar–1st week Nov from 10, closing time subject to change
Thrill-seekers pursuing that ultimate white-knuckle ride will head
for the excitement of Alton Towers, which claims to have a roller
coaster ride for everyone. Here you can loop, swoop, speed and
soar at terrifying speeds on rides with such frightening names as

The Blade, Nemesis and Nemesis Sub-Terra, Ripsaw, Submission and Oblivion, the world's first vertical-drop rollercoaster, and Th13teen, the world's first freefall-drop rollercoaster. A new feature at the Alton Towers Resort is CBeebies Land, based on the popular BBC TV childrens' channel. The former Gothic seat of the Earls of Shrewsbury is now far better known as one of Britain's premier theme parks.

▶ Ashford in the Water   MAP REF 274 B1

Ashford in the Water is not the Peak District Venice its name
perhaps makes it sound. Only when the River Wye – the 'water'
that Ashford's in – infrequently floods does it live up to that
intriguing name. But if you want to escape the crowds in
Bakewell (see page 71), a quiet interlude leaning over the
ancient Sheepwash Bridge in Ashford, watching the trout
glide effortlessly in the crystal-clear current, is highly
recommended. You should spot both the native brown trout,
with its spotted flanks, the star of Izaak Walton and Charles
Cotton's *Compleat Angler*, and the rainbow trout, an American
import, able to tolerate warmer and more polluted water.

Ashford itself is one of the most attractive and interesting of
the Peak District's villages, sited on a sweeping bend of the

▼ Sheepwash Bridge, Ashford in the Water

Wye, and thankfully bypassed by the busy A6 Buxton road. Many of the wonderful stone houses and cottages on the main triangle of lanes at the village centre date from the 17th and 18th centuries and there was also once a corn mill, a candle-maker and several stocking mills. This has given Ashford a distinctive character: part pretty English village, part quirky Peak District jumble of architecture.

In the middle of Ashford, the green space known as Hall Orchard was once part of the grounds of Neville Hall, a medieval hunting lodge which stood on the eastern side. The space is now a playing field but there are some tall trees, notably limes, and around the rest of the village the eponymous ash trees continue to offer shelter and shade.

A local saying is that 'Oak won't grow in Ashford', and this has proved accurate in the lime-rich soil of the village over the years.

On Church Street, between Hall Orchard and the Wye, is a 17th-century tithe barn (now a private house) and the beautiful old parish church of the Holy Trinity. Most of the structure of the church is restored Victorian but just above the porch, in its original position, is a Norman tympanum. The Normans apparently were not as expert as the Saxons at carving animals, so there is some doubt about what the stone slab depicts. It may be a tree of life with a boar on one side and a lion on the other, or it may be meant to represent the ancient Royal Forest of the Peak, with a boar and a wolf.

Henry Watson's former black marble quarry works, opened in 1784, on the northern edge of the village. Black 'marble' was in fact an impure local limestone which only turned a shiny black when polished. After the death of her beloved Prince Albert, the mourning Queen Victoria made anything black highly fashionable, and Ashford black marble was used for everything from vases to fire-surrounds. There are some fine examples in the church, and a great collection in the Buxton Museum and Art Gallery (see page 94).

Four rare but tattered 18th-century virgin 'crants', or crowns, hang in the chancel of Ashford parish church. These were funeral garlands, carried at maidens' funerals and then hung on beams or from the roof of the church. They are made of white paper attached to a wicker frame, and in the middle is a paper glove, bearing the name of the girl. The tradition of virgin crowns was once widespread across England, but rarely do any of the fragile garlands survive to tell their sad tale.

Close to the idyllic village cricket field, the bridge on the closed road carries an inscription 'M. Hyde 1664', a memorial to the unfortunate Rev Hyde, who was thrown from his horse and drowned in the river below. Upstream, on the former Portway packhorse trail, is the attractive Sheepwash Bridge. It gets its name from the stone fold on one side, which was where the sheep were held before being plunged into the river and made to swim across, washing their fleeces in the process.

EAT AND DRINK

The Ashford Arms

ashford-arms.co.uk
Church Street, Ashford in the Water
DE45 1QB | 01629 812725
The Ashford Arms is a traditional village inn dating from Napoleonic times, and eating here is a real treat. The varied menu uses plenty of local, fresh produce. Award-winning chef Robert Muxlow gained his reputation at The Tavern and Merlin's in Matlock, and maintains a warm country pub atmosphere while creating top quality, fresh food. The menu caters for everyone's

palate – from home-made, tasty savoury pies to mouth-watering à la carte dishes. Steak nights feature Robert's famous 'sizzling sauces'. You can either eat in the bar, which is a great meeting place, or enjoy the relaxed ambience of the comfortably furnished restaurant in the conservatory.

The Bull's Head

bullsheadashford.robinsonsbrewery.com

Church Street, Ashford in the Water DE45 1QB | 01629 812931

In Debbie Shaw's family for 60 years, this popular 17th-century coaching inn has an abundance of oak beams, as well as open fires, carved settles, and jazz playing quietly in the background. While they've been at this Robinson's Brewery-owned house, landlords Debbie and husband Carl have picked up a number of impressive accolades. Carl is also the chef, producing not just the meals but the breads, chutneys and even the cheese biscuits, everything in fact that might accompany or follow a meal. The new Supper Club offers a choice of seven dishes if ordered before 7pm. A snack in the attractive beer garden, followed by a game of boules, could be fun.

The Monsal Head Hotel
see page 229

Monsal View Café

Monsal Head, Ashford in the Water, DE45 1NL | 01629 640346

Overlooking magnificent Monsal Dale, this friendly, stone-floored cafe with a roaring fire in winter offers filling fare, from snacks to restaurant meals and Derbyshire cream teas.

The Riverside House Hotel

riversidehousehotel.co.uk

Fennel Street, Ashford in the Water, DE45 1QF | 01629 814275

Set beside the River Wye, the comfortable Riverside House Hotel has ambience aplenty and is the perfect spot for celebrating a special occasion. Enjoy an excellent three-course lunch or dinner, or a quick snack in the Conservatory.

▶ **PLACES NEARBY**

Southwest of Ashford, on the limestone plateau, is **Sheldon**, a small mining village, located close to the famous Magpie lead mine (see page 213). The main shaft of the mine was 728 feet deep and water had to be pumped

▼ Ashford in the Water

up to a sough, which carried it to the Wye on the curve below Great Shacklow Wood. In 1966, the roof of the sough collapsed and there was an explosion of pent-up mud and rocks, the resulting tsunami rushing into the Wye. The debris can still be seen today.

▶ Ashover MAP REF 275 D2

One writer described the Amber Valley as 'the valley of silence and wild flowers', and it's certainly a little gem of unspoilt and little-visited scenery, just to the east of the Peak. Viewed from the rocky ridge known as The Fabric (apparently so named because it provided the 'fabric' for much local building), with the upstanding monolith of Cocking Tor in the foreground, the prospect of Ashover shows a scattered village unobtrusively filling the pleasantly wooded valley.

At the centre of the village is the 15th-century All Saints church. One of its great treasures, apart from the Decorated-style windows, tower and spire, is the Norman font, made from the abundant local lead. Described by Pevsner as 'the most important Norman font in the county', it is oddly the only one made of lead in this lead-rich district. Of the many monuments in the church, especially impressive is the alabaster tomb chest of Sir Thomas Babington, who died in 1518, and his wife, which has been called 'the best in Derbyshire'. There are also brasses to James Rolleston (1507) and his wife and children, and a priest, which dates from 1510.

Next to the church is the flower-decked Crispin Inn, which claims to date from 1416, but is more likely to date from the 17th century, as do most of the other houses in the village. The name of the inn reflects one of Ashover's traditional trades, because St Crispin is the patron saint of shoemakers and cobblers.

The Ashover Show, held every August, is one of a fast-disappearing number of truly local agricultural shows. The Ashover Agricultural and Horticultural Society traces its origins back to 1924, when a meeting was held in Kelstedge to resurrect the agricultural events that had been held locally in both Ashover and Kelstedge, in the form of small village shows and ploughing matches before World War I. Some of those were recorded back into the 1880s.

The first Ashover Show was held on the Rectory Fields in September 1925, and it has continued there ever since. It became so popular that the former Ashover Light Railway ran special trains from Clay Cross, when the show was fixed to coincide with the Wakes Week Holiday.

EAT AND DRINK

The Crispin Inn
qualitypubs.co.uk/
thecrispininnashover
Church St, Ashover, S45 0AB
01246 590911

Beautifully situated in the heart of the village opposite the church, The Crispin is a Grade II listed inn and a great place to eat and drink.

▷ Bakewell   MAP REF 274 B1

If you happen to visit Bakewell on a Monday, you'll understand why it styles itself the 'Capital of the Peak' (a fiercely contested title, incidentally, also claimed by Chapel-en-le-Frith – see page 106). All roads into the town are jammed with convoys of livestock lorries, tractors and trailers as farmers from the surrounding villages bring in their animals to buy and sell at the futuristic new Agricultural Business Centre and market.

And it's not just the farmers who flood into Bakewell on a Monday. Their wives and partners also take the opportunity to come to town, to visit the street market or supermarket to stock up with food, and catch up with the neighbours they probably don't see all week. Bakewell Market has been a fixture in the social and business calendar for the population of the Peak for over 700 years – and long may it remain so. Without the weekly market, Bakewell would become just another tourist trap, like Castleton (see page 98).

▼ All Saints Church, Bakewell

With a population of 4,000, this bustling little town is the largest inside the National Park. Even in the depths of winter, it's almost always busy with visitors and local people, and its streets are never free of traffic and bustle. But if that's the price you have to pay for a town which is still a thriving, working community in addition to being a tourist hotspot, then you just have to accept it.

Bakewell was granted its market charter and a 15-day fair by Henry III as long ago as 1254, and it still exudes the atmosphere of a town twice its size and importance. There are a number of fine 17th-century buildings in the town, such as the formerly arched Old Market Hall, which now serves as the Peak District National Park Information Centre (see page 75), and the old Town Hall up the Monyash road, now, like so many Bakewell businesses, an antique shop.

The commanding parish church of All Saints lords it over the town, with outstanding views over the Wye valley. Like many Derbyshire churches, it is broad and low, but All Saints has an elegant spire as sharp as a 3H pencil. Inside you will find some fascinating fragments of Saxon and Norman stonework, and the famous monument to Sir John Manners and his wife Dorothy, who are reputed to have eloped together from Haddon Hall in 1558. The waist-high miniature monument to Sir Godfrey Foljambe and his wife is dated 1385, and is one of the oldest in the region.

▼ The River Wye in Bakewell

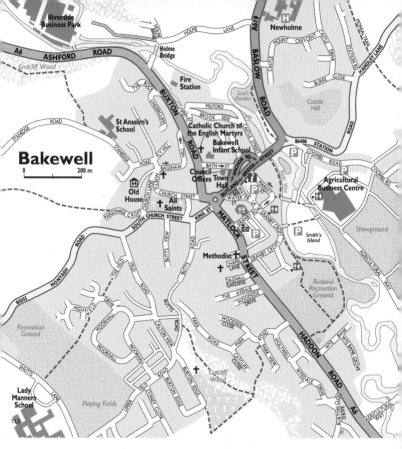

Outside in the churchyard stand the shafts of two Saxon stone preaching crosses, beautifully decorated with interlacing vine scrolls and figures, and inside the south porch is one of the finest collections of Anglo Saxon and Norman stonework in the country. Near the church is Cunningham Place and The Old House, a 16th-century building which once housed Richard Arkwright's tenants from the nearby cotton mill, and now serves as one of the best local museums in the country.

The River Wye runs like a living, flowing artery through the town, and is crossed by a venerable, five-arched 14th-century bridge, which somehow still seems able to cope with the stresses of thundering modern traffic. Watching over the bridge from the east is wooded Castle Hill, the site of a Norman motte and bailey castle and now of a high-class residential development. Upstream from the town bridge is Holme Bridge, a narrow packhorse bridge with low parapets designed to accommodate packhorse trains with their swinging panniers.

A favourite pastime for visitors to Bakewell is to feed the ducks and swans along the pleasant riverside walks, and it's always entertaining to see the trout contesting with the ducks for the breadcrumbs.

Bakewell began life as a Saxon settlement at this vitally important crossing of the Wye. King Edward the Elder established a Mercian fort, or *burh*, in AD 920 in the fields to the south of the modern town, where he received homage from various other northern kings. The original name of *Badecan wiellon* means the springs or wells of a Saxon named Badeca or Beadeca, and in the town park there is still a warm, iron-bearing spring, which may even have attracted the spa-loving Romans.

GO TO THE BAKEWELL AGRICULTURAL SHOW

The town's annual show is held at the town's idylli showground, backed by the wooded ridge of Manners Wood, and is one of the oldest agricultural shows in the UK. It is also the most important single event in the Peak's social calendar, and a meeting place for the whole of the rural community. Enjoying nearly 200 years of history, the show is held on the first Wednesday and Thursday of August, and has taken place every year (apart from the war years) since 1819. It even opened (without the animals) during the disastrous outbreak of foot-and-mouth disease in 2001. The show has evolved

▼ The Old Original Bakewell Pudding Shop

from being a purely agricultural event into the diverse and entertaining family event that it is today.

TRY A PUDDING

Ask most people what they know about Bakewell, and they'll say it's the home of the Bakewell tart – more correctly known as a pudding. The fame of the Bakewell pudding has spread so far that it is now exported all over the world, and has become a favourite British pud. According to tradition, the recipe was the result of an error that emanated from the kitchen of the Rutland Arms Hotel in around 1860. The cook, flustered by a special order to prepare a strawberry tart for some very important guests, put the jam in first, then poured in the egg mixture designed for the pastry on top. Far from being a disaster, the new invention was hailed as a culinary triumph and became a regular item on the menu.

Incidentally, don't ask for a Bakewell 'tart' – they are always known here as 'puddings', and are nothing like the Mr Kipling variety.

VISIT THE MUSEUM
Old House Museum
oldhousemuseum.org.uk
Cunningham Place, DE45 1DD
01629 813642
This originally Tudor house is so-named because it is thought to be the oldest house in Bakewell. It was used by

5 street markets

▶ **Bakewell,** page 71 (held on a Monday)

▶ **Ashbourne,** page 59 (Thursday and Saturday)

▶ **Chesterfield,** page 117 (Monday, Friday and Saturday)

▶ **Buxton,** page 88 (Tuesday and Saturday)

▶ **Chapel-en-le-Frith,** page 106 (Thursday)

Richard Arkwright to house tenants from his nearby mill and is now an award-winning local museum. It features a Victorian kitchen and changing displays of local history, toys and lace.

CHECK OUT THE VISITOR CENTRE
Bakewell Visitor Centre
peakdistrict.gov.uk/ visiting/ ic/ ic-bakewell
Old Market Hall, Bridge Street, DE45 1DS | 01629 816558
The 17th-century gritstone Old Market Hall in Bridge Street in the centre of Bakewell serves as the Peak District National Park Information Centre. It is fully accessible and ideally placed to welcome you to Bakewell and the wider Peak District as you arrive. The mezzanine floor houses a photographic gallery featuring work by local landscape photographers, and offering visitors the opportunity to experience the dramatic landscapes of the Peak District

National Park. The centre is a joint venture between the Peak District National Park Authority and Derbyshire Dales District Council.

PLAY A ROUND
Bakewell Golf Club
bakewellgolfclub.co.uk
Station Road, DE45 1GB
01629 812307
A hilly, parkland course with plenty of natural hazards, which also enjoys magnificent views across the Wye Valley.

EAT AND DRINK
The Old Original Bakewell Pudding Shop
bakewellpuddingshop.co.uk
The Square, DE45 1BT
01629 812193
Above the shop where Bakewell's famed recipe was allegedly first re-created, this comfortable tea room has exposed beams reminiscent of a medieval barn. Indulge in sandwiches and pastries, afternoon tea o a more filling meal, but don't miss out on a generous helping of Bakewell pudding. You can buy a range of baked goods from the shop, too.

Piedaniel's ⌘
piedaniels-restaurant.com
Bath Street, DE45 1BX
01629 812687
Located near Bakewell's town hall, Piedaniel's offers a warm welcome from a husband-and-wife team and bistro-style cooking that doesn't go too far down the modernist road. The stone-built half-timbered look suggests a traditional country inn, but this appealing venue has an air of contemporary chic about it, with its smartly dressed tables and the whitewashed stone walls.

▶ PLACES NEARBY
Haddon Hall
see page 165

▶ Bamford   MAP REF 278 B5

The story of Bamford, lying at the heart of the Dark Peak below the serrated crags of Bamford Edge, is inescapably linked to the nearby Ladybower Reservoir and Upper Derwent Valley Dams (see page 136).

When the Howden and Derwent Dams were built in the early years of the 20th century, the valley of the Upper Derwent was flooded and many farms submerged under the rising waters. The 1,000 or so navvies working on the project, and their families, were housed at Birchinlee, a temporary village of corrugated iron shacks which was known to locals as 'Tin Town'. Then the third and largest reservoir, the Ladybower, was built between 1935 and 1943, involving the inundation of the two villages of Derwent and Ashopton.

The dead from the church at Derwent were re-interred in the churchyard of St John the Baptist, Bamford, and the living rehoused in the purpose-built hamlet of Yorkshire Bridge, below the earthen embankment of the Ladybower Dam.

Bamford's elegant needle-spired church was designed by the famous church architect William Butterfield in 1861, and Bamford Mill, just across the road by the river, was built as a cotton mill in 1820 and later made electrical furnaces before being converted to high-class residential accommodation.

In 1943, the RAF's crack 617 Squadron, known as the Dambusters, used the Howden and Derwent reservoirs for testing Barnes Wallis's famous bouncing bombs, later used to destroy two important German dams in the heart of the Ruhr. The reservoirs were chosen because of their resemblance to those in the Ruhr valley, and the area was later used in the 1953 film starring Richard Todd and Michael Redgrave. Various anniversaries of the raid, involving flypasts by the last flying Lancaster bomber, have attracted thousands into the valley.

Bamford is also the home of one of the most famous of the Peak District sheepdog trials, held annually in spring.

GO TO THE CARNIVAL
Bamford's annual festival is a hugely popular event with locals and visitors alike. Held on a Saturday every July, the event includes a well dressing, a fell race and a parade.

TAKE OFF
Peak Airsports
peakairsports.com
Joan Lane, S33 0AW | 01246 768193
Paragliding and tandem hang-gliding over the beautiful Upper Derwent Valley.

GO FISHING
Ladybower Reservoir
01433 651254
Fly-fishing permits are available.

PLAY A ROUND
Sickleholme Golf Club
sickleholme.co.uk
Saltergate Lane, S33 0BN
01433 651306 | Open daily all year

An undulating course in the lovely Derwent Valley, with stunning scenery.

EAT AND DRINK
The Angler's Rest
anglers-rest.co.uk
Taggs Knoll, Hope Valley, S33 0BQ
01433 659317
The Angler's Rest is a unique pub, and a real hub of village life. It became the first community pub in Derbyshire in 2013 when, threatened with closure, it was purchased collectively by the community, and is now run for their benefit. The Angler's, as it is affectionately known, offers something for everyone: a traditional village pub, The Rest Café and the village Post Office, along with many other facilities including a large car park and secure bike parking. By visiting The Angler's, you are helping to sustain a community.

Yorkshire Bridge Inn

yorkshire-bridge.co.uk
Ashopton Road, S33 0AZ
01433 651361

Named after the old packhorse bridge over the River Derwent, this early 19th-century free house is only a short distance away from the Ladybower Reservoir. Inside, views from the beamed and chintz-curtained bars take in the peak of Whin Hill, making it a jolly good spot for enjoying a pint of the unique Bombs Gone, specially brewed for the inn at the Bradfield Brewery, and good-quality pub food made with fresh local produce. Sandwiches are all freshly prepared with hot and cold fillings. A rousing beer and cider festival is held in mid-May.

▶ PLACES NEARBY

Across the A57 from Bamford, the visitor centre at Fairholmes (see page 138), below the wall of the Derwent Dam, tells the story of the drowned villages of Derwent and Ashopton, the Dambusters and the rest of the popular valley.

▶ Baslow MAP REF 278 C6

The 18th-century turnpike road from Sheffield crossed the River Derwent next to St Anne's parish church in the oldest part of Baslow, which is called Bridge End. A modern bridge now spans the river a short distance to the south, making it possible to enjoy the 17th-century triple-arched bridge and take a closer look at the little toll house (the doorway is just 3.5 feet high) which guards it.

Further along the lane on the west bank of the river stands Bubnell Hall, which is as old as the bridge, while on the east bank, above the main road, Baslow Hall, an early 20th-century copy, has been converted into a luxury hotel.

On the far side of Baslow is **Nether End**, almost a village in itself, gathered around its own little Goose Green and with a row of pretty thatched cottages, which overlook the Bar Brook. Thatched cottages are now rare in the area, although 'black thatch' (heather or turf) may once have been more widespread. Nether End marks the northern entrance to the Chatsworth estate (see page 109), and there is a touch of sophisticated comfort about everything; this applies equally to the nearby Cavendish Hotel, which contains some fine antiques from 'the Big House'.

Further east along the Sheffield road, the Bar Brook cuts a nick in the dramatic gritstone scarp, with **Baslow Edge** on one side and **Birchen Edge** on the other. A sea of bracken laps the footings of the rock faces, while the moorland above the edge is a lonely wilderness of heather, the home of merlin and grouse.

In the Bronze Age, when the climate was a little kinder, it was the home of farmers too. It is astonishing to find field systems still visible from more than 3,000 years ago. Below Baslow Bar, just out of Nether End, it is also possible to see narrow fields separated by drystone walls that follow the old reversed-S pattern, the sign of ox-ploughing in medieval times.

EAT AND DRINK
Cavendish Hotel ⊚⊚
cavendish-hotel.net
Church Lane, DE45 1SP
01246 582311

On the Chatsworth estate, the Cavendish Hotel is a supremely civilised place to stay and eat. There's been an inn on this spot for a good while (even local historians aren't sure when it first opened its doors, but it was a long time ago), and today's incarnation has plenty of period charm. It's been done out extremely tastefully by the Duke and Duchess, with lots of antiques and original paintings. The Gallery is a traditional, elegant dining room, with smartly laid tables and great service. Expect ambitious, creative food based on good local ingredients.

▼ Baslow Edge

Fischer's Baslow Hall ⊛⊛⊛
fischers-baslowhall.co.uk
Calver Road, DE45 1RR
01246 583259

Reaching the 25-year landmark here in 2013, Max and Susan Fischer have turned this Edwardian country house into a restaurant with rooms of the highest order. It is special. Even driving down the winding tree-lined driveway lowers the blood-pressure, and it falls lower still when the house, built in the style of a 17th-century manor, comes into view. The garden is a joy to behold and even pays its dues by contributing vegetables, fruits and herbs for the table. Inside, it's a class act, too, with a soothingly traditional demeanour, plenty of period character, and everything from paintings to furniture chosen with a keen eye. The team in the kitchen – headed up by Rupert Rowley – has really put Fischer's on the map: this is a kitchen that really does embrace the new, respect the old, and put the ingredients centre stage. There's craft, balance and intelligence to the food here. The 'Classic Menu' is supported by a 'Taste of Britain' tasting menu that puts first-class seasonal, regional ingredients to the fore, and the vegetarian menu delivers punchy, enticing flavours, too.

▸ Beeley MAP REF 274 C1

The over-reaching influence of nearby Chatsworth (see page 109) can be felt everywhere you go in Beeley. For over two centuries it has been an estate village belonging to successive Dukes of Devonshire, part of the wider Chatsworth estate which also included the villages of Edensor (see page 147) and Pilsley (see page 113), as well as numerous farms. Latterly, many of the properties at Beeley have been sold off, but the handsome village pub, inevitably called The Devonshire Arms, has now been brought back into the Duke's control. It was formerly three separate cottages, knocked together in 1747, and Edward VII and Charles Dickens are both said to have stayed there.

Nearly all the buildings are constructed from a honey-coloured gritstone, giving Beeley a picturesque and harmonious feel, more like the Cotswolds than Derbyshire. A tannery once stood beside the brook, and there was an estate-built school and a barn to house the coal wagons that supplied the Chatsworth estate glasshouses with fuel.

There has been relatively little modern development in and around the village, which is probably due to 250 years or so of ducal ownership; and it also helps that the main road effectively bypasses the village, leaving the streets relatively quiet and traffic-free. Many current and former Chatsworth employees still live in Beeley.

Beeley Moor is an intriguing place, little-visited compared to the better-known moors further north, which is surprising given its proximity to Chatsworth. But that doesn't mean that there's nothing to see. If you walk beyond the plantations of Hell Bank towards the top of Beeley Brook and out on to Harland Edge you'll come to Hob Hurst's House, a Bronze Age burial mound, square in shape rather than the usual round.

GET OUTDOORS

Of all the heather moorland in the Peak, the expanse above Beeley is one of the best for wildlife. This is partly due to its isolation and lack of access, but now it is possible to explore several of its finest areas without damaging the most sensitive ecological sites. You don't have to walk very far to find the wildlife as the roadside walls are one of the best places to look. Lichen-coloured moths, such as the grey chi and glaucous shears, sit on the stone walls, while the full-grown caterpillars of emperor and northern eggar moths like to sun themselves on the tops of bilberry and heather clumps.

TAKE YOUR PICK

Purple bird droppings on moorland walls are a sign that it is bilberry time. Bilberry (blaeberry in Scotland and blueberry in America) grows on the drier slopes and along the road verges of places like Beeley Moor. The small, bell-shaped flowers give way to glorious dark purple berries in July and despite being rather inconspicuous, the fruit bushes are quickly stripped by grouse, foxes and other wild animals. But just 30 minutes of gathering should produce enough fruit for a small pie, and the taste really is delicious.

EAT AND DRINK

The Devonshire Arms at Beeley ◉
devonshirebeeley.co.uk
Devonshire Square, DE4 2NR
01629 733259

This handsome, 18th-century former coaching inn often welcomed Charles Dickens and, so rumour has it, King Edward VII often entertained his mistress, Alice Keppel, here. The original part of the inn is much the same as they would remember it, with low-beamed ceilings, wooden settles, flagstone floors and open fires in winter. Far more 21st century are the floor-to-ceiling windows in the bright, stripey-chaired Brasserie, which overlooks a brook and the village square, while up a few steps in the Malt Vault is the 'big table', ideal for family get-togethers. The modern British dishes are noteworthy for their focus on superb local produce.

▶ Birchover MAP REF 274 C2

The main street of Birchover climbs gently up from the weird outcrops of Rowtor Rocks, at the foot of the village behind the Druid Inn, towards the heights of neighbouring Stanton Moor. The name accurately describes this hillside village, and means the 'birch-covered steep slope'.

Birchover was the home of father and son JC and JP Heathcote, who systematically investigated the monuments and barrows on nearby Stanton Moor (see page 242) and kept a fascinating private museum in the old village post office in the main street. The extensive Heathcote collection is now in Sheffield's Weston Park Museum.

Outside Birchover, the nearby **Rowtor Rocks** are said to have been used for Druidical rites. Whether they were or not is open to question, but the village vicar, the Rev Thomas Eyre, who died in 1717, was certainly fascinated by them. It was he who built the strange collection of steps, rooms and seats which have been carved out of the gritstone rocks on the summit of the outcrop. It is said that he took his friends there to admire the view across the valley below – a view now sadly obscured by trees. More recently, prehistoric cup-and-ring marks have been discovered carved into the rocks, which also once boasted a 50-ton rocking stone, balanced on a sandstone pivot.

Thomas Eyre lived at the Old Vicarage in the village below the rocks and built the charming little church known as the Jesus or Rowtor Chapel beneath the rocks. The chapel had been demoted to the village cheese store before Eyre's restoration, and it now features, among fragments of Norman work, strange carvings and decorations, including modern stained glass by Brian Clarke, the internationally famous artist who lived at the Vicarage for a time in the 1970s.

EAT AND DRINK

The Druid Inn
druidinnbirchover.co.uk
Main Street, DE4 2BL
01629 653836
A gastro pub with four dining areas, all housed in a 17th-century building. The daily menu is set out on blackboards.

▶ PLACES NEARBY

Robin Hood and the Hermit
Nearby are the strange water-eroded outcrops of **Robin Hood's Stride** (also known as Mock Beggar's Hall from its resemblance, in certain lights, to a ruined mansion) and Cratcliff Tor, at the foot of which a medieval Hermit's Cave, complete with crucifix, can still be found hidden behind a venerable yew. The atmospheric remains of Nine Stones Close stone circle can be seen from Robin Hood's Stride, which itself once appeared in *The Princess Bride*.

▶ Bleaklow MAP REF 277 E3

There are no drifting sand dunes under a broiling sun to be found here but, nonetheless, Bleaklow – at 2,060 feet (628m), the second-highest summit in the Peak – has been called one of Britain's only true deserts. It is a vast expanse of virtually featureless moorland, where the dunes are the chocolate-brown banks of bare peat, known here as hags, and deep drainage channels, which are known as groughs (pronounced 'gruffs').

The celebrated fell-wanderer Alfred Wainwright didn't much like it here when he visited back in the 1960s: in his *Pennine Way Companion* (1968), he complained, 'Nobody loves Bleaklow. All who get on it are glad to get off.' But this is seriously underselling this unique landscape, which at the time was going through a difficult period in its long history – as the rambler-botanist John Hillaby described, it was an example of 'land at the end of its tether'. And in his *Journey through Britain* (1968), he wrote: 'All the life has been drained off or burnt out, leaving behind only the acid peat.' Nothing could be found like it anywhere else in Europe, he claimed.

Thanks to enlightened management by owners like the National Trust, and moorland restoration projects by the Moors for the Future Partnership, things are changing now though, and Bleaklow is enjoying something of a green revival. A 14-mile fence enclosing nine square miles around the summit plateau was erected in 2003 by what was then known as English Nature (now Natural England). Erected to keep sheep, not people, out, the results have been astonishing.

In summer, drifts of the waving cotton-wool fruiting heads of cotton grass now cover the once-bare moorland, and the rare cloudberries – a sort of upland raspberry – and, most importantly, the peat-forming sphagnum mosses have all returned. It's a conservation success story unmatched elsewhere in Britain's shrinking peat moorlands, which are an important store of carbon and as internationally rare as the Amazonian rainforest.

The more dramatic side of Bleaklow is the extraordinary outcrops of weathered gritstone, here known as tors. Probably most famous are the Wain Stones, otherwise known as the Kissing Stones, on Bleaklow's summit. Viewed from a certain angle, and with a little stretch of the imagination, these twin stones look like a couple about to kiss. Bleaklow Stones, the pockmarked Grinah Stones, and lofty Higher Shelf Stones on the western scarp are all dramatic natural sculptures created by aeons of snow, frost, wind and rain, and vitally important landmarks to the dedicated Bleaklow bogtrotter.

Bonsall MAP REF 274 C3

Bonsall is a charming former lead-mining village that clusters around a ball-topped 17th-century cross, encircled by 13 gritstone steps, in the steeply sloping market square. Set in a steep-sided dale beneath Masson Hill, Bonsall was famous as a mining centre, and many of the fields and meadows around are still littered with the remains of 't'owd man's' work.

Beside the cross stands The King's Head Inn, which dates from 1677 and is said to be haunted. The other pubs in the village reflect the traditional occupations of its residents: the Pig of Lead and the Barley Mow. Above the village centre stands the battlemented church of St James, with its distinguished Perpendicular pinnacled tower and spire. Most of the church was built in the 13th century, and a beautiful clerestory lights the nave.

The delightfully wooded road up from Cromford (see page 126) is known as the Via Gellia, but it is not Roman as many people suspect. It was named after the Gell family of nearby Hopton by Philip Gell, who first built the road in the 1790s to carry lead and stone from his mines and quarries to the Cromford Canal. The name was later adapted to 'Viyella' by the owners of the former Hollin Mill when they invented a new brand of hosiery.

▼ Market Cross, Bonsall

GO ROUND THE GARDENS
Cascades Gardens
derbyshiregarden.com
DE4 2AH | 01629 822813
Open mid-Apr to Sep Wed, Sat, Sun
& BHs 10–5 and by arrangement
A beautiful 4-acre public garden
surrounding the ruins of an old
corn mill. There's a wide variety
of plants, including a great
range of perennials.

EAT AND DRINK
The Barley Mow
barleymowbonsall.co.uk
The Dale, DE4 2AY | 01629 825685
The friendly landlord tells
tales of UFOs, ghosts and
ghouls at this old village pub,
with its warm winter fires,
grand, home-cooked food,
locally brewed beers and an
unspoiled interior.

▸ Bradwell   MAP REF 278 B5

Bradwell – often abbreviated (in the way of many Peak District
villages) to 'Bradder' – is a charming little limestone village
sheltering under the glider-haunted escarpment of Bradwell
Edge. Yet again, it owes its fortune to the lead mining industry
of the 18th and 19th century, when it was at the centre of a rich
mining area.

Most Peak District lead miners also wore a Bradwell
product. The hard, black, brimmed hat into which they stuck
the candles to light their way underground were universally
known as 'Bradder beavers', and were allegedly the model
for World War I soldiers' helmets. Another Bradwell claim to
fame is that it was the birthplace in 1815 of Samuel Fox, the
inventor of the folding-frame umbrella – a useful accessory in
the often damp climate of the Peak. Bradwell has also made
cotton goods, telescopes and spectacles during its long
industrial past.

The village's long and fascinating history goes back at
least as far as the Romans, who, during the first century AD
built the small, playing card-shaped fort known as Navio on
the banks of the River Noe north of the village, probably to
defend their lead mining interests in the area. There is a
persistent local legend, originating from Castleton, that the
people of Bradwell were Roman slaves, and this may be a
long-held folk memory of the civilian *vicus* which once existed
outside the walls of Navio.

During the troubled period after the Romans left the region,
the mysterious Grey Ditch – a broad fortification north of the
village – was built, perhaps to defend Bradford Dale and
the village against the Hope Valley. But no one really knows
why it was built or by whom. Another local legend is that
Bradwell was the scene of a Dark Age battle after which the
Saxon King Edwin was murdered by being hung from a tree.

The local place name of 'Eden Tree' is said to get its name from the mysterious events that happened in this spot.

A mile south of the village at the head of the rock-rimmed Bradwell Dale is Hazelbadge Hall, a lovely old stone-built manor house which dates from 1549 and which was part of the dowry which Dorothy Vernon of Haddon Hall (see page 165) gave to her new husband, John Manners.

TAKE OFF

Derbyshire Flying Centre

d-f-c.co.uk

S32 5QD | 0776 2729663

The Peak District is reckoned to be one of the best places in the country to learn to paraglide and hang-glide, with its unpredictable weather producing highly skilled and knowledgeable pilots. The Derbyshire Flying Centre takes you through the BHPA qualifications and opens up new horizons for you to share the ability to fly as free as a bird. It is open year round for all courses and lessons. The DFC was established in 1987, and holds the BHPA Merit Award.

EAT AND DRINK

The Samuel Fox
Country Inn ◉◉

samuelfox.co.uk

Stretfield Road, S33 9JT

01433 621562

If you've had cause to put up a folding umbrella during your time here in the wild hills of the Peak District, say a word of thanks to Samuel Fox, the local man who invented the device. The old village boozer that bears his name has been revamped to good effect in recent years in a fresh, modern style, with an airy open-plan layout and lovely views of the Hope Valley through the windows. The kitchen sources the best materials it can lay its hands on and takes a creative modern approach that has firmly established the place on the local foodie scene. Dishes score highly on their unfussy attitude and full-on flavours – it is pub food that's full of generous, hearty appeal.

▸ **PLACES NEARBY**

Abney

Nearby Abney's fortunes are all about its altitude. The frequent strong winds experienced here, high on the gritstone moors, created the draught needed for smelting the precious lead ore, and Abney's situation made it well placed to become a leading lead smelting centre in the 18th and 19th centuries. The lead was obtained from the nearby White Peak limestone plateau.

Abney and its associated hamlet of Abney Grange are still airy, isolated settlements, guarding the upper reaches of the Highlow Brook. First recorded as *Habenai* in the Domesday Book, Abney was owned by William Peverel, the bastard son of the Conqueror, who built Peveril Castle at nearby Castleton. One of Abney's most famous sons was William Newton, the so-called 'Minstrel of the Peak', who was born here in 1750. A carpenter by trade, Newton became a popular and accomplished poet.

The delightfully contradictory Highlow Hall, to the east, is a fine, battlemented 16th-century manor house built by the Eyre family, with a ball-topped gateway and stone dovecote.

▶ Brassington   MAP REF 274 C3

Evidence of 't'owd man' – the local name for the former lead miners – is found everywhere in and around Brassington. The hill-top village boasts some fine 18th-century stone-built cottages and lies in the heart of lead mining country, and the landscape all around is littered with the remains left by the miners. The bumps and hollows in the green meadows tell of 200 years of underground industry in pursuit of the precious galena – or lead ore – but they now flower with lead-tolerant flowers such as mountain pansy, spring sandwort and orchids.

The oldest 'resident' of Brassington is the relief carving high on the west wall on the inside of the Norman tower of St James' church. It depicts a naked man with one hand over his heart. The carving may be Saxon in date, but most of the rest of the church is Norman, with a fine south arcade and Perpendicular windows, heavily restored by the Victorians. Nearby is the Wesleyan Reform Chapel, one of the so-called 'Smedley Chapels' built in 1852 by the local millowner, Mr Smedley, a keen Revivalist. Of the two other chapels in the village, one now serves as the village hall and the other is a private house.

EAT AND DRINK

Ye Olde Gate Inn

oldgateinnbrassington.co.uk

Well Street, DE4 4HJ

01629 540448

Sitting beside an old London-to-Manchester turnpike in the heart of Brassington, this venerable inn dates back to 1616. It's a tremendous old pub – haunted of course – with low, dark beams (reputedly salvaged from an Armada ship), old blackened ranges, quarry-tile floors, old settles and pews and a superbly atmospheric snug. There's also grand local fodder and several real ales to enjoy.

▶ PLACES NEARBY

Rainster and **Harborough Rocks** are pockmarked and heat-affected brownish dolomitic limestones, in whose caves and crevices have been found evidence of prehistoric man.

▶ Buxton MAP REF 277 D6

If only it had a kinder climate and had been a few feet lower in altitude, Buxton might have been a spa to rival Bath or Cheltenham. But the 18th-century dream of the fifth Duke of Devonshire to create a grand northern spa was never fully realised, and Buxton today carries an air of faded elegance and an aura of what might have been.

Having said that, as you drop down from the high moors to the west into the bustling town, you can find yourself blinking in disbelief as you emerge from the surrounding wilderness into tree-covered parks, gardens and grand, Palladian-style buildings.

As usual, it was the Romans, with their passion for bathing, who first established a watering place here in the days of Agricola at their spa of *Aqua Arnemetiae* – which has been translated as 'the spa of the goddess of the grove'. They discovered the natural warm springs of pale blue, slightly effervescent waters which emerged from the limestone rocks in eight thermal springs at a constant temperature of 82° Fahrenheit.

▼ Buxton

Buxton

The Palace Hotel

St Thomas More School

Superstore

University of Derby (Buxton Campus)

BUXTON STATION

STATION ROAD

Cavendish Arcade

The Springs

St John the Baptist

Old Hall Hotel

The Pump Room

St Ann's Well

Buxton Opera House and Pavilion Arts Centre

Buxton Miniature Railway

Town Hall

St Annes RC

Buxton Infant School

Police Station

Courts

Pavilion Gardens

The Slopes

Buxton Museum & Art Gallery

Football Ground

Mill Cliff

St Anne's

St Mary the Virgin

Buxton Community

Cote Heath Park

Council Offices

Buxton Community School

TLS

Superstore

BAKEWELL RD

DUKE'S DRIVE

0   200 m

▲ The Pavilion Gardens

Later, the apparently miraculous health-giving properties of the waters made them extremely popular with pilgrims, to the extent that Henry VIII ordered them to be closed. One of the most famous personalities who came to Buxton to 'take the waters' was the imprisoned Mary, Queen of Scots, who allegedly left a message scratched onto the glass of a window in what is now the Old Hall Hotel.

By the 18th century, Buxton was set firmly on the then-fashionable spa trail. The fifth Duke of Devonshire of nearby Chatsworth (see page 109) was responsible for the main wave of new building at Buxton – impressed in the 1770s by the Royal Crescent at Bath, he had money to spend in Buxton thanks to the enormous profits he made from his successful Ecton copper mines in the Manifold Valley (see page 217).

The elegant, sweeping semicircle of The Crescent, designed by John Carr of York, was built in 1784 and was originally three hotels, complete with 42 Doric pilasters and 378 windows. The Great Stables and Riding School, with its central court and Tuscan columns, followed in 1790 to cater for the visitors' horses.

▲ Buxton Opera House

In the 19th century, the sixth and seventh Dukes of Devonshire continued the work, so that by late Victorian times the spa in the valley had completely eclipsed the old market town, centred on the market place on the slope above. The Great Stables became the Devonshire Hospital, 'for the use of the sick poor', and was given a massive domed roof 156 feet across. At the time, it was the largest unsupported dome in the world, and now forms part of the University of Derby. Elegant terraces of hotels, such as The Palace, and many more modest guest houses sprang up to cater for the influx of visitors to the Thermal and Natural Baths.

The coming of the railway in 1863 marked the zenith of Buxton's popularity, and in 1871, the beautiful Pavilion Gardens and Serpentine Walk were laid out on the banks of the Wye. In 1905 the magnificently baroque gilded Opera House opened, designed by Frank Matcham and home now to the Buxton Festival.

Perhaps the best way to soak up the town's authentic atmosphere is to park at the marketplace in the old town (it vies with Alston in Cumbria in its claim to be the highest

▲ Baroque gilded Opera House

in England) and walk past the town hall, down a path across the grassy dome called The Slopes towards The Crescent. Opposite The Crescent is the famous twin-domed old Pump Room, where smart visitors once took their prescribed mineral waters. It is currently under long-term redevelopment plans.

Nearby stands a modest fountain known as St Ann's Well, one of the original Wonders of the Peak (see page 34) and which is still the source of the famous waters and of Buxton's continued prosperity.

Local people still queue up at St Ann's Well to fill plastic containers with the tepid water, claiming it makes the best tea in Britain. If you are feeling brave enough, try it straight from the well. It was good enough for Mary, Queen of Scots, after all, and it was this tepid water that brought the Romans to Buxton in the first place.

Few places in England evoke such a comfortable, Georgian sense of town and country as Buxton does. An abundance of shopping arcades and visitors keep the streets lively and local businesses thriving. Weekly markets and a programme of seasonal events ensures there's always something to enjoy when visiting the town.

▶ **Pavilion Gardens** MAP REF 277 D6

paviliongardens.co.uk
St John's Road, SK17 6BE | 01298 23114 | Open daily 9.30–5

A natural focal point forming a significant part of the Victorian splendour of Buxton, the 23-acre Pavilion Gardens are in the very heart of the town. The main building, built in 1871 by Edward Milner, pupil of Sir Joseph Paxton, contains The Pavilion Gift Boutique, which incorporates the Tourist Information Centre and The Gallery in the Gardens, home of the High Peak Artists and Craft Workers' Association.

In addition to the extensive conference and exhibition facilities, a restaurant, cafe and the Buxton Swimming and Fitness Centre, the beautiful gardens include lakes, flower beds and shaded walks. There is an extensive children's play park, an adventure playground, outdoor gym equipment and a miniature railway. The Pavilion Arts Centre, Buxton's newest theatre venue, can be reached through the Pavilion Gardens.

▼ Pavilion Gardens Conservatory

VISIT THE MUSEUM
Buxton Museum and Art Gallery
derbyshire.gov.uk
Peak Buildings, Terrace Road,
SK17 6DA | 01629 533540
Open Tue–Fri 9.30–5.30, Sat 9.30–5,
also Easter–Sep Sun and bank
holidays 10.30–5

An excellent local museum and art gallery, featuring the award-winning Wonders of the Peak gallery. You time-travel through seven time zones to return to when there were sharks, hippopotamuses and rhinoceroses, bears and hyenas roaming the Peak District.

As well as discovering the geology, archaeology and history of the Peak and admiring the museum's fine collection of Ashford black marble and Blue John ornaments, you can see the re-created study of the Victorian antiquarian William Boyd Dawkins (1837–1929).

The museum also hosts a variety of exhibitions of art, craft, photography and local history throughout the year, and has a busy programme of events and workshops. The shop stocks fascinating fossils, colourful minerals and gifts made from decorative stones.

GO ROUND THE GARDENS
Pavilion Gardens
see highlight panel on page 93

GET OUTDOORS
Poole's Cavern & Buxton Country Park
see highlight panel on page 96

WALK THE HIGH ROPES
Go Ape! Buxton
goape.co.uk/buxton
Poole's Cavern, Green Lane,
SK17 9DH | 0333 331 7158
See website for availability
(pre-booking advised)

Go Ape! is all about getting out in the open, having fun and being adventurous. You are kitted out with harnesses, pulleys and karabiners, given a 30-minute safety briefing and training before being let loose into the forest canopy, free to swing on a high wire through the trees.

SADDLE UP
Buxton Riding Centre
fernfarmcottages.co.uk
Fern Farm, SK17 9NP
01298 72319
Explore on horseback.

PLAY A ROUND
Buxton & High Peak Golf Club
bhpgc.co.uk
Buxton, SK17 7EN | 01298 26263
Open daily all year

This bracing, well-drained meadowland course is the highest in Derbyshire. This is a challenging but extremely enjoyable course.

Cavendish Golf Club
cavendishgolfcourse.com
Watford Road, SK17 6XF
01298 79708 | Open Mon–Fri,
Sun all year

This parkland and moorland course with its comfortable clubhouse lies below rising hills. Generally open to the prevailing west wind, it is noted for its excellent surfaced greens which contain many deceptive subtleties. Designed by Dr Alister MacKenzie, the course has skilfully managed to preserve the character of his original design.

EAT AND DRINK
BEST WESTERN
Lee Wood Hotel ⊛
leewoodhotel.co.uk
The Park, SK17 6TQ | 01298 23002
Refurbished style exudes from every pore of Lee Wood, a Georgian grey, stone manor house. Dining goes on in an expansive conservatory room with fronds of hanging foliage overhead and refreshing views of the grounds all about. The young service team runs the show with admirable efficiency, delivering modern brasserie cooking that scores some hits and a tempting array of desserts.

▶ PLACES NEARBY
The Goyt Valley (see page 156), just to the west of Buxton, is a very popular place for walking. Two reservoirs, the Errwood and the Fernilee, flood the valley to provide clean, fresh water to nearby Stockport, while the surrounding moors are as bleak and challenging as any found in the Peak. The area was once ruled by the wealthy Grimshaw family, whose palatial Italianate home of Errwood Hall was demolished when the Errwood Reservoir was constructed in 1938, and only the romantic ruins remain.

▼ Waterfall at the Pavilion Gardens

▶ Poole's Cavern & Buxton Country Park MAP REF 277 D6

poolescavern.co.uk

Green Lane, SK17 9DH | 01298 26978 | Open daily 9.30–5, tours leave every 20 mins, last tour begins at 4.30

Limestone rock, water and millions of years created this natural cavern containing thousands of crystal formations. A 45-minute guided tour leads the visitor through chambers used as a shelter by Bronze Age cave dwellers and Roman metal workers, as well as a hideout by the infamous robber Poole. Attractions include the underground source of the River Wye, the Poached Egg Chamber, Mary, Queen of Scots Pillar (she was an early visitor), the Grand Cascade and underground sculpture formations. Set in 100 acres of woodland, Buxton Country Park has leafy trails to the Grinlow viewpoint and panoramic Peakland scenery.

▶ Calver MAP REF 278 C6

Calver (pronounced 'Carver'), on the west bank of the River Derwent, achieved national fame when its Napoleonic cotton mill appeared in the popular 1970s BBC TV series *Colditz*, standing in for the grim Saxony castle which served as a prisoner of war camp during World War II.

Calver Mill is a magnificent, six-storeyed structure built in 1805 to replace the original building built by Richard Arkwright in 1785 but destroyed by fire. It once employed 200 people. Internally it has cast-iron pillars holding up the floors, which were originally of wood. There is a preserved wheel house from the original mill. Cotton was produced here until 1923, when the mill was bought by a Sheffield company which specialised in stainless steel products. The mill has now been converted to high-class residential apartments.

Calver lies on the River Derwent in the lee of the limestone White Peak. A bridge built in the 18th century links Calver with Curbar (see page 133), but this is bypassed by a crossing just downstream.

Calver Sough and the former Calver Sough Mine are at the northern end of the village, and recall the days when lead mining was such an important plank of the local economy. (A 'sough' – pronounced 'suff' – is an underground canal constructed to take water away from lead mines.)

VISIT THE GALLERY
Derbyshire Craft Centre
derbyshirecraftcentre.co.uk
Calver Bridge, S32 3XA
01433 631231
On the A623 between Baslow and Stoney Middleton, the Centre has a well-stocked shop, gallery and restaurant. Founded by local bookshop owner David McPhee, it is a popular attraction for visitors, and offers a wide range of goods, many produced by local craftspeople and artists.

▶ Carsington Water MAP REF 274 C3

New reservoirs usually take years to blend with their landscapes, and sometimes they just never do. But the still waters of the 741-acre Carsington Reservoir, opened by HRH the Queen in 1992, somehow look completely at home in the gently rolling hills southwest of Wirksworth.

Most of the Peak District's 50 reservoirs gather their water from acid-rich moorland, so they are low in nutrients, and this in turn means they are poor for aquatic plants and animals. However, Carsington is quite different: it is filled largely by water pumped from rivers and so makes an excellent home for wildlife. In the winter there are wildfowl by the thousand, including wigeon, pochard and tufted duck; in the summer there are great crested grebes and dabchicks; and in the spring and autumn, at migration time, all sorts of waders and seabirds use the reservoir as a rest and refuelling stop.

One of Carsington Water's most controversial residents is the American ruddy duck. Just 50 years ago this little duck, with its big blue bill, white cheeks, reddish back and stiff, upright tail, was quite unknown outside Wildfowl Trust reserves. But it escaped and is now so widespread that it is threatening to overrun Europe, diluting the genes of its close relative, the European white-headed duck, in the process.

A third of the Carsington shore is set aside as a conservation area, but the rest is accessible by footpath, bicycle and horse. The main Visitor Centre is on the west shore, with an extensive car park off the B5035. Here you can hire a bike or a boat, go fishing, or just enjoy the walk around the shores of the reservoir.

GET ACTIVE
Carsington Water
stwater.co.uk
01629 540696
You can hire a boat, go fly-fishing or take part in a range of water sports at this reservoir. Land lovers can hire a bike or enjoy a walk from the Carsington Water Visitor Centre, which also features fascinating exhibitions.

▶ Castleton MAP REF 277 E5

Castles and caves seem to cast a potent spell, and Castleton, which has both, can sometimes suffer from a surfeit of tourists. But there is so much of interest in this busy little village at the head of the Hope Valley that it is impossible not to be drawn to it, or at least to use it as a base from which to explore this fascinating landscape at the boundary of the White and Dark Peaks.

The curtain of high hills which encloses the head of the valley rises to 1,695 feet (517m) at Mam Tor (see page 214), two miles northwest of the village. Unstable bands of shale and gritstone on the heavily landslipped east face of the hill give it the local name of 'the Shivering Mountain'. The whole hillside is gradually slumping down into the valley, taking the former main road to Chapel-en-le-Frith with it.

The road was once the most expensive to maintain in Derbyshire, and was finally closed in 1979. The steep road

▶ Winnats Pass, near Castleton

through the Winnats Pass took its place. The crumbling road under Mam Tor looks like it has been struck by an earthquake, and now draws as many sightseers as the more conventional tourist attractions in the area. The name Mam Tor is very old, and probably means 'mother mountain'.

Mining for lead ore was a major industry in the Castleton area for the best part of 2,000 years, and it has left its scars. Grassy mounds and tree-lined ditches hide old spoil heaps and rakes or veins, and at Odin Mine, in the shadow of Mam Tor, is one of the oldest lead mines in the Peak. Across the now-closed road is a stone circle and wheel used to crush the lead ore.

Many of the spoil heaps were reworked for other minerals, such as fluorspar and blende, and natural limestone caves were enlarged. The area west of Castleton, known as Treak Cliff, and up the winding road to the Winnats Pass, is famous for its Blue John, a rare deep purple to yellow semi-precious form of fluorspar.

Castleton's caverns – Treak Cliff, Speedwell, Peak and Blue John – are all open to the public, and offer exciting glimpses into the Peak's underworld. Of these, Treak Cliff, a former lead mine, probably has the finest formations and is rich in veins of Blue John, which is still worked on site, while the Speedwell Mine is different because the main chambers, including the so-called 'Bottomless Pit', can only be reached by boat, floating along an underground canal. Peak Cavern, in the centre of Castleton (which recently reverted to its old, more

▲ Castleton

robust, name of the Devil's Arse), is set into Castle Hill and has what is claimed to be the largest natural cave entrance in Britain. A mighty 100 feet across and 50 feet high, the cave entrance was once home to a community of rope-makers that, it is claimed, never saw the sun. Rope-making demonstrations are still held in the vast entrance.

Castleton owes its name and very existence to Peveril Castle, perched on Castle Hill. Peveril was built by William de Peverel, the bastard son of William the Conqueror, in 1076. All mineral rights belonged to the king, who therefore had good reason to set a relative up with an overview of the lucrative lead-mining area. The castle was also in the heart of the Royal Forest of the Peak, which was prime hunting country for the king and his cohorts. The Normans evidently liked to mix profit with pleasure.

Peveril Castle, one of the earliest stone keeps in the country, is managed by English Heritage and open to the public. The footpath up to it from town is steep and winding, but the views from the curtain wall are exceptionally good, across to hillfort-topped Mam Tor and the Lose Hill ridge, and down the sylvan Hope Valley to the gritstone hills of the Eastern Edges beyond. Cave Dale, a sheer-sided limestone gorge, forms a natural defence to the castle to the south and east, while the Peak Cavern gorge serves the same purpose to the west.

TAKE IN SOME HISTORY
Peveril Castle
english-heritage.org.uk
Market Place, S33 8WQ
01433 620613 | Open daily in
summer, weekends only in winter,
check times online

The steep climb to Peveril
Castle to enjoy the wonderful
views over the Hope Valley is a
highlight of a day out in
Castleton. The romantic ruins
of this Norman fortress are
situated high on a rocky crag
overlooking the village, and the
views of the surrounding Peak
District are truly breathtaking.
Mentioned in the Domesday
Book, Peveril is one of
England's earliest Norman
stone fortresses – built I in
1176. You can explore the
remains of the keep, including
the garderobe (a medieval
lavatory), which sits somewhat
scarily over the gaping void
of Cave Dale beneath. Displays
in the visitor centre tell the
story of Peveril as the
administrative focus of the
Royal Forest of the Peak. Sir
Walter Scott featured the castle
in the opening lines of his novel
Peveril of the Peak.

SEE A LOCAL FESTIVAL
'Pudding in a Lantern'
Oak Apple Day, 29 May, is
celebrated in Castleton by
the ancient Castleton Garland
Ceremony, a glorious pub
crawl involving a procession
led by a 'King' and 'Queen',
both on horseback and
dressed in Restoration
costume. The King is
completely encased in a great
wooden cone stuffed with
wildflowers, which is later
hoisted to the top of the church
tower. A silver band plays the
traditional tune *Pudding in a
Lantern*, which bears a
remarkable similarity to the
Cornish Floral Dance and was
probably brought to the area by
Cornish lead miners. Local
schoolchildren, all dressed in
white, dance through the
streets, and everyone welcomes
the summer.

This is Garland Day; obscure,
colourful and intoxicating. The
words of the song capture
the event's spirit:

> *Thou doesno' know, and I*
> *dono' know*
> *What they han i' Brada*
> *(Bradwell);*
> *An owd cow's head, and a*
> *piece o' bread,*
> *And a pudding baked in a*
> *lantern.*

CHECK OUT THE VISITOR CENTRE
Castleton Visitor Centre
see highlight panel on page 104

GO UNDERGROUND
Peak Cavern
see highlight panel on page 104

Blue John Cavern & Mine
see highlight panel on page 104

Speedwell Cavern
see highlight panel on page 105

Treak Cliff Cavern
see highlight panel on page 105

EAT AND DRINK
The Peak Hotel

peaksinn.com

How Lane, S33 8WJ

01433 620247

Here's where to aim for after climbing Lose Hill, or walking along the Hope Valley. Standing below Peveril Castle, this 17th-century stone building is a real magnet, seducing visitors with its leather armchairs, open log fires and locally brewed cask beers, real ciders and wines by the glass; alternative places to recover are the restaurant/coffee shop and raised sun terrace. Regional ingredients are used to good effect in a range of tasty and well-cooked dishes.

Rose Cottage Café

visitcastleton.co.uk

Cross Street, S33 8WH

01433 620472

Staff at the Rose Cottage Café are used to hungry walkers and climbers dropping in and provide all kinds of home-cooking to sample inside or to take into the pretty rustic garden. There are 10 different varieties of tea alongside a light lunch menu of snacks, sandwiches and set teas. Specialities include a Rose Cottage sandwich. Also cream teas and snacks.

Ye Olde Nags Head

yeoldenagshead.co.uk

Cross Street, S33 8WH

01433 620248

Close to Chatsworth House and Haddon Hall, this traditional 17th-century coaching inn is situated in the heart of the Peak District National Park. The owner continues to welcome thirsty travellers, and the miles of wonderful walks and country lanes favoured by walkers and cyclists means that there are plenty of them willing to occupy the cosy bars warmed by open fires. The interior is a successful mix of contemporary and traditional, a theme also reflected on the menu, with lighter bites, such as pizza and sandwiches, as well as main meals. There's also a beer festival in the summer.

▼ Peveril Castle

▶ Castleton Visitor Centre & Show Caves MAP REF 277 E5

peakdistrict.gov.uk/visiting/ic/ic-castleton

Buxton Road, S33 8WN | 01629 816572

Open Apr–Dec daily 10–5 (Dec weekends until 6), Jan–Feb 10.30–4.30, Mar 10.30–5

If you want to experience the view from Mam Tor, feel what it's like to hang-glide over the Hope Valley, or cling to a rockface on Stanage Edge, then Castleton Visitor Centre may be the place for you. Located in the centre of the village, it's the main hub for exploring Castleton and the Hope Valley, a centre from which to explore the northern National Park, and also a Tourist Information Centre and the location of the Castleton Village Museum, home of many local treasures, some dating back to prehistoric times.

Peak Cavern

peakcavern.co.uk

S33 8WS | 01433 620285 | Open Apr–Oct daily 10–5, Nov–Mar limited tours, check online for times

Peak Cavern – one of the original Wonders of the Peak and now once again known by its ancient name of the Devil's Arse – is said to be the largest natural cave entrance in Britain. Its huge, yawning entrance was once the site of a community of rope-makers, who lived in ramshackle cottages inside the cave. Rope-making demonstrations still take place there. Inside the cave, you have to stoop to pass through the appropriately named Lumbago Walk before you enter to hear the amazing acoustics of the Orchestral Gallery and the perpetual cascading water of Roger Rain's House.

Blue John Cavern & Mine

bluejohn-cavern.com

Mam Tor, S33 8WA | 01433 620638

Open all year, daily 9.30–5 (or dusk in winter); guided tours of approx 1hr every 10 mins

A remarkable example of a water-worn cave, over a third of a mile long, with chambers 200 feet high. It contains eight of the world's 14 veins of Blue John, a very rare mineral, and has been the major source of this unique form of fluorspar for nearly 300 years.

▲ Peak Cavern

Speedwell Cavern

speedwellcavern.co.uk

Winnats Pass, S33 8WA | 01433 623018 | Open Apr–Oct daily 10–5,
Nov–Mar 10–4; last tour one hour earlier than closing time

You have to descend 105 steps to a narrowboat that takes you on
a one-mile underground exploration of floodlit caverns, part of
which was once a lead mine. The hand-carved tunnels open out
into a network of natural caverns and underground rivers. Your
journey ends at the Bottomless Pit, a huge subterranean lake in
a vast, cathedral-like cavern.

Treak Cliff Cavern

bluejohnstone.com

S33 8WP | 01433 620571 | Open all year daily from 10 (last tour
Mar–Oct 4.15 & Nov–Feb 3.15); tours may be cancelled during quiet periods,
call ahead to check times

Treak Cliff Cavern is an underground world of stalactites,
stalagmites, flowstone, rock and cave formations, minerals and
fossils. There are rich deposits of the rare and beautiful Blue John
stone, including The Pillar, the largest piece ever found. Chambers
include the Witch's Cave, Aladdin's Cave, Dream Cave and
Fairyland Grotto. These caves contain some of the most impressive
stalactites in the Peak District. Visitors can also polish their own
Blue John stone (in school holidays) and purchase Blue John stone
jewellery and ornaments in the gift shop. Carols by Candlelight are
held during weekends in December.

▶ Chapel-en-le-Frith   MAP REF 277 D5

In competition with Bakewell, the busy little town of Chapel-en-le-Frith proudly announces itself on entrance road signs as 'The Capital of the Peak'. Its name comes from the Royal Forest of the Peak, which extended over much of the Peak District during the Middle Ages and was used by medieval kings and princes for hunting. Chapel's name comes from Norman French and literally means 'the chapel in the forest'.

Chapel-en-le-Frith has been described as one of the best-kept secrets of the Peak, and it certainly hides its charms away from the fleeting passer-by. The opening of the Chapel-en-le-Frith A6 bypass in 1987 meant that even more people miss this charming and ancient market town as they rush between Buxton and Stockport.

The first chapel was built here for the foresters in 1225, and later it was dedicated to St Thomas Becket, as the present mainly 14th-century parish church still is. But the first medieval church was extensively modernised in 1733, creating the crumbling but still dignified Georgian exterior, with its classical porch topped by a sundial, we see today. The interior of the building features 19th-century box pews and the monument to William Bagshawe of nearby Ford Hall, who was known as 'the Apostle of the Peak' for his evangelistic work as a non-Conformist minister during the latter part of the 17th century. Most of what is visible today is from the 18th-century refurbishment, but there are hints of antiquity all around; the shaft of a Saxon cross and the weathered sundial.

In the churchyard is a simple slab marked by the letters PL and engraved by the outline of an axe. It is tempting to think that this so-called 'Woodcutter's Grave' marks the burial place of one of the original foresters of the Royal Forest of the Peak.

The main road through the town, Market Street, passes below the sloping, cobbled Market Square. This is the real centre of Chapel and a delightful place, surrounded by a range of interesting old inns and buildings and watched over by a medieval cross, which may have stood there for over 500 years, and the recently renovated village stocks. Except on market day (Thursday) this is a quiet and out-of-the-way place, perfect for a cup of tea and a wander. Church Brow, which leads down from the church to Market Street, is a charming thoroughfare, steep and cobbled, and looking as though it might have been transported from the West Country.

One episode in Chapel's history casts a long and morbid shadow. In the Civil War, following the Battle of Ribbleton Moor in 1648, 1,500 Scottish soldiers were imprisoned in the church for 16 days. The conditions must have been appalling because it became known as 'The Black Hole of Derbyshire'. By the time they were released to start a forced march north, 44 men were dead. They were buried in the churchyard, a testament to more brutal times.

Chapel's modern fortune is based on the huge Ferodo brake linings factory to the west of the town, founded a century ago by local man Herbert Frood, who first developed a brake block for the horse-drawn carts which then plied across the steep Derbyshire hills. Chapel was formerly a centre of the boot and shoemaking industry, which strangely enough gave rise to the modern term 'brake shoes'.

PLAY A ROUND

Chapel-en-le-Frith Golf Club

chapelgolf.co.uk

The Cockyard, Manchester Road, SK23 9UH | 01298 812118 | Open daily all year

A scenic parkland course surrounded by hills and bordering Combs Reservoir.

▶ PLACES NEARBY

Buxworth

What's in a name? Well, the villagers of Bugsworth, just off the A6 near Whaley Bridge, evidently thought there was quite a lot. The village now known as Buxworth was formerly known as 'Bugsworth' or 'Buggesworth'. But apparently in 1929, the parish council grew tired of being the butt of jokes and had the name changed to Buxworth – presumably to be associated with the more upmarket Buxton just down the road.

During the 19th century, Buxworth (then Bugsworth) was a busy little inland port, the terminus for the Peak Forest Tramway and the Peak Forest Canal, which were built in 1806 to convey limestone from nearby upland quarries to Manchester, and linked to the River Mersey. Up to 70 narrowboats a week carrying coal, limestone and slates used the Bugsworth Basin. The extraordinary tramroad and canal interchange has now been lovingly and tastefully restored.

The Parish Church at Buxworth built in 1874 is worth a visit too.

Chestnut Centre

chestnutcentre.co.uk

Castleton Road, SK23 0QS

01298 814099

This Conservation and Wildlife Park is set in 50 acres of landscaped grounds and is an otter and owl sanctuary, where rarely seen animals and birds can be experienced at close quarters. It includes Europe's largest collection of otters, 16 species of owls and other indigenous wildlife, all kept in natural surroundings. The Centre's South American giant otters, an endangered species, and their cubs, are a special delight.

Navigation Inn

navigationinn.co.uk
Brookside, Buxworth, SK23 7NE
01663 732072

In Bugworth Basin, you'll enjoy fine real ales from far and wide and tasty, traditional English cooking at this friendly inn. The building itself is more than 200 years old.

Chinley

Once described as 'one of the greatest monuments to Victorian Industrial England', the twin curved Chinley Viaducts which sweep over the A6 and A624 are by far the most impressive structures in this small village on the western edge of the Peak District.

The lines from Derby to Manchester and Sheffield joined here, making Chinley Station, built in 1902, a key junction for passengers to Manchester, Liverpool, London and Sheffield. At one time, up to 180 trains a day passed through the station, which had five waiting rooms (each apparently with a roaring fire), a bookstall and a refreshment room.

Chinley Chapel, built in 1667, is a rare survivor of a 17th-century independent place of worship. From the outside, this two-storey building looks like any other house, but behind its mullioned windows is a stately, galleried chapel. The Methodist Church – known locally as 'The Preaching Room' – dates from 1862, and replaced a shop at Chinley End, where John Wesley was once entertained.

Combs

The village of Combs, southwest of Chapel-en-le-Frith, has stone-built cottages centred on the welcoming Beehive Inn. A short walk away is Combs Reservoir, which has a sailing club and is also a popular spot for coarse fishing and birdwatching. Overlooking the reservoir on a steep promontory of Combs Edge is the important Iron Age hillfort known as Castle Naze.

Dove Holes

Anywhere less like the more famous Dove Holes in Dove Dale (see page 139) would be hard to imagine, but the village shop in the *other* Dove Holes still regularly gets visitors thinking they are in the famous limestone dale near Ashbourne.

This bleak, one-street village high on what used to be the moors north of Buxton is surrounded by quarries and lime works and always seems to wear an air of weary desolation. The small Victorian Gothic parish church, chapel and rows of quarrymen's cottages line up along the A6 as it heads between Buxton and Chapel-en-le-Frith.

The Bull Ring Henge, to the east of the village behind the church, dates from the Late Neolithic, the same period and about the same size as the better-known Arbor Low (see page 57) and Stonehenge. But even this had its standing stones removed in the 18th century for building material.

Chatsworth MAP REF 274 C1

chatsworth.org
DE45 1PP | 01246 565300
Open mid-Mar to Dec 11–5.30 (last entry 4.30)
Not for nothing is Chatsworth, Derbyshire, the seat of the
Dukes of Devonshire, known as 'the Palace of the Peak'. It is a
veritable treasure house of works of art from all over the world,
set in 'Capability' Brown's glorious landscaped parkland, and is
one of Britain's best-loved and most-visited stately homes. A
favourite backdrop for film-makers, the gilded Palladian west
front of Chatsworth is instantly recognisable to millions.

Towards the end of the 17th century, William Cavendish, the
4th Earl of Devonshire, soon to be made the 1st Duke, decided
his Elizabethan mansion, originally built by the legendary Bess
of Hardwick, needed a radical new look. For a while he tinkered
with alterations, but finally knocked everything down and
started again. Demolishing one great historic house to build
another might seem an odd investment of a lifetime, but in
those days great families were judged by their homes and
gardens, and fashion and taste were everything.

▲ Chatsworth House

The Chatsworth that rose from the rubble was in the then-fashionable classic Palladian style, to the duke's own design, with advice from Thomas Archer. It took about 30 years to complete and it set the seal on his new status – even some of the window frames were gilded on the outside. The irony is that he never saw it at its best. Great houses needed great gardens and grounds, and these took decades to establish. In the middle of the 18th century, Lancelot 'Capability' Brown and James Paine laid the foundations of what we see today by changing the course of the River Derwent, moving roads, building bridges and setting out the woodland vistas.

The house is bursting with great works of art in the most superb settings; the Painted Hall is a work of art in itself, with huge, swirling scenes from the life of Julius Caesar by Louis Laguerre on the ceiling and upper part of the walls. Splendour follows splendour as you progress through the house, but one of the most engaging features that stays in the memory of visitors long after they have departed is the wonderful *trompe l'oeil* painting of a violin on the inner door of the Music Room.

There are no less than 17 staircases in the house, but the Grand Staircase leads to the 1st Duke's state rooms on the second floor. The 6th Duke – known as the Bachelor Duke because he never married – thought them all 'useless display'

▲ The library, Chatsworth House

and wanted to make bedrooms out of the whole lot. But these were never rooms for relaxed living. Instead, they display the awesome wealth and power of the Cavendishes, with superb carved panelling, lavishly painted ceilings and priceless objects at every turn. The overall impression is of polished wood, gold leaf and rich fabrics.

The chapel looks just as it did three centuries ago, and you can almost see the curly wigged courtiers of Charles II sitting on the stiff-backed chairs; the library, once the Long Gallery, took shape in the 1830s, and prepares you for the enormous dining room – like an outpost of Buckingham Palace – and the 6th Duke's Sculpture Gallery, a rather chilly assembly of beautiful neoclassical marble figures.

No one can deny the sheer magnificence of the house itself, but the real secret of Chatsworth is surely in its glorious setting. From any direction it looks majestic, and from the southwest, approaching Edensor on a sunny evening, it can be breathtaking. On the horizon to the east are the high gritstone moors; in the middle distance are tiers of woodland, melting into ribbons and stands of beech and oak and rolling parkland; and in the foreground winds the River Derwent. The front of the house reflects the golden glow of evening sunlight to perfection; around it are superb formal gardens and the fine Emperor fountain, created for a visit by the Tsar of Russia who, ironically, never arrived. This is a view the 1st Duke never saw, and could only have dreamed about.

The current 12th Duke of Devonshire and his wife are keen patrons of the arts, so don't be surprised to come across some strikingly modern sculptures by artists like Damian Hurst and Anthony Gormley in the formal landscaped gardens at Chatsworth.

The Chatsworth estate stretches far and wide and includes grouse moors, working farmland and neat little estate villages like Pilsley, Edensor (see page 147) and Beeley (see page 80).

▼ The Cascade

ENTERTAIN THE FAMILY
Chatsworth Farm and Adventure Playground
chatsworth.org
Chatsworth, DE45 1PP
01246 565300 | See website for opening times

Kids can see cows being milked, chicks hatching, piglets being fed, trout rearing and much more at the Chatsworth Farm and Adventure Playground. Opened in 1973, it was designed for children of all ages to learn how the land is used, where their food comes from, and why and how the estate keeps cows and sheep. There are animal demonstrations all year round and a newly refurbished guinea pig village allows children to get up close to guinea pigs in daily animal handling sessions. There's also a climbing forest, suitable for children over six and adults alike, right in the heart of the spectacular woodland adventure playground. Regular craft sessions are held in the Oak Barn, and trailer rides take you into the trees of Stand Wood.

MEET THE LIVESTOCK
A visit to Chatsworth's glorious parkland can give the impression of a Derbyshire version of the African Serengeti, with cattle, sheep and deer instead of wildebeest and impala. The deer at Chatsworth are both native red and fallow deer, which were introduced into Britain by the Normans to grace their hunting forests.

EAT AND DRINK
Cavendish Restaurant
chatsworth.org
DE45 1PP | 01246 565390

Hundreds of thousands of visitors come to see Chatsworth House, its gardens and its park every year, and are refreshed at these wonderful rooms. They're housed in the old stables, which were refurbished by the Dowager Duchess of Devonshire with a luxurious new look and equine theme. Serving British and European dishes, the Cavendish also has a choice of teas, including their own house blend. The menu lists afternoon teas, freshly baked cakes and desserts. You can book for afternoon tea online.

▶ PLACES NEARBY
Pilsley
One of the Chatsworth estate villages, Pilsley is only a mile to the west of the 'big house' and most of the warm, gritstone

▶ Tea and cakes at Chatsworth

6 stately homes

cottages are still occupied by estate workers. Like those of nearby Edensor, many of the cottages were designed by Joseph Paxton, Chatsworth's head gardener and later designer of London's Crystal Palace. Unlike Edensor however, several are much older and date from the 18th century. Most notable of these is the village pub, almost inevitably named The Devonshire Arms. The village's colourful well dressings are held in July. Pilsley is also home to the famous Chatsworth Farm Shop where you buy a range of locally produced goods and its own microbrewery.

Chatsworth Farm Shop
chatsworth.org
Pilsley, DE45 1UF | 01246 565411
Winner of Farm Retailer of the Year 2009 and 2011 and Best On-farm Butchery 2009 at the FARMA awards, the popular Chatsworth farm shop offers quality produce fresh from the estate, tenant farms, Derbyshire suppliers and small food producers. Just a mile and a half from Chatsworth, in the village of Pilsley, traditional butchers will guide you through the vast array of meat, poultry and game. Delicious home-cooked meats and pies are available from the delicatessen counter, and the bakery provides wonderful fresh bread and cakes.

The Devonshire Arms
devonshirepilsley.co.uk
High Street, Pilsley, DE45 1UL
01246 583258
Set in an estate village amid the beautiful rolling parkland that surrounds Chatsworth House, the 'Palace of The Peaks', this fabulous old stone pub is an ideal base for visiting Matlock Bath and Castleton. There are open fires, Peak Ales from the estate's brewery and meats, game and greens from the adjacent estate farm shop, all sourced from these productive acres at the heart of the Peak District. After a day's exploration, classics like fish pie; ham, egg and chips; or steak and ale pie followed by Eton Mess will hit the spot.

▶ Chelmorton MAP REF 273 E1

Affectionately known locally as 'Chelly', the hillside village of Chelmorton is one of the highest villages in the whole country. Twin burial mounds on the airy, 1,463 feet (446m) summit of Chelmorton Low watch over the village, showing that its history stretches back at least into the Bronze Age.

The stream which runs down from the Low and through the centre of this one-street, linear village has the delightful name of Illy Willy Water. The medieval strip field systems of Chelmorton, 'fossilised' by enclosure-period drystone walls running back from the village crofts, are a nationally famous historic landscape, now protected by the Peak District National Park.

The church of St John the Baptist, built into the side of the hill, is one of the most interesting in the Peak, and the elegant, 15th-century spire recessed onto its 13th-century tower is topped by a weathervane in the form of a golden locust – a reminder of John the Baptist's time spent in the wilderness. Parts of this lovely old church, including the south arcade, date from the early 13th century and it boasts the real rarity of a complete 14th-century Perpendicular-style stone chancel screen. In the stone-vaulted south porch is a gallery of early sculptures and grave slabs, some of which may date from Saxon times, like the broken shaft of an old cross in the steeply sloping churchyard.

EAT AND DRINK
The Church Inn
thechurchinn.co.uk
Chelmorton, SK17 9SL
01298 85319
The Church Inn has been here since 1742 when it was an alehouse called the Blacksmith's Arms, but it was renamed The Church Inn in 1884. Serving a range of tasty meals from a varied menu at lunchtimes and in the evenings, The Church Inn also has a warm, welcoming bar, with an excellent range of beers, wines and spirits. It's been in the CAMRA Good Beer Guide for the last 10 or so years, and has a loyal following.

▶ PLACES NEARBY
King Sterndale
The pretty village of King Sterndale was threatened by the expansion of the Topley Pike Quarry, until the news that it was eventually to close. The great faces of the enormous quarry had almost reached the village street but thankfully are hidden from view behind rows of beeches. It remains a charming little limestone hamlet in the hills high above Ashwood Dale, in the valley of the Wye, two miles east of Buxton. The road to the village ends beyond the village green, which has the battered remains of the village cross. The

intimate little parish church was designed by Bonomi in the Gothic style and built in 1847. It has a bellcote, lancet windows and dormer lights in the roof. There is a commemorative brass to Miss Ellen Hawkins from nearby Cowdale, who founded the church, and there are other memorials to the Pickford family, including the judge, William Pickford, who became Lord Sterndale, Master of the Rolls, and died in 1923.

▶ Chesterfield MAP REF 275 E1

It's sad but true, the bustling market town of Chesterfield is best known nationally only for the bizarrely twisted, corkscrew spire of its parish church. Even its League Two football club, recently moved to the shiny new Proact Stadium on the Sheffield Road, is known as the Spireites.

The irony is that the 228-foot-high spire of St Mary and All Saints Church would have tapered to an elegant pencil-point had its timbers been properly seasoned when it was built at the end of the 13th century. It is thought that the twisting occurred as a result of the effects of the sun (it must have been warmer in the Middle Ages) warping the lead-covered, unseasoned timbers. No one is quite sure when the spire took on its eccentric, and from certain viewpoints alarming, twist but a local legend says it was caused when the Devil got his forked tail caught on the spire while flying over the town. Now it stands crooked and twisted, a unique landmark – famous for the wrong reasons.

Modern Chesterfield is a hard-working, industrial town. Its heart still beats in time with the surrounding former coalfields, but it is worth visiting if only for its old inns and coalfield humour. It lies just outside the Peak District, but serves as an important eastern gateway from Junction 29 on the M1.

Chesterfield, as the name suggests, has a history which goes back to Roman times. Derbyshire's second-biggest town began life as a Roman fort, protecting the important lead-mining interests of the Peak – part of the story of the town which is effectively told in the town's excellent museum and art gallery.

Medieval Chesterfield was a prosperous town of craftsmen's guilds. It was full of fine buildings and aspired to have a church that was worthy of its status. Many of these medieval buildings still exist behind modern, ironically mock-Tudor shopfronts, and occasionally still reappear when renovation takes place.

In any other place, Chesterfield's mainly 14th-century church of St Mary and All Saints would surely rank cathedral status; such is its size and grandeur. This testifies to the prosperity of the town's many tradesmen's guilds during the 13th and 14th centuries. The cool, usually dark interior includes many fine monuments, especially those to the local Tudor Foljambe family at the east end of the Lady Chapel.

The centrepiece of Chesterfield is its splendid Market Place, which is filled with colourfully awninged stalls every Monday, Friday and Saturday and watched over by the tall, red-brick clock tower of the Market Hall, which was built in 1857. Dating as far back as 1165, when its charter was granted, Chesterfield's is one of the largest open-air markets in England. Fortunately saved from unsuitable modern development by an upsurge of local public opinion in the 1970s, it attracted national recognition, and a prestigious European Casa Nostra award, for its sensitive redevelopment.

The former Peacock Inn in Low Pavement, a medieval, half-timbered building, was scheduled for demolition but was saved and now enjoys a new life as the Peacock Tourist Information Centre. Important modern buildings in the town centre include the stylish new County Library and the striking circular, multi-gabled Court House. The commanding and handsome red-brick and stone Town Hall, dignified by its gracious portico, was built in in 1938.

Chesterfield is well served with cultural facilities. The Pomegranate Theatre in Corporation Street is a delightful Victorian 546-seat proscenium arch theatre housed in the Grade II listed (George) Stephenson Memorial Hall. Established in 1949, this claims to be the country's oldest civic theatre. Its name paying tribute to the town's coal-mining past, The

▶ St Mary and All Saints Church

Winding Wheel theatre in Holywell Street is another Grade II-listed venue, built in 1923 as a cinema known as The Picture House. Chesterfield Borough Council purchased and refurbished the building in 1987, keeping the art deco internal decor intact, but removing the fixed seating and constructing a dance floor above the stalls.

Many of the town centre streets have names which reflect their medieval history, such as The Shambles, but most of the mock half-timbered shops in Knifesmithgate and Glumangate date from between the wars. There are some good 18th-century terraced houses in Saltergate, a name which is a reminder of the valuable product which was brought across the Pennines from Cheshire by packhorse trains.

Of the many other Chesterfield churches, the most important is probably Holy Trinity in Newbold Road, a 19th-century Victorian Gothic structure which was the last resting place of one of Chesterfield's most famous sons, the steam power pioneer George Stephenson, of 'The Rocket' fame. Stephenson lived for the last years of his life at Georgian red-brick Tapton House, northwest of the town centre.

The lovely wooded surroundings of Queen's Park close to the town centre are still occasionally used by Derbyshire County Cricket Club, and it is reached from the town centre by a footbridge formed by a graceful arch of pre-stressed concrete.

VISIT THE MUSEUM

Chesterfield Museum and Art Gallery

chesterfieldmuseum.co.uk

St Mary's Gate, S41 7TD

01246 345727 | Open all year

Mon, Thu–Sat 10–4

The Chesterfield Museum tells the story of Chesterfield from its beginning as a Roman fort to the building of the 'Crooked Spire' church and its growth as a market town. Chesterfield's most famous Victorian resident, George Stephenson, dubbed the 'Father of the Railways', is also featured. The displays continue the story of the town to the present day. There is a small art gallery in the museum and a full programme of events.

Chesterfield Visitor Information Centre

visitchesterfield.info

Rykneld Square, S40 1SB

01246 345777

This purpose-built centre provides all manner of useful information on Chesterfield, Derbyshire, the Peak District and the UK. It also sells a range of tickets, from theatre seats for the Pomegranate Theatre and Winding Wheel in Chesterfield, to local and national events.

WATCH A MATCH

Chesterfield Cricket Club

chesterfield.play-cricket.com

Queen's Park, S40 2BF

01246 273950

Queen's Park has hosted Chesterfield Cricket Club matches since 1894.

SADDLE UP
Alton Riding School
S42 6AW | 01246 590267
Learn to ride at this riding school and livery yard.

PLAY A ROUND
Chesterfield Golf Club
chesterfieldgolfclub.co.uk
Walton, S42 7LA | 01246 279256
Open all year Mon–Fri
A varied and interesting parkland course with picturesque holes and views.

Grassmoor Golf Centre
grassmoorgolf.co.uk
North Wingfield Road, Grassmoor, S42 5EA | 01246 856044 | Open daily all year
An 18-hole heathland course with challenging and interesting water features, testing greens and par 3s.

Stanedge Golf Club
stanedgegolfclub.co.uk
Walton Hay Farm, S45 0LW
01246 566156 | Open daily all year
A moorland course in hilly situation open to strong winds. Some tricky short holes with narrow fairways.

Tapton Park Golf Club
taptonparkgolfcourse.co.uk
Tapton Park, Tapton, S41 0EQ
01246 239500 | Open daily all year
A municipal parkland course with some fairly hard walking. The 625 yard (par 5) 5th is a testing hole.

EAT AND DRINK
Casa Hotel ◉◉
casahotels.co.uk
Lockoford Lane, S41 7JB
01246 245990
Casa gives Chesterfield a chunk of architectural modernity with a Spanish theme. The Cocina restaurant is entirely in keeping, a large über-chic space with pale wood, white chairs and floor-to-ceiling windows. The menu is as likely to appeal to grazers as to trenchermen, with a sizeable selection of salads and tapas, running from a board of Spanish charcuterie to a croquette of hake, cheese and chives with tartare dressing.

Northern Tea Merchants
northern-tea.com
Crown House, 193 Chatsworth Road, Brampton, S40 2BA | 01 246 232600
This tea and coffee tasting shop is owned and run by an old established company of tea merchants – it doesn't get much more specialist than this. A family firm of tea blenders and tea bag manufacturers, which supplies stately homes and restaurants with their favourite brew, offers casual visitors the chance to sample the same quality fare. From Formosa Oolong to Russian Caravan and a range of flavoured teas, each one is clearly described, and served on its own or with a traditional afternoon accompaniment such as cucumber sandwiches, home-made cake, or scone with

jam and cream. The less exotic teas and a choice of five house blends are also listed. Tours and tastings can be arranged and there's a shop too.

Red Lion Bar & Bistro ⊛⊛
peakedgehotel.co.uk
Darley Road, Stone Edge, S45 0LW
01246 566142

Dating back to 1788, the Red Lion has seen many changes but it has retained much of its character. Located on the edge of the beautiful Peak District National Park, the original wooden beams and stone walls are complemented by discreet lighting and comfy leather armchairs which add a contemporary edge. Striking black-and-white photographs decorate the walls, while local bands liven up the bar on Thursday evenings. Meals are served in the bar and bistro, or beneath umbrellas in the large garden. Seasonal produce drives the menu and the chefs make everything, from sauces to the chips.

▸ PLACES NEARBY

Barrow Hill Roundhouse Railway Centre
barrowhill.org
Campbell Drive, Barrow Hill,
S43 2PR | 01246 472450
Open Sat–Sun 10–4

The Barrow Hill Roundhouse Railway Centre, just outside Chesterfield, is the last surviving operational roundhouse engine shed in Britain, and a unique example of 19th-century railway architecture. A group of rail enthusiasts known as the Barrow Hill Engine Shed Society rescued the site from dereliction in 1991, and now run special events on the site, featuring working steam and diesel locomotives, which are often joined by a variety of modern diesels. Trade stands, catering and a free bus service from Chesterfield railway station for these special events make for a great day out. But no trip to the Roundhouse would be complete without a ride on a train, and rides from the Roundhouse Halt, a purpose-built platform, take visitors around the depot and up the Springwell branch line, pulled by either a steam or diesel locomotive.

Bolsover Castle
english-heritage.org.uk
Castle Street, Bolsover, S44 6PR
01246 822844 | See website for opening times

For the first time in almost 400 years, from the spring of 2014 visitors to the splendid hilltop 17th-century Bolsover Castle, six miles east of Chesterfield, will be able to take the high-level wall walk. The wall walk was originally built for Cavendish family guests as a platform from which to admire the stunning landscape, which stretches west for over 10 miles across the Vale of Scarsdale towards what is now the modern intrusion of the constant buzz of the M1.

It's all part of a £1 million restoration project by English Heritage for what is known as the Little Castle at Bolsover, which is recognised as one of the most important Jacobean buildings in the country. It is perhaps best known for its exquisite interiors, which comprise an opulent ensemble of decorative finishes, including gilded panelling, carved stonework and wall paintings, some of which have recently been restored by a team of conservation specialists.

Bolsover Castle was built by William Cavendish, Duke of Newcastle, a courtier to King Charles I, as a retreat for entertainment, cultural pursuits and horse-training facilities in the superb Riding School, deep in the Derbyshire countryside. Cavendish and his father Charles wanted to create a unique complex of buildings where they could impress their visitors. The new restoration offers visitors the chance to take a closer look at the surviving architecture and appreciate the vision and background to a cultured nobleman's life from four centuries ago.

The Herb Garden

theherbgarden.co.uk
Hardstoft, Pilsley, S45 8AH
01246 599977 | Open Mar to
mid-Sep Wed–Sun 9.30–4.30; see
website for exact dates

The Herb Garden at Pilsley claims to be one of the most important in the country. Its rare and unusual herbs, the historical interest of its physic garden and the sweet-scented lavender and pot-pourri gardens have made it a favourite destination in the area for over 30 years. Established in 1983, it was relaunched by its new owners, Enable Housing Association, in 2011. A tea shop offers refreshments including tempting home-made cakes.

Poolsbrook Country Park

poolsbrookcountrypark.org.uk
Pavilion Drive, Poolsbrook,
Staveley, S43 3WL
01246 470579

Once the derelict and abandoned site of the former Ireland Colliery, Poolsbrook has been transformed into a wildlife-rich country park. The 180-acre country park includes 23 acres of lakes, 85 acres of woodland and 42 acres of grassland.

There is a purpose-built visitor centre which houses a ranger base, toilets, community meeting rooms and a cafe. Also in the park are a children's adventure play area, picnic sites, sledging slopes, four miles of trails for cycling, horse riding and walking, and lakes for angling, canoeing and model yachting. Poolsbrook has also become an important and diverse site for wildlife, and birdlife includes great crested grebes, cormorants, mute swans, pink-footed geese, wheatears and yellow wagtails.

Revolution House

visitchesterfield.info

High Street, Old Whittington,

S41 9JZ | 01246 345727

Open Apr–Sep weekends and bank holidays only, 10–4

To the north of Chesterfield lies the village of Old Whittington, where a group of daring conspirators led by the Earl of Devonshire met in 1688 to hatch a plot to overthrow the Catholic King James II. The plot was a success; the country welcomed William of Orange and the course of history was changed.

The meeting took place in a little thatched inn called the Cock and Pynot, now known as Revolution House and a modest tourist attraction, furnished in 17th-century style and telling the story of the Revolution. Just two miles away is Newbold Moor, where the tiny Norman Chapel was attacked in the same year by a mob of Protestants. The chapel has a simple weather-beaten charm. Nearby is Tapton House, the home of George Stephenson, the pioneering railway engineer.

Congleton MAP REF 272 B2

Recent surveys have suggested that the small market town of Congleton, in the Cheshire Plain about six miles to the west of the Peak District, is one of the wealthiest places to live in the country, with the best quality of life. Conveniently situated close to the M6 and within an hour's drive of Manchester, Liverpool, Birmingham and Stoke-on-Trent, it is an ideal base for commuters to those cities.

This is not to suggest that Congleton is merely a commuter town, without a distinguished history of its own. It was mentioned in the Domesday Book when it was owned by the Earls of Chester. It was granted a market charter in 1272, enabling it to hold fairs and markets, elect a mayor and ale taster, have a merchant guild and – rather bizarrely – to have the power to behead known criminals.

Congleton became notorious in the 17th century when bear-baiting was a popular sport. The story goes that the town was unable to attract large crowds to its bear-baiting contests and lacked the money to pay for a new, more aggressive bear. The town used the money it had saved to buy a Bible to buy a new bear, and replenished the Bible fund with the income from the increased number of bear-baiting spectators. It earned the town the nickname 'Beartown'. The chorus of the modern folk song *Congleton Bear*, by the Derbyshire folk singer John Tams, recalls the legend:

Congleton Rare, Congleton Rare
Sold the Bible to buy a bear.

By the 18th century, Congleton, like its near neighbour Macclesfield, had become an important centre of textile production, especially of silk, cotton and lace. The earliest silk throwing mill, known as the Old Mill, was built by John Clayton and Nathaniel Pattison in 1753. More cotton and silk mills followed, but the town's prosperity depended on the tariffs imposed on imported silk. When those tariffs were removed in the 1860s, the empty mills were converted to fustian cutting. A limited silk-ribbon weaving industry survived into the 20th century, and woven labels were still produced in the 1990s. Most mills now survive as industrial or residential units. Congleton's imposing red-brick town hall was designed in the Gothic style by Edward William Godwin, and opened in 1866.

▶ **PLACES NEARBY**

Biddulph Grange Garden
nationaltrust.org.uk
Grange Road, Biddulph, ST8 7SD
01782 517999 | See website for opening times
You can take a journey around the world in this amazing hillside Victorian garden, created by James Bateman for his worldwide collection of plants. Discrete planting areas take you on a global journey from classical Italy to the pyramids of Egypt via a Victorian vision of China, and a re-creation of a Himalayan glen. The garden also features collections of rhododendrons, summer bedding displays, a dahlia walk (stunning in late summer), and the oldest surviving golden larch in Britain, brought from China in the 1850s. In the recently restored Geological Gallery you can see how Bateman tried to reconcile geology and theology, and travel back through time as the chronologically arranged geological specimens attempt to depict the creation story.

▼ Little Moreton Hall

▲ Mow Cop Castle

Little Moreton Hall

nationaltrust.org.uk

CW12 4SD | 01260 272018

See website for opening times

The building surveyors who inspected the crazily tilted and ominously leaning black-and-white timber-framed Little Moreton Hall, four miles south of Congleton, in 1990 could not believe their eyes. 'Logically',they reported, 'it should not still be standing up!' But the moated 16th-century manor house of Sir Richard de Moreton has defied logic – and gravity – for over 500 years, and continues to delight visitors and attract period location-seeking film producers.

The interior of the house has been left unfurnished by the National Trust, in order to allow visitors to appreciate its structural eccentricities – the sloping floor of the Long Gallery can still seem a little alarming at first sight. The manicured knot garden, restored in the 1980s, is at the back of the house, where you'll also find the herbs and vegetables that the Tudors would have used in their cooking and medicines. Seasonal produce from the garden is used in Mrs Dale's Pantry and the Little Tea Room, where a delicious selection of home-made cakes, light lunches and afternoon teas is served daily.

Attractive Little Moreton Hall was used as the backdrop to ITV's depiction of the saucy *Moll Flanders*, in 1996, and in the 1986 film *Lady Jane*, starring Helena Bonham Carter.

Mow Cop Castle

nationaltrust.org.uk

Mow Cop

This picturesque folly, standing proud on a 1,100 foot hilltop overlooking the Cheshire Plain, was built in 1754 by Squire Randle Wilbraham of nearby Rode Hall as an elaborate summerhouse. At first sight, it looks like a medieval fortress with its two-storeyed round tower, but this is merely sham Gothic – a Georgian attempt to catch the eye.

The 'castle' was given to the National Trust in 1937, and in that same year over 10,000 Methodists met on the hill to commemorate the first Primitive Methodist Camp Meeting. This was held at Mow Cop by Potteries wheelwright Hugh Bourne and his friend William Clowes in 1807, and a commemorative plaque serves to remind of the event. The area around the Cop was famous for the quarrying of high-quality millstones (or querns) used in watermills. Excavations at Mow Cop have found querns dating back to the Iron Age, but the most striking feature of the quarries left today is the free-standing pinnacle known as the Old Man of Mow.

Cressbrook   MAP REF 278 B6

Tucked away in the steep-sided and winding valley of the River Wye just upstream from Monsal Head, Cressbrook is a perfect little gem of a village. It was largely founded by the enlightened mill manager William Newton, who was responsible for building the village school and the charming row of lattice-windowed cottages which face the magnificent Cressbrook Mill (private) and look down on it from above.

The mill, which stands in a stunningly beautiful setting at the junction of the River Wye with Ravensdale, gives a much better impression of a Georgian country mansion than a cotton mill. It is surely one of the Peak's finest monuments of industrial archaeology. With its classical, 12-bay pedimented facade and neat little cupola (which once contained a bell to summon its workers) on its hipped roof, the current mill was built in 1815 to replace Richard Arkwright's earlier building, which had been destroyed by fire in 1785.

William Newton, the so-called Minstrel of the Peak and a self-educated carpenter born at Abney (see page 86), became a partner and manager of the mill after the original building burned down. He proved to be a shining example of the humane treatment of the child apprentices who worked there, in sharp contrast to the deprivations suffered by those employed by Ellis Needham at Litton Mill, a mile upstream. Their tragic story was told in the *Memoir of Robert Blincoe*, published in 1832, which became an important piece of propaganda in the movement towards factory reform.

After many years of neglect, Cressbrook Mill has now been sensitively restored and converted into fancy apartments. The Victorian mock-Gothic Cressbrook Hall is now a hotel.

Crich MAP REF 275 D3

Perched atop a limestone anticline, the monument on Crich Stand glows from a distance looking like a lighthouse set on alabaster cliffs above a shadowy green sea. Three beacon towers have stood here, but each time they were destroyed by lightning strikes. The present structure dates from 1921 and is a memorial to the men of the Sherwood Foresters Regiment killed in the service of the Crown. The 63-foot (19m) tower is open to the public and offers views across eight counties.

Below the Stand lies a busy working quarry, still eating away at the hill. In its early years George Stephenson built a narrow-gauge railway so that the limestone could be carried to kilns at Ambergate. Today the worked-out shelf of the quarry is the location of Crich Tramway Village (see highlight panel opposite), where more than 40 trams from all over the world are housed. Many are in working order and run every few minutes through a period street and up onto open countryside.

Along the street is the Georgian facade of the Derby Assembly Rooms, relocated here in 1972 after the original building in Derby's Market Place had been badly damaged by fire. Other attractions here include an enormous exhibition hall and the high-tech sound and vision experience *Tracks in Time*.

Crich village is a quiet little place; many of the houses date back to the 18th or early 19th century and were once the homes of stockingers, working on knitting frames by the light of top-storey windows. The Jovial Dutchman pub dates from about the same period.

Cromford MAP REF 274 C3

River, road, railway and canal are all crammed into the valley of the Derwent and run side by side south of Cromford. At first sight it is hard to understand why transport was so important to the place, as until 1771 it had been little more than a cluster of small cottages around an old packhorse bridge.

Then the pioneer industrialist and former Preston wig-maker Richard Arkwright arrived in Cromford and set to work building the world's first successful water-powered cotton mill. His sources of power were abundant and plentiful, in the shape of Bonsall Brook and Cromford Moor Sough (a drainage canal from the nearby lead workings), and there was a ready supply of cheap labour due to the decline in the lead mining industry.

Within 20 years Arkwright was fabulously rich – he boasted he could liquidate the national debt from his personal fortune – and the village had become a cradle of the Industrial Revolution. It is no exaggeration to say that were it

▶ Crich Tramway Village   MAP REF 275 D3

tramway.co.uk
DE4 5DP | 01773 854321
Open Apr–Oct daily 10–5.30

Here you can experience a mile-long scenic journey through a
period street to open countryside with panoramic views. You can
enjoy unlimited vintage tram rides, and the exhibition hall houses
the largest collection of vintage electric trams in Britain. The
George Stephenson Discovery Centre opened in 2011. The village
street contains a bar and restaurant, tea rooms, a sweet shop, ice
cream shop, and police sentry box, among others. There is also
a Workshop Viewing Gallery where you can see the trams being
restored. Ring for details of special events.

▼ Crich Tramway Village

▲ Cromford from Black Rocks

not for the apparent remoteness of Cromford at the time, it could well have become a manufacturing centre like Manchester or Sheffield.

An enlightened employer, Arkwright built three mills and lines of three-storey, solidly built gritstone-faced terraced houses in places like North Street. These accommodated his hardworking workforce who, for the first time, laboured for long hours in factories rather than in their own homes. He also built the village school, in the main part of the village west of the A6 across the limestone cutting known as Scarthin Nick. And in Greyhound Square, which has a spacious, urban feel about it, he provided, in 1778, the Greyhound Inn, with its grand facade, as somewhere for his workers to relax after work. For good and ill, Arkwright's 'Satanic Mills' were the birthplace of the urban working class.

Cromford village is made much prettier by its large millpond behind Greyhound Square, known as The Dam. The pond was originally one of the impounding reservoirs built to hold water from the Bonsall Brook, but now it is a tranquil spot away from

▲ Waterfall on Bonsall Brook

the rushing traffic, and the home of ducks and nesting swans. David Mitchell's rabbit warren of a bookshop, Scarthin Books, on the grandly titled Promenade by the pond, provides a fascinating diversion to while away an hour or so.

Arkwright also built for himself the mock-Gothic Willersley Castle, just over Cromford's famous 15th-century bridge, which with its rare bridge chapel and 18th-century Fishing Pavilion. Unfortunately for him, he didn't live long enough to enjoy his Gothic stately home, for he died in 1792, before it was complete. Below Willersley Castle stands St Mary's church, built on the orders of Arkwright. It is mainly in the Perpendicular style and contained the tomb of the man who put Cromford so firmly on the map.

Cromford Canal was built in the early 1790s to link up with the Erewash Canal which ran southeast to Nottingham. Cromford Wharf marked its northern terminus, near the mill. A turnpike road (now the A6) was opened up through Scarthin Nick in 1817. In the 1830s, the Cromford and High Peak Railway was constructed up and over the challenging White Peak landscape, joining the Cromford Canal with the Peak Forest Canal at Whaley Bridge, thus linking the Trent with the Mersey.

In its early years this busy 33-mile wagonway employed horses on the level stretches and a clever, continuous-cable balancing system, later replaced by steam winding engines such as that at Middleton Top, on the inclines. The Middleton or Sheep Pasture Incline, running up from Cromford Wharf at a gradient of up to one in eight, to Middleton Top, still has a runaway wagon stuck in its emergency catchpit halfway up. At the time it was built, the railway was considered an extension of the canals, and the stations were actually called wharfs. But by the middle of the 19th century, the age of steam had arrived and the Midland Railway was extended north from Ambergate to meet the High Peak line.

The Cromford and High Peak Railway was closed by Dr Beeching's axe in 1967 and is now a popular multi-use walking and riding recreational trail known as the High Peak Trail. The Pennine Bridleway also follows part of it.

Cromford and the rest of the Derwent Valley down to Derby received international recognition for its unique position as a cradle of the Industrial Revolution when it was inscribed as a UNESCO World Heritage Site in 2001. Cromford Mill is still undergoing an extensive restoration programme by the Arkwright Society, which aims to create a lasting monument to his extraordinary genius. There are guided tours, and a visitor centre on the site interprets the mill's heyday.

The Cromford Canal, now an SSSI and a Derbyshire Wildlife Trust nature reserve famous for its water voles (see page 132), is popular for family picnics, and there is a pleasant walk along the tow path to the High Peak Junction, where there is another visitor centre.

GET INDUSTRIAL
Cromford Mills
arkwrightsociety.org.uk
Mill Lane, Cromford, DE4 3RQ
01629 823256 | Open daily 9–5
Cromford Mills site presents a remarkable picture of an early textile factory complex. The site is part of the Derwent Valley Mills World Heritage Site. Visitors may be students of the Arkwright story, here to explore the shops, or view the exhibitions in the gallery.

Masson Mills
massonmills.co.uk
Cromford, Matlock Bath,
DE4 3PY | 01629 581001
Textile Museum open Jan–Nov
Mon–Sat 10–4, Sun 11–4, closed
Dec; Shopping Village open daily
throughout the year, Mon–Sat
10–5.30, Sun 11–5
Sir Richard Arkwright's
1783 Masson Mills, between Cromford and Matlock Bath, are the finest surviving and best-preserved example of

▲ Cromford Mill

an Arkwright cotton mill. Machinery demonstrations happen twice a day subject to availability. In addition to a working textile museum illustrating Arkwright's legacy, there is a Shopping Village, restaurant, conference centre and on-site parking facilities.

High Peak Junction Visitor Centre
derbyshire.gov.uk
Cromford, DE4 5HN | 01629 822831 | Open Easter–Oct daily 10–5, Nov–Easter weekends only 10.30–5
High Peak Junction, at the meeting of the Cromford Canal

and the High Peak Trail, was once the hub of transport activity but is now a haven of heritage and wildlife. A mile southeast of Cromford, it forms part of the Derwent Valley Mills World Heritage Site. There are buildings and workshops from the former Cromford and High Peak Railway. This was one of the first railways to be built on canal principles.

The High Peak Junction Visitor Centre offers a warm welcome, refreshments, gifts and a variety of maps, walk leaflets and books. Just a few minutes' walk away is the canal aqueduct over the River Derwent and the superb Leawood Pump House, a steam-powered beam engine which operates some summer weekends and bank holidays.

High Peak Junction Workshops

derbyshire.gov.uk
Cromford, DE4 5HN
01629 822831 | Open Easter–Oct daily 10–5, Nov–Easter weekends only 10.30–5

Claimed to be among the world's oldest surviving railway workshops, the High Peak Junction Workshops were built around 1830 and are now faithfully restored to how they would have looked in the 1880s. Standing at the junction of the Cromford Canal and the High Peak Trail, a mile southeast of Cromford village and in the beautiful Derwent Valley Mills World Heritage Site, it is now a haven for wildlife and an ideal spot for a stroll or a heritage or nature walk. An audio guide takes you back to the days of steam on the former Cromford and High Peak Railway.

GET OUTDOORS

Derbyshire Wildlife Trust's Cromford Canal nature reserve is an interesting example of how nature can reclaim what was once an industrial landscape. Famous for its colony of the now rare and nationally threatened water vole (or 'Ratty' in Kenneth Grahame's 1908 children's classic *The Wind in the Willows*), the overgrown canal is now a haven busy with wildlife, including dragonflies, damselflies, kingfishers, frogs and grass snakes. The surrounding woodlands ring with the songs of wood warblers, redstarts and pied flycatchers. On certain summer weekends, you can enjoy a leisurely Shire horse-drawn trip in a canal narrowboat from Cromford Wharf.

EAT AND DRINK

Bookshop Café

scarthinbooks.com
Scarthin Books, The Promenade, DE4 3QF | 01629 823272

This rabbit warren of a bookshop crammed into three floors also provides on-site arts and crafts exhibitions, and a quirky little vegetarian cafe. Homebakes and tea bread, nine kinds of tea and thick soups made from home-grown vegetables are on offer.

▶ Curbar   MAP REF 278 C6

The 18th-century turnpike to Chesterfield winds steeply east out of Curbar in the Derwent Valley, heading for the gap, known as Curbar Gap, in the gritstone escarpment on the skyline. This is a famous and easily attainable viewpoint from the car park, with the vista extending south down towards Chatsworth (see page 109), and east across the White Peak limestone plateau. To the north stretch a succession of 'edges' heading towards the greater hills of the Dark Peak.

Curbar village itself is a quiet and pretty exclusive place on the banks of the Derwent below the edge, very popular with Sheffield commuters and business people. Among the older features of the village are a circular pinfold or stock-pound, where stray livestock were kept until claimed; a covered well and circular trough, and a lock-up with a conical roof. These structures survived because they were fashioned in stone and were built to last. Apparently in the 18th century, nobody could foresee a time when sheep wouldn't stray, horses wouldn't be thirsty and men wouldn't get drunk.

Great gritstone slabs were easily won from the edge and were used in the area for more than just millstones. On the tussocky pasture close to the village lies a small group of gravestones marking the final resting place of the Cundy family, who died of the plague in 1632 – more than 30 years before the more famous Eyam outbreak (see page 149). Further up, several natural slabs of rock bear biblical references, the work of a molecatcher-cum-preacher, Edwin Gregory, who worked on the Chatsworth estate a century ago.

Finally, as the road straightens and heads southeast over the Bar Brook, there are drystone walls, guideposts and a clapper bridge, dating back to the packhorse era long before the road was made a turnpike in 1759.

▶ The Dark Peak   MAP REF 278 B3

Enclosing the limestone White Peak plateau (see page 256) like the remaining hair on a balding man's head, the Dark Peak is the generic name given to the millstone grit moorlands and shale valleys which lie to the north, east and west. For some, it's a forbidding, even threatening, landscape of inhospitable, brooding moors which end abruptly in sharp, steep walls of gritstone known as 'edges', and punctuated by eccentrically shaped tors eroded by aeons of wind, rain, snow and frost.

Under the moors lie broad, green shale valleys where villages and the great houses of Chatsworth and Haddon Hall were built.

The northern Dark Peak lies on the watershed of England. From the gritstone outcrops and peaty morasses of the moors tumble well-fed streams, the source of great rivers like the Derwent, which eventually reaches the North Sea via the Trent and Humber, and the Goyt and Etherow, which feed into the Irish Sea via the Mersey. This abundance of clean, fresh water resulted in many valleys being dammed to create about 50 reservoirs designed to slake the insatiable thirst of the surrounding cities. Virtually all the Dark Peak valleys except Edale contain a reservoir, and many, as is the case in Longdendale and the Upper Derwent, have several along their length.

Perhaps the most dramatic of these reservoir-filled valleys is the Upper Derwent, where the great battlemented dams of Howden, Derwent and Ladybower and their associated reservoirs supply clean, fresh water to Sheffield, Leicester and Nottingham. Vast acres of rough farmland and, in the case of the Ladybower, two villages, were depopulated and flooded to make what is now a series of breathtaking waterscapes.

The Dark Peak moors, visible from the homes and workplaces of the people in the surrounding cities, were unsurprisingly the cradle of the access battles of the 1930s. These culminated in the celebrated Mass Trespass on Kinder Scout in 1932, when five ramblers were imprisoned for walking on the moors (see page 191). Pioneering access agreements followed, but the Dark Peak remains the heartland of the English rambling tradition.

To the west and east, the moorland areas of Staffordshire, such as around The Roaches, and the Eastern Moors, which give Sheffield its prized 'Golden Frame', are lower than the reigning 2,000-foot (610m) summits of Kinder Scout and Bleaklow, but can be just as challenging to the walker, here known for very good reason as a 'bogtrotter'.

Even on a sunny day, the weather can quickly take a dramatic turn for the worse on the Dark Peak moors, and navigation can become more problematic as walkers are engulfed in impenetrable mist and cloud. The average rainfall is around 60 inches on the high points of Kinder and Bleaklow, and heavy, drifting snow is not uncommon in the winter.

The great glory of the Dark Peak are the heather moors, which turn the landscape a regal purple in August. We have to thank one plump, furry-footed gamebird for this spectacular display. The moors are managed almost exclusively for the red grouse, which is ritually shot after the 'Glorious Twelfth'.

There are three kinds of heather on the Dark Peak moors – the common ling found on drier ground; cross-leaved heath found on wet or boggy ground, and bell-heather which prefers dry, rocky slopes. Both these last two plants have bigger flowers than ling, but they don't attract as many bees. Heather honey is a local speciality, and in summer, you'll often come across hives stationed around the edge of the moors.

▶ Darley Dale   MAP REF 274 C2

The administrative ties which bound together four settlements along the River Derwent under the name of Darley Dale a century ago were never strong enough to give the place a real identity. The ever-busy A6 replaced the former Midland Railway as the artery of the community, but it also tore out its heart.

Darley Dale's most important claim to fame was that it was the home of Sir Joseph Whitworth, the man who invented the Whitworth screw thread. Munitions (which included a rifle that fired hexagonal bullets), nuts and bolts, and machine tools soon made him very rich, and he bestowed much of his wealth on the local community by building not only a Whitworth Hospital but also Whitworth Hotel, a Whitworth Park and an Institute.

Victorian benefactors liked to have their good deeds recognised, but in Whitworth's case his generosity won him few friends and he wasn't popular. He lived at Stancliffe Hall (private), guarding his privacy behind walls and hedges, and when he died in 1887 his dreams of a model village died too.

Hidden by trees beside the A6 lies Stancliffe Quarry. Gritstone from here was sent to London, where it was used to pave Trafalgar Square and the Embankment.

▼ Darley Dale

The old, original part of the village known as Churchtown lies to the west, close to the River Derwent, and clusters protectively around the wonderful St Helen's church, which in turn is protected by Darley Dale's famous and massive yew tree. Estimates of the yew's age range from 600 to 4,000 years, and the stone tablets which surround its enormous gnarled old trunk – 33 feet in circumference – record moments in history which it has lived through.

The church itself is cruciform shape and dates mainly from the 13th and 14th centuries, but there is evidence of a much earlier, Norman, establishment. There are 12th- and 13th-century sepulchral stones built into the walls, and the shaft of a highly decorated Saxon cross. Following a 19th-century restoration, some fine and colourful stained glass by William Morris and Edward Burne-Jones in the Arts and Crafts style was inserted in the south transept. The scenes depicted are from the Song of Solomon, the chunky figures were by Burne-Jones and the angels probably by Morris. Victorian stained glass doesn't get any better. Also in the church is the medieval tomb of Sir John de Darley (with his heart in his hands), and the private pew of the reclusive Sir Joseph Whitworth.

VISIT THE MUSEUM
Working Carriage Museum
Red House Stables, Old Road, Darley Dale, DE4 2ER | 01629 733583
Open Mon–Sat 10–5 (4 in winter), Sun 10–3 (2 in winter)
The Working Carriage Museum has one of the finest collections of original horse-drawn vehicles and equipment in Britain. In constant demand for the many film and TV period costume dramas which have been set at nearby Haddon Hall (see page 165) and Chatsworth (see page 109), the Red House Stables also provides visitors with the chance to drive in a coach-and-four through 'Capability' Brown's parkland.

Derwent Dams MAP REF 278 B4

It's a funny thing about scenery. To most people, large lakes surrounded by trees are beautiful, even if, as in the case of the Upper Derwent valley, both features are entirely unnatural. Water engineers had their eyes on the Upper Derwent for decades before work began on the **Howden Dam** in 1901. It was the perfect spot; a long deep valley through solid millstone grit, bleak rain-soaked moors all around, and only a few scattered farming communities to relocate.

After Howden came the **Derwent Dam**, built in a similar, battlemented Gothic style, which was completed in 1916. **Ladybower**, the last and largest, was inaugurated in 1945, flooding two miles of the Derwent Valley and drowning the villages of Derwent and Ashopton. Their houses were dismantled and the villagers transferred to a new housing estate at Yorkshire Bridge at Bamford (see page 76).

Ladybower now holds about 6,000 million gallons of water, the others slightly less. More than a third of the water is piped to Leicester, another third to Sheffield, and the rest is shared between the East Midland cities of Derby and Nottingham.

The sheer scale of the engineering works is impressive, especially when water overflows the Howden and Derwent Dams in winter in an awesome, scintillating waterfall. But the Canadian Rockies-style landscape still draws visitors with extensive views over great sheets of water, surrounded by dark curtains of conifers planted for water purity. There are still a few wildlife surprises in the Upper Derwent's forests. In good seed years the local chaffinches are joined by flocks of crossbills, and a threatened and diminishing population of goshawks are sometimes to be seen in early spring, when they soar high in their display flights over the wooded cloughs.

When there is a drought, thousands of people flock to see the few revealed stones and walls of drowned Derwent and Ashopton. The only structure to cheat the flood was the ancient packhorse bridge at Derwent, which was dismantled and rebuilt further up the valley to span the infant river at Slippery Stones after the Ladybower Reservoir was opened. It is dedicated to the pioneering Sheffield rambler and guidebook author John Derry.

The resemblance of the Derwent Dams to those in the Ruhr caused the legendary 617 Dambusters Squadron to practice here before their famous raid in 1943. Anniversaries of the raid have attracted huge crowds into the valley to watch flypasts by the last flying Lancaster bomber and other aircraft from the Battle of Britain Memorial Flight. And it's said that one of the first flights new pilots in their Tornado jets in the former 617 Squadron had to do was over the Derwent Dams.

Just above Derwent Reservoir at Birchinlee, the valley road passes beside the site of 'Tin Town', which was a settlement of corrugated-iron houses provided for the navvies who built the upper two reservoirs of Howden and Derwent. For a decade at the beginning of the 20th century it was a self-contained community 1,000 strong, with its own school and railway station. Now all that remains are a few grass-covered terraces and the foundations of the tin huts.

Car parks and cycle hire facilities make it easy to explore the western side of the Derwent Valley, through the forest along the shores of all three reservoirs.

GET OUTDOORS

Fairholmes Visitor Centre
peakdistrict.gov.uk
Fairholmes, Derwent, Bamford,
S33 0AQ | 01433 650953 | See
website for opening times
Situated below the wall of the
Derwent Dam, the centre acts
as a natural focus for the two
million visitors who journey to
this beautiful valley each year.
It's an ideal base from which to
explore the Upper Derwent
Valley and surrounding
moorlands. From majestic
reservoirs and quiet forests to
wild open spaces, there's
something for everyone. The
experienced and welcoming
team advise on how to make the
most of your visit to this
beautiful valley and spectacular
surrounding moorland.

EXPLORE BY BIKE

Derwent Cycle Hire
peakdistrict.gov.uk
Fairholmes Car Park, S33 0AQ
01433 651261
Cycle hire and mobility scooters
for exploring the hills.

▶ **PLACES NEARBY**

The Old Hall Hotel
see page 186

The Peak Hotel
see page 103

The Samuel Fox Country Inn
see page 86

Ye Olde Nags Head
see page 103

Yorkshire Bridge Inn
see page 78

▶ Dove Dale   MAP REF 273 E3

If you want to enjoy the heady mix of the crystal-clear trout stream and amazing rock formations of Izaak Walton's 'princess of rivers', you will avoid Dove Dale on a bank holiday or summer weekend. Because then it seems as if the world and his wife are queuing to cross the famous Stepping Stones (recently somewhat controversially restored and levelled by the National Trust) under Thorpe Cloud.

Dove Dale and its Stepping Stones appear on thousands of postcards and attract over a million visitors every year, and it sometimes seems as if they're all queuing to cross the gin-clear waters of the Dove at the same time. The National Trust does a heroic job to manage this part of its South Peak Estate, but it really is a good idea to keep away from the place on sunny Sundays. Try it on a winter's morning, when the surrounding trees sparkle with iridescent diamonds of frost – and you'll have the place to yourself.

The Dove flows for 45 miles, but for only a short section is it called Dove Dale. Above Viator's Bridge it successively becomes Mill Dale, then **Wolfscote Dale** and finally **Beresford Dale**. But it's to the southernmost Dove Dale that most visitors flock.

▼ Bunster Hill, Dove Dale

Within the space of a few miles of easy riverside walking on a broad, level path, there are superb craggy rocks and spires, such as the Twelve Apostles, Tissington Spires, Ilam Rock and Pickering Tor, rising out of dense ash woodland. There are also sweeps of open pasture with banks of flowers, dark caves such as Reynard's under a natural arch and the gaping Dove Holes, and fine cascades of sparklingly clear water.

As with most Derbyshire dales, there is no road through Dove Dale, and the main path follows the east (Derbyshire) bank. It is not even necessary to cross the Stepping Stones upstream from the car park on the Staffordshire side of the river, because there's a footbridge a few yards away.

It was Victorian fashion which first blighted Dove Dale. Its undoubted beauties were praised by every famous romantic writer from Byron to Tennyson, and it soon became almost as popular as Switzerland. Donkey tours and guided expeditions once ferried people up the path to view the scenery, and an extensive programme of footpath restoration eventually saved the dale from its own popularity. Of more enduring merit were the earlier words of Izaak Walton and his co-writer Charles Cotton, from nearby Beresford Hall, who loved the Dove and put their heads and hearts into *The Compleat Angler* in 1653.

EAT AND DRINK
Bentley Brook Inn

bentleybrookinn.co.uk
Fenny Bentley, DE6 1LF | 01335 350278

Located in scenic Fenny Bentley (see page 152) just a short distance from the many glories of Dove Dale, this eye-catching black-and-white country property was constructed over 200 years ago on the footprint of a medieval farmhouse. It became a pub only in the 1970s. Many period features remain, including a splendid central log fireplace. Outside are several acres of landscaped gardens which host the World Toe-Wrestling Championship every summer. From this you may deduce that real ales play an important part in the daily life of the inn: Leatherbritches (which originated here), Marston's and Falstaff brews are all on offer. Service starts with breakfast at 8am (8.30am in winter), but check the inn's diary if you're planning an evening out – the week is dotted with special attractions such as the tasty Chinese buffet on Thursdays. With a menu proffering popular pub meals, there's something for everyone: from tandoori chicken skewers to scampi in a basket. Children and dogs are made very welcome, and the Sunday carvery lunch is popular with walkers and families.

▼ The Stepping Stones, Dove Dale

Dovestone Reservoirs   MAP REF 277 D2

On the doorsteps of the busy industrial towns of Oldham and Mossley, the Dovestone Reservoirs and surrounding moors have provided a wonderful escape from the grimy, back-to-back terraces and mills of Lancashire for over a century.

The first of the four reservoirs collectively known as Dovestones was **Yeoman Hey**, constructed in 1880, and followed by **Greenfield** in 1902. When **Chew Reservoir** was built on Dove Stone Moss, 10 years later, it was the highest in Britain at around 1,600 feet (488m) above the sea. **Dovestone Reservoir,** the largest of the group, was completed in 1967.

Sailing and windsurfing take place on Dovestone Reservoir, and the thriving sailing club (see below) holds regular regattas. On the adjoining hillside there are two terrific orienteering routes – look out for the small posts with helpful coloured markings and numbers. Swimming in the reservoir is forbidden, because of the deep water and outlet pipes that can cause dangerous undercurrents.

The two-and-a-half-mile track constructed by United Utilities around Dovestone Reservoir has been made suitable for wheelchair users, while the numerous paths and bridleways that explore the surrounding moors include the Oldham Way, which runs high and straight across the hillside to the south, on the route of a former steam tramway that was built 100 years ago to aid the construction of Chew Reservoir.

GET ON THE WATER
Dovestone Reservoir
Sailing Club
dovestonesc.org.uk
Club House, Dovestone Reservoir,

Greenfield, Oldham,
OL3 7NE | 01457 873000
A great place to hire a boat and get out on the water. You can also get sailing lessons.

Earl Sterndale   MAP REF 273 E1

In the shadow of the spectacular reef limestone peaks of High Wheeldon, Hitter, Chrome and Parkhouse Hills (some of the only true 'peaks' in the Peak District) and at the less-frequented, northern end of the Dove Valley, Earl Sterndale is one of the Peak's hidden treasures. It stands at over 1,100 feet (335m) above the sea and is surrounded by a number of farms called 'granges' – a reminder that during the Middle Ages, much of this land was owned by Basingwerk Abbey in far-off Flintshire, and these were its outlying farms.

Earl Sterndale's usual claim to guidebook fame is its pub, the 400-year-old Quiet Woman, in the main village street. The strictly sexist sign shows a headless woman with the caption

'Soft words turneth away wrath', and is said to illustrate the sad fate of a former landlord's wife, who apparently talked too much. The pub was in the hands of the Heathcote family, still a common local surname, for nearly 300 years.

The small early 19th-century parish church of St Michael has the unusual distinction of being the only church in Derbyshire to suffer a direct hit from a bomb during World War II. It was rather unluckily struck by a jettisoned bomb intended for nearby Manchester. The church was restored and refurbished in 1952 but retains its Saxon font.

EAT AND DRINK
The Quiet Woman
Earl Sterndale, SK17 0BU
01298 83211
If you ignore the decidedly non-PC name, you'll find a good, old-fashioned pub in The Quiet Woman. There is no canned music here, just the hum of conversation over home-made pork pies washed down with Marston's ale and a couple of guest beers. Behind the pub is a smallholding with friendly stock to keep the kids entertained.

▶ Edale MAP REF 277 E4

For hardened ramblers and bogtrotters, the real Peak District starts at Edale. This broad green shale valley tucked beneath the ramparts of Kinder Scout to the north and the Great Ridge of Mam Tor, Back Tor and Lose Hill to the south, provides a beautiful, sylvan introduction to the highest ground in the Peak.

Five ancient farming communities, all known as 'booths' (a Tudor word meaning a shelter for livestock), are scattered along the northern slopes of the valley of the River Noe, tucked in beneath the Kinder plateau. These booths have grown into the modern hamlets of Upper Booth, Barber Booth, Grindsbrook Booth, Ollerbrook Booth and Nether Booth, which are all linked by green meadows and twisting lanes.

Grindsbrook Booth, usually known as Edale village, is the largest, and lies at the heart of the dale. On a sunny Sunday, it is thronged with booted, rucksacked and anoraked ramblers heading for the hills, many of whom have disembarked from the 'Ramblers' Route' Hope Valley railway line, which links Sheffield with Stockport.

Edale also marks the starting point of the Pennine Way, Britain's oldest and toughest national trail (see page 144). Sitting outside the Old Nag's Head Inn, the official starting point, and watching a constant tide of well-equipped and seriously keen walkers disappearing up the path track can be a little daunting. But in fact most visitors heading for Kinder are only there for the day and doing a circular walk of a few miles.

For those intending to walk the whole 256 miles of the Pennine Way, the sodden peat bogs of Kinder Scout (see page 189) and Bleaklow (see page 83) offer the first really testing challenge of the whole walk. Having said that, the going is much easier than it used to be, because much of the worst of the Kinder and Bleaklow bogs has been tamed by the laying of paving slabs, rescued from former cotton mills in the surrounding cities, across the boggiest ground along the route.

The official route of the Pennine Way follows a paved track opposite The Old Nag's Head, and westwards along an old packhorse trail. This now well-established route takes you through Upper Booth and up Jacob's Ladder, a heavily reconstructed and carefully paved zigzag route cut into the hillside. The medieval Edale Cross, now somewhat incongruously enclosed by a wall, marks the meeting of the three wards of the Royal Forest of the Peak. From there it is only a few hundred yards north to Kinder Low and Kinder Downfall, the scenic highlight of the Kinder plateau. This 100-foot waterfall is the highest in the Peak, and is famous for sometimes being blown back uphill in the teeth of the frequent western gales. This means uniquely you can get wet simultaneously from above and below. It's a stiff walk, but worthwhile – the views to the west over the outskirts of Manchester and the Cheshire Plain are pretty fabulous.

WALK (A LITTLE BIT OF) THE PENNINE WAY

In Depression-torn 1930s England, Tom Stephenson, outdoors correspondent for the *Daily Herald*, told his readers of his dream – to create 'a long, green trail' up the backbone of England. The southern starting point would be Edale, and his hidden agenda was that it would serve to open up the then-forbidden moors of the Peak to walkers. It took 30 years of patient negotiations and an Act of Parliament to achieve, but in 1965 the Pennine Way was finally opened. Running 256 miles from Edale to Kirk Yetholm, just over the Scottish border, it was Britain's first official long-distance path and is still the toughest. Go to Edale any Friday night and you'll see eager-eyed Pennine Wayfarers in the Edale campsite making their last-minute preparations, or in The Old Nag's Head, poring over maps or looking through Alfred Wainwright's little buff-covered guidebook.

GET OUTDOORS
The Moorland Centre
peakdistrict.gov.uk
Fieldhead, Edale, S33 7ZA
01433 670207
This highly sustainable circular building has a living roof of sedum turf, enlivened by a waterfall tumbling over glass panels into a pool at the entrance. The turf acts as an eco-friendly insulator, and the building is also fuelled by an energy-saving ground-source heat pump. Headquarters of the Moors for the Future Partnership, the Edale centre provides a national focus for moorland research, and an inspirational experience for visitors to Edale and the Peak District National Park. The Moorland Centre's design and interactive exhibitions reflect its upland setting in the shadow of Kinder Scout.

GET ACTIVE
YHA Activity Centre
yha.org.uk
Rowland Cote, Nether Booth, S33 7ZH | 01433 670302
Try climbing, abseiling, kayaking, canoeing, caving, orienteering, high ropes, hill walking or archery at YHA Edale.

EAT AND DRINK
The Old Nag's Head
the-old-nags-head.co.uk
Edale, S33 7ZD | 01433 670291
Situated at the traditional southern starting point of the Pennine Way, The Old Nag's Head dates back to 1577 and appears in lists of the 100 greatest pubs in England. It is surrounded by some of the best and toughest walking country in the Peak, with fantastic views of Kinder Scout and the surrounding countryside. With authentic and welcoming log fires, the pub is child, pet and muddy-boot friendly. It offers a wide range of lagers, ciders and draught, and even has its very own ale – 'The Nags 1577'.

The Penny Pot Café
Station Approach, Edale, S33 7ZA
01433 670293
This superb little cafe welcomes walkers and is the perfect place for a bacon butty or a bowl of home-made soup before or after a day in the hills.

The Rambler Inn
theramblerinn.com
Edale, S33 7ZA | 01433 670268
The second of Edale's walkers' pubs is The Rambler Inn, formerly known as The Church Inn, and offers a comfortable refuge after a day of rambling on Kinder and the neighbouring hills. The bar carries real ales, traditional ciders and a large variety of whiskies and spirits. Hot and cold food is served daily in all of the four dining areas, with a large variety of meals available as well as the Chef's Daily Specials. There is an open bar area as well as a large beer garden, so you can enjoy your surroundings while you enjoy The Rambler's warm hospitality.

Edensor MAP REF 274 C1

Edensor (pronounced 'Ensor') is the village which the 6th Duke
of Devonshire transplanted lock, stock and barrel when he was
redesigning Chatsworth – allegedly because it spoiled the view.
With the help of his brilliant gardener, Joseph Paxton, and his
architect, John Robertson of Derby, the Duke chose to build
every house with completely different design details,
from Swiss chalet to Tudor cottage, so that no two in this
pretty little model village are exactly the same. Only one house
of the original village remains, called Park Cottage but known
at one time as Naboth's Vineyard. The biblical reference relates
to the owner in 1838 who is supposed to have refused to sell or
be relocated.

The effect of the hotchpotch of styles is surprisingly
pleasing, and the village is watched over by the graceful spire
of St Peter's, built in 1867 to the design of Sir George Gilbert
Scott. Inside are monuments to the Cavendish family, and in
the churchyard is the ducal burial ground where lies, among
others, Kathleen Kennedy, sister of US President John F.
Kennedy, who died in an aircrash soon after her husband, and
Lord Hartington, the present Duke's uncle, who was killed in
World War II. Also buried in the churchyard is Joseph Paxton,
the talented Chatsworth gardener who went on to design
London's Crystal Palace, which he based on his designs for
Chatsworth's greenhouse.

EAT AND DRINK
Tea Cottage
Edensor, DE45 1PH
01246 582315
This charming little tea room
and licensed cafe is tucked
away just behind the village
church, hidden amid the
peaceful byroads of the
estate village. Expect quality
cream teas and dainties, snacks
and soups, many made using
Chatsworth estate produce, and
served with decorum.

Elton MAP REF 274 B2

The numerous bumps and hollows in the fields around Elton,
lying high on the White Peak limestone plateau, give away its
industrial history. It is surrounded by the remains of centuries
of lead mining during which, according to the celebrated
landscape historian WG Hoskins, 'no stone was left unturned'.

Many of the good limestone cottages in the village street
date from the heyday of the lead mining industry in the 18th
century, when most of the occupants were engaged in the dual
economy of mining and farming. Elton Hall, which has a date
stone of 1668 in a semicircular pediment above the door, was

▲ Robin Hood's Stride

once a Youth Hostel but is now in private hands, and the village has become a popular centre for walking in the White Peak.

All Saints church stands in the centre of the village and was completely rebuilt in 1812 after the collapse of the old steeple onto the previous medieval church. The font is a copy of the original 12th-century Norman one which the villagers, not realising its worth, allowed to go to nearby Youlgreave (see page 267). Here it was recognised for its antiquity and was 'rescued' from the vicarage garden and now occupies pride of place in Youlgreave's All Saints church. Rather galling for the parishioners of Elton.

GET OUTDOORS

Hermit's Cave and Robin Hood's Stride

A popular four-mile walk heading north from Elton leads to a small, railed-off medieval hermit's cave, hidden behind an ancient yew beneath Cratcliff Rocks. Carved into the back of the cave is the weathered figure of Christ on the cross. The tottering towers of the unusual rock formation known as Robin Hood's Stride, or Mock Beggar's Hall, and the Bronze Age stone circle known as Nine Stones (now only four) are also nearby, across the ancient Portway track.

▶ Eyam MAP REF 278 B6

Death from disease was a fact of life in medieval England, and many Peak villages suffered the horrors of the Black Death. What made the weaving village of Eyam (pronounced 'Eem' as in 'stream', incidentally) different was the attempt by the local rector, William Mompesson, and his Nonconformist predecessor, Thomas Stanley, to keep the 1665 to 1666 outbreak within the confines of the community and not let it be carried elsewhere. They persuaded the whole village to effectively put itself into quarantine, and as a result 259 villagers perished, including, in some cases, entire families. Eyam became a byword for tragedy and epic self-sacrifice.

According to tradition, the deadly virus was introduced into the village by a tailor called George Viccars, who brought some infected cloth from London. He was lodging with Mary Cooper at what is now called Plague Cottage near the church, where he died a few days after arriving in Eyam. A fortnight later Mary's son Edward died and the whole community braced itself for disaster. The young rector quickly sent his own children away, but stayed with his wife to care for the sick and organise the quarantine, conducting services outdoors under the limestone crag known as Cucklett Delf. Over the months, through 1665 and into the autumn of 1666, most of the population died, including Mompesson's wife Elizabeth. Her table-top tomb is in the churchyard, close to a magnificent, though truncated, Saxon preaching cross. Among the other features in this fascinating church are medieval wall paintings, good Jacobean woodwork and an elaborate 18th-century sundial over the south door.

▼ Sundial, Eyam church

There's little doubt that the death toll in Eyam would have been considerably lower had the quarantine not been imposed. But this was the 17th century, when little was known then about medical hygiene and disease prevention. The heroic efforts of the village were successful, and the epidemic did not spread outside Eyam. The names of those who died are recalled on individual cottages in the village, and in the parish register held in the restored 13th-century parish church of St Lawrence.

Eyam has kept its unique place in history because you can stand beside victims' homes, read about their lives and look across to their graves. Their story is graphically told in the village museum housed in the former Methodist Chapel in Hawkhill Road. Award-winning exhibits and displays tell the harrowing story of the 'visitation' of the plague.

The modern Eyam is neither a sad place nor somewhere which dwells on its tragic past. It stands on the hill brow between Middleton Dale and Eyam Moor, as self-contained and aloof as ever. Visitors come to enjoy the traditional well dressing and the sheep roast in late August. But the folk-memories of the plague still manage to send a shiver down the spine.

TAKE IN SOME HISTORY
Eyam Hall and Craft Centre
nationaltrust.org.uk
Eyam, S32 5QW | 01433 639565
Check online for opening times
Behind ornate iron gates and opposite the village green, Jacobean Eyam Hall, which was in the Wright family for over 300 years, was built in 1671 as survivors came together after the devastation of the plague. The Hall, recently taken over by the National Trust, is a wonderfully unspoilt example of a 17th-century manor house. Inside, visitors can enjoy family portraits, furniture belonging to

▼ Riley Graves, Eyam

each generation, and the wonderful Tapestry Room, hung with examples of several different periods, including a 15th-century Flemish one. Several have been unceremoniously cut up to fill the walls, like draught-proof wallpaper. The Craft Centre, built in the Hall's former stable yard, offers a vibrant hub from which to explore the wider village of Eyam and its captivating stories. Here you will also find a collection of locally run craft units, an independent cafe and a National Trust shop.

VISIT THE MUSEUM
Eyam Museum
eyam-museum.org.uk
Hawkhill Road, Eyam, S32 5QP
01433 631371 | Open mid-Mar to Oct Tue–Sun and BHs 10–4.30
Eyam Museum is the ideal place to start your exploration of 'The Plague Village'. The main public car park, with toilets, lies directly opposite, and a free car park lies behind and above the council one. The museum tells the story of the development of the community from prehistoric to modern times, including the harrowing story of the bubonic plague, how it reached Eyam and was heroically contained there. The story of the village's subsequent social and industrial history and its fascinating geology and prehistory is also unfolded piece by piece in the award-winning displays.

5 top museums

▶ **Old House Museum**, Cunningham Place, Bakewell, page 75

▶ **Buxton Museum & Art Gallery**, Terrace Road, Buxton, page 94

▶ **Chesterfield Museum & Art Gallery**, St Mary's Gate, Chesterfield, page 118

▶ **Eyam Museum**, Hawkhill Road, Eyam, see below

▶ **Peak District Lead Mining Museum**, The Pavilion, Matlock Bath, page 224

EAT AND DRINK
Eyam Tea Rooms
eyamtearooms.co.uk
The Square, Eyam, S32 5RB
01433 631274
This friendly tea room and ice cream parlour serves various teas and coffees, breakfasts until 11.30am, light lunches, assorted freshly baked cakes and cream teas and lots of lovely ice cream.

Miners' Arms
theminersarmseyam.co.uk
Water Lane, Eyam, S32 5RG
01433 630853
This welcoming 17th-century inn and restaurant was built just before the plague hit Eyam. It gets its name from the local lead mines, which go back to Roman times. Now owned by Greene King, there's always the option to pop in for a pint of their IPA or Ruddles Best bitter, or enjoy a meal. A beer festival is held three times a year.

▶ Fenny Bentley MAP REF 274 B4

Bisected by the busy A515 Ashbourne–Buxton road, Fenny Bentley is often overlooked by the tourists rushing north to the next Peak District 'honeypot'. But this pretty little village on the Bentley Brook rewards those who take a longer look.

The most interesting building in the village is Cherry Orchard Farm (private), once known as Bentley Hall. The squat, medieval defensive tower of the hall dates from the late 15th century when the building was the seat of the Beresford family. The heavily restored church of St Edmund across the road from the hall probably dates from the 14th century and contains an ornate screen, which may have come from the Beresford Chantry, which was founded in 1511. The most impressive internal feature is the alabaster Beresford tomb, which represents Sir Thomas, his wife Agnes, and their 21 children, all enclosed in shrouds. You'll never see another like it. Thomas Beresford fought with one of his sons alongside Henry V at Agincourt in 1415.

EAT AND DRINK

Bentley Brook Inn
see page 141

The Coach and Horses Inn
coachandhorsesfennybentley.co.uk
Fenny Bentley, DE6 1LB
01335 350246
A cosy refuge in any weather, this family-run, 17th-century coaching inn stands on the edge of the Peak District National Park. Besides the beautiful location, its charms include stripped wood furniture and low beams, real log-burning fires plus a welcoming air. Expect a great selection of real ales and hearty home cooking that uses the best of local produce.

▶ Flash MAP REF 273 D1

The terms 'Flash Harry' and 'flash money' entered the English language as a consequence of events in the bleak village of Flash which, at an altitude of 1,518 feet, claims to be the highest village in England.

It gained the dubious honour of giving its name to sharp practice when a group of peddlers known as 'Flash men' living near the village travelled the country hawking ribbons, buttons and other goods. They initially paid for their purchases with hard cash but after establishing credit, vanished with the goods and moved on to another supplier. Their name became associated with ne'er-do-wells in taverns, who helped people drink their money and were never seen again, and was immortified in an 18th-century song, 'Flash Company'. Flash money also referred to counterfeit banknotes, manufactured in the 18th century by another devious local gang. They were finally captured when a servant girl exposed them to the authorities, and some were hanged at Chester.

Flash was the ideal location for avoiding the law because of its proximity to the borders of three counties in the days when police in one county could not pursue miscreants into another. An old packhorse bridge and local beauty spot called Three Shire Heads, in the heart of the moors about a mile northwest of the village, is the meeting place of Derbyshire, Cheshire and Staffordshire. Illegal bare-knuckle fights were held here and when the police arrived, the participants simply crossed the bridge and continued their bout on the other side.

While all this lawlessness was going on, the more peaceable inhabitants of Flash formed the Tea Pot Club. Originally a fund to help members who were sick, the Flash Loyal Union Society still has an annual Tea Pot Parade each June from the church to Flash Bar.

SADDLE UP
Northfield Farm Riding & Trekking Centre
northfieldfarm.co.uk
Flash, SK17 0SW | 01298 22543

A range of rides to suit all abilities are available at Northfield. Rides are usually two hours in length, and are fully supervised.

▶ Foolow MAP REF 278 B6

It is often the source of amusement to visitors that just to the west of Foolow is the small dry valley known as Silly Dale. In fact, the name of Foolow has nothing to do with the intelligence of its inhabitants – it comes from Old English and probably means 'multicoloured hill'. And the prefix of the nearby dry dale has the delightful meaning of 'happy' or 'prosperous'.

This small village on the limestone plateau between Eyam (see page 149) and Tideswell (see page 248) clusters around its village pond or 'mere', which in turn is watched over by a crocketed medieval cross. Foolow is another candidate for one of the prettiest villages in the Peak, for the large green is surrounded by some fine 17th- and 18th-century cottages, the most important of which are the bay-windowed, 17th-century Manor House, and the Old Hall.

During this time of the village's heyday, lead mining combined with farming as the major occupation of the inhabitants, and there is still much evidence of their spoil heaps and shafts in the surrounding meadows. The village well dressings take place in late August.

The small parish church has an unusual dedication to St Hugh, and was built in 1888. The Wesleyan Reform Chapel was built in 1836 and has a grand, Tuscan-style porch and thin, lancet side-windows.

EAT AND DRINK
The Bull's Head Inn
thebullatfoolow.co.uk
Foolow, S32 5QR | 01433 630873
This 19th-century former coaching inn is the epitome of the English country pub, with bags of atmosphere and character which are in part due to its open fires, oak beams and flagstone floors but also its good food and beer. The bar serves Black Sheep and Peak Ales, lunchtime snacks and sandwiches, in addition to a wide choice of main meals.

▶ Froggatt   MAP REF 278 C6

The Froggatt Show, held every August Bank Holiday Saturday, is the highlight of the year in this small, rather exclusive village which lies beneath the frowning gritstone escarpment of Froggatt Edge on the well-wooded banks of the Derwent. The show has agricultural roots and was founded in the 1930s as an offshoot of the village 'Cow Club', but its exhibits are now mainly horticultural, reflecting the change in village society.

The bridge over the River Derwent dates from the 17th century and is unusual in that it has a large central arch nearer to the village and a smaller one on the other side, which probably formed part of the original bridge constructed when the river was narrower and before the Derwent was dammed downstream for the mill at Calver.

The Wesleyan Reform Chapel is the major building of note in the village, which uses All Saints parish church at nearby Curbar (see page 133) for its Church of England services.

EAT AND DRINK
The Chequers Inn ®®
chequers-froggatt.com
Froggatt Edge, S32 3ZJ
01433 630231
Walk, cycle or drive to this 16th-century pub, standing on a wooded hillside below the gritstone escarpment of Froggatt Edge. You won't be disappointed. Wooden floors, antiques and blazing log fires create a welcoming interior that's perfect for a pint of Peak Ales Chatsworth Gold, brewed on the nearby estate of the Duke of Devonshire. The kitchen's loyalty to local produce and suppliers is reflected in the pub menu of main meals. In addition, there's a range of lunchtime sandwiches and an ever-changing selection of blackboard specials, including vegetarian options.

▶ Glossop MAP REF 277 D3

Although firmly and proudly situated in Derbyshire, Glossop always gives the impression of a Lancashire mill town. That's because at the turn of the 19th century, there were more than 56 mills in the eight townships which make up Glossop, sheltering beneath the moors at the foot of the A57 Snake Pass (see page 240) from Sheffield. Most were cotton mills, but there were also paper mills, ropewalks and woollen mills. Not many survived, and those that did moved with the times and converted to power looms, which were steam-driven and needed more water and more coal.

The original Saxon settlement expanded rapidly in the early 19th century under the patronage of the Duke of Norfolk, who owned much of the land and moors hereabouts, and at one time part was named Howard Town after the family name and to distinguish it from Old Glossop, the more ancient village to the east. The Anglo-Saxon name Glossop came from *glott hop*, 'hop' being a valley and 'Glott' probably the name of a much earlier lord of the manor.

But it was the Howards who left the most indelible mark on the new town and who were responsible for most of the important buildings, such as the colonnaded Market Hall and the Railway Station, complete with a statue of the Norfolk armorial lion over its entrance. The beating heart of Glossop is still Norfolk Square, which retains a certain elegance and is surrounded by interesting shops.

Glossop suffered disastrously when the cotton industry collapsed in the 1920s, and it took decades to recover. Overspill housing from the 1960s has affected the character of the town too, but there are some fascinating nooks and crannies, hidden away in the fabric of the place.

Just beyond the vast housing estate of Gamesley lies the remains of the Agricolan Roman fort of Melandra Castle, while to the north of the town, near Howard Park, is Mouselow or Castle Hill, with important Bronze Age and Iron Age associations and the site of a motte and bailey castle built by Castleton's William Peverel.

Glossop's roads to the east lead to Longdendale (see page 203) and over the notorious Snake Pass, while a few miles to the west lies the M67 and the urban sprawl of Manchester.

EXPLORE BY BIKE
Peak Tours
peak-tours.com
SK13 7SH | 01457 851462
Cycle hire.

GO FISHING
Arnfield Reservoir
arnfield-fly-fishery.com
Tintwistle, SK13 1HP
01457 856269

PLAY A ROUND
Glossop & District Golf Club
glossopgolfclub.co.uk
Hurst Road, Off Sheffield Road,
SK13 7PU | 01457 865247 (club
house) | Open Mon–Fri, Sun all year
A course on the edge of the
moors, with excellent natural
hazards, and a difficult closing
hole (the 9th and 18th).

EAT AND DRINK
The Bull's Head
bullsheadglossop.robinsonsbrewery.
com | 102 Church Street, SK13 7RN
01457 237240
Patronised by stars from
Coronation Street and other
celebrities, the Bull's Head is
also prized for its superb Indian
cuisine, which is prepared by
chefs trained on the famous
'Curry Mile' in Rusholme,
Manchester. It's claimed to be
the oldest pub in Glossop and
attracts locals and visitors.

The Chocolate & Coffee Shop
Henry Street, SK13 8BW
01457 864604
It may be a little cramped
inside, but the characterful
Venetian-windowed Chocolate
& Coffee Shop more than
makes up for it with its
delicious coffee, cakes and
other treats. There is also a
wide range of handmade
chocolate treats, designed
to tempt even the most
ardent dieter.

Mettrick's Butchers
mettricksbutchers.com
20–22 High Street West, SK13 8BH
01457 852239
You can enjoy a delicious range
of mouth-watering home-
cooked lunchtime snacks,
including sandwiches, burgers,
meat pies and wraps, from this
multi-award-winning butcher's
shop. Mettrick's are different
from most modern butchers
because all their free-range
meat and produce is sourced
from local farms and processed
in their own abattoir. No wonder
John Mettrick is one of only
10 butchers in the UK to have
been awarded the accolade
Master Butcher.

Goyt Valley MAP REF 277 D6
The ever-popular Goyt Valley has accurately been described as
the Dark Peak in microcosm. It has everything you might
expect to find in a typical Dark Peak valley – wild peat and
heather moorland enclosing still reservoirs embowered in dark
ranks of alien conifers.

The River Goyt flows from south to north, rising in the bogs
of Whetstone Ridge on Axe Edge Moor, a wild and windswept
place with a reputation for attracting some of the worst of the
weather. The river eventually joins the River Tame in Stockport
to create the famous River Mersey and empties into the Irish

▶ The River Goyt

Sea at Liverpool. Its upper and middle reaches cleave a deep, gorge-like valley through some of the most unspoilt moorland in the Peak District. In late April and May golden plovers and curlews add their voices to those of pipits and larks, and this is also the breeding ground of the twite, a small finch with a pink rump.

This is an area that is threaded by old packhorse trails and the old railway track of the former Cromford and High Peak line. It is also the place where Cheshire meets Derbyshire, amid a blaze of heather and bilberry-carpeted uplands.

Originally, the Goyt was as natural an upland valley as any in the Peak, but the river was impounded and meadowlands and farms flooded to create the **Fernilee** and **Errwood** reservoirs for the citizens of nearby Stockport. Fernilee was the first to be completed in 1938, and the Errwood followed relatively recently in 1967. The original scatter of ancient oaks was replaced by dense conifer plantations, planted in the interests of water purity. The other victim of the flooding of the valley was the Italianate mansion of Errwood Hall, built by the prosperous Grimshawe family in 1830. Only its evocative arched ruins remain, surrounded by banks of rhododendrons and azaleas, originally planted by the Grimshawes.

The combination of reservoir and forest, cobalt and viridian beneath the deep magenta of the heather moorland, rising to the highest point in Cheshire at nearby **Shining Tor**, 1,834 feet (559m), makes the Goyt Valley a colourful place to be in late summer. There are parking and picnic sites around the

reservoir shores and some facilities are available at **Derbyshire Bridge**, at the upper end of the valley. The walks through the woodlands draw so many walkers and visitors that there is a one-way system up the narrow road to Derbyshire Bridge – on summer Sundays and bank holidays this road is closed to traffic. Near the source of the river is the Cat & Fiddle Inn, at 1,689 feet the second-highest pub in England.

GO FISHING

Simpson's Tackle

simpsonstackle.co.uk

Whaley Bridge, SK23 7HS

01663 734220

Day tickets and membership of local clubs are available at this shop, alongside the usual fishing equipment.

EAT AND DRINK

Cat & Fiddle Inn

catandfiddleinn.com

Buxton Road, SK11 0AR

01298 78366

Like many other high-altitude hostelries such as The Snake Pass Inn (see page 241), the Cat & Fiddle was built in the turnpike era at the beginning of the 19th century. It is still a very welcome sight for traffic on the sinuous A537, much-loved by speeding motorcyclists. But be warned, it's considered to be a dangerous road so take care. There are no other buildings to be seen for miles around, and on a dark and foggy winter's night, it stands out like a beacon of light for travellers between Buxton and Macclesfield or Congleton to the west.

▼ Errwood Reservoir, the Goyt Valley

▶ Great Hucklow MAP REF 278 B5

Nowhere was Jaques's claim in Shakespeare's *As You Like It* that 'All the world's a stage, and all the men and women merely players' truer than in the isolated village of Great Hucklow. It's hard to believe, but this bleak former lead-mining village tucked under Hucklow Edge was once renowned all over the country for its outstanding amateur dramatic group, known as the Hucklow Players.

The group was the inspiration of Dr Laurence du Garde Peach, a well-known author, playwright, broadcaster and dramatist, who lived at nearby Housely and whose father had been the local minister. The Players, all of whom were local people, performed in the Unitarian Holiday Home in the village until 1938, when they moved to a converted cupola barn which became the new playhouse. Plays were often performed in the Derbyshire dialect, which may have made them sometimes difficult to understand to audiences which came from as far away as Stratford-upon-Avon and Harrogate. To aid local people, plays were often put on to coincide with the full moon, because most of the audience had to walk home in the dark to the neighbouring villages after the performance. The playhouse is now used as a Scout centre for visiting groups.

Great Hucklow's Primary School was built in 1873 on a lead mine hillock – another reminder of the days when the village was yet another important centre of the lead mining industry.

At Camphill Farm, high on Hucklow Edge, the Derbyshire and Lancashire Gliding Club (see below) has its headquarters, and gliders often fill the skies above the village. The club was founded in 1935 and occupies one of the most spectacular launching sites at over 1,360 feet above the sea.

TAKE OFF
Derbyshire and Lancashire Gliding Club
dlgc.org.uk
Camphill, Great Hucklow,
SK17 8RQ | 01298 871270
Take to the skies with expert instruction and intuition. By appointment only.

EAT AND DRINK
The Queen Anne Inn
queenanneinn.co.uk
Great Hucklow, SK17 8RF
01298 871246

This lovely old inn dates from 1621 – a licence has been held for over 300 years and the names of all the former landlords are known. The sheltered south-facing garden enjoys wonderful open views, and it's an ideal space for al fresco dining and families during the warmer months. Inside you'll find an open fire in the stone fireplace, an ever-changing range of cask ales, and a short menu of popular pub dishes.

▶ Grindleford MAP REF 278 C6

Undoubtedly the most spectacular way to arrive in Grindleford
is by train, either from Sheffield to the east, bursting through
the three-and-a-half-mile-long Totley Tunnel (the second
longest in the country), or from the west, down the line from
Edale along one of the prettiest sylvan stretches of the Hope
Valley line. Before the railway came in 1898, Grindleford was
little more than a turnpike crossing (the toll house still stands
next to the bridge over the Derwent). The nearby settlements
of **Upper** and **Nether Padley** were small enough to be lost
among the trees.

The village prospered with the coming of the railway, and
most of the large houses jostling on the surrounding slopes
and terraces, with their attractive wooded backdrop, were built
by the resulting wave of commuting Sheffielders.

Grindleford Station is actually in Upper Padley. A few
hundred yards down towards the Derwent, over Burbage Brook
and past the converted watermill, lie the ruins of Padley Hall.
Very little remains of the 14th-century mansion except for its
foundations. It was once the proud home of the FitzHerbert
family, who were Roman Catholics and had the misfortune to
be caught harbouring priests in 1588, at a time when it was
illegal to celebrate mass. In fact the timing could not have been

▼ Padley Chapel

worse; the Spanish Armada had just set sail and the country was on the alert for spies. The two priests, Nicholas Garlick and Robert Ludlam (local men who had been trained in France), were arrested and taken to Derby where they were hung, drawn and quartered. John FitzHerbert died in the Tower of London 30 years later.

Padley Hall then became the home of one of Elizabeth I's chief priest-catchers before becoming a farm. The gatehouse, which had survived as a barn, was restored in 1933 and is now a peaceful chapel and the site of an annual pilgrimage in memory of the Padley Martyrs each July.

In the other direction, following the Burbage Brook upstream, runs a lovely network of paths through **Padley Gorge**. The boulder-strewn slopes of the gorge are covered in mosses and ferns, thriving in the damp shadows of the ancient oak wood. The trees are sessile rather than pedunculate oaks, the most obvious difference being that the acorns are 'sessile' – meaning they don't have stalks. Acorns provide an autumn bonanza for birds and animals; badgers and squirrels, jays and woodpigeons all make the most of the easy pickings. The spring bonus is the plentiful crop of caterpillars, gathered from the emerging leaves by migrants such as the striking black-and-white pied flycatchers, for which Padley Gorge is justly famous, and wood warblers.

Padley Gorge is part of the National Trust's **Longshaw Estate**. Longshaw Lodge, built in 1827 as a shooting lodge for the Duke of Rutland, stands beside the B6521 in attractive grounds. The grounds are also home to what is claimed to be the oldest sheepdog trials in the country, originating in 1898 and held every September since, apart from the war years. Longshaw is also the core of a country park, from where there is access to the moorland above Froggatt Edge. To the east rises White Edge on Big Moor, running south to Swine Sty, a Bronze Age settlement in a 'fossilised' landscape of prehistoric fields, picked out among beds of bracken and heather.

GET OUTDOORS
Longshaw Visitor Centre
nationaltrust.org.uk
Longshaw Estate, Longshaw, S11 7TZ
01433 637904 | See website for
opening times
A wonderful place to enjoy spectacular views of the Peak District, with plenty of ancient woodland, parkland and heather moorland to explore. The super shop at Longshaw sells gifts, including framed prints of local landscapes by Martin Decent. You can also buy Longshaw trail maps, a wide

range of Peak District walking leaflets together with walking accessories, wildlife products and books.

SEE A LOCAL CHURCH
Padley Chapel
hallam-diocese.com
Padley, Grindleford, S32 2JA
01433 650352 | Open Sun
& Wed 2–4 during the summer;
for private group visits, call the
custodian

The former gatehouse of Padley Hall, which now serves as a Roman Catholic chapel, is two storeys high with wooden floors and is a good example of a 14th-century medieval building. The ruins of the hall, although in many areas little more than foundations, are preserved in good condition. There is clear evidence of a range of buildings covering an area of about 20 acres arranged around the four sides of a small courtyard.

The annual joint Hallam and Nottingham Diocesan Pilgrimage – in honour of the Padley Martyrs – takes place on the Sunday nearest 12 July and is usually well-attended.

EAT AND DRINK
The Grindleford Spring Water Company
Station Approach, Grindleford,
S32 2JA | 01433 631011
Known to generations of walkers and cyclists, this venerable cafe is tucked next to the west portal of Totley Tunnel, on the Sheffield to Manchester line. Enjoy the full breakfasts, snacks and pint mugs of tea or coffee, all to be had in the company of like-minded customers.

The Maynard ⊚⊚
themaynard.co.uk
Main Road, S32 2HE
01433 630321
A number of attractions lie within easy reach of this stone-built former coaching inn, including Chatsworth House (see page 109), the Blue John Cavern (see page 104), the wooded crags of Froggatt Edge (see page 154).

Although decorated in a contemporary style, the Maynard's attractive interior retains plenty of original features and character, while local artists are invited to display their work on the walls, alongside photographs of Peak District scenes.

The Longshaw Bar, with its leather sofas and log fires, is a snug retreat and the place to enjoy a pint of Abbeydale Moonshine or Peak Ales Bakewell Best – brewed on the Chatsworth Estate.

The Maynard's contemporary restaurant overlooks the gardens and countryside, where seasonal menus might offer starters of a pork tasting plate, or crisp sea bass fillet; and desserts of home-made Yorkshire parkin with spiced rum custard.

The large beer garden offers panoramas across the moorland and river valley. Dogs are welcome.

▶ Haddon Hall MAP REF 274 C1

haddonhall.co.uk
Bakewell, DE45 1LA | 01629 812855 | Hall and gardens open May–Sep
daily 12–5, Oct Sat–Mon; see website for more information

For three centuries, Haddon Hall slumbered like Sleeping
Beauty's fairy-tale castle. It was kept ticking over and repaired
where necessary, but as the fashions for baroque, Palladian,
neoclassical and Victorian Gothic laid their sometimes heavy
hand on other houses, Haddon remained unchanged. Its grey
medieval towers, with their blanket of ivy, floating magically
over the River Wye, as if waiting for their Prince Charming to
appear and breathe life into them once again.

▼ The River Wye and Haddon Hall

And like all the best fairy stories, Haddon's tale has a happy ending, for Prince Charming did come – though he was a duke rather than a prince. John Manners, the ninth Duke of Rutland, while still the Marquis of Granby, came back to Haddon from the favoured family seat at Belvoir Castle in Leicestershire at the beginning of the 20th century, and began its painstaking restoration. The care with which it had been kept since the 1700s meant that his task, which he carried out with enormous sympathy, not just for the structure of the house but also for its unique atmosphere, was less daunting than it might have been. The Duke (he succeeded his father in 1925) insisted on two things – that as much as possible should be preserved in the house, and that, where it was necessary to replace, the highest standards of craftsmanship were to be used. Work began in the 1920s, and by his death in 1940 he had seen beauty awaken at Haddon once again.

Haddon Hall was originally owned by the Vernon family from 1170 until 1567 and passed to the Manners family by marriage. Over all those years the house was extended gradually; the Peveril Tower in the 12th century, the cross-wing in the 14th, battlements in the 15th, a gatehouse and courtyard in the 16th and the Long Gallery early in the 17th century. The chapel dedicated to St Nicholas was completed in 1427. For generations, layers of whitewash concealed and protected the its pre-Reformation wall paintings, which are now revealed and

▼ Gardener's Cottage at Haddon Hall

feature, among other subjects, St Christopher carrying Christ across the river on his shoulders.

Important and aristocratic families always had their own ancestral emblems or devices, which accounts for the curious animal shapes that appear on the gutters and in the ironwork of Haddon Hall. The boar represents the Vernon family and the peacock the Manners family; they appear alternatively around the architrave of the Long Gallery and all over the estate, perhaps most spectacularly as carefully clipped and maintained topiary figures in the huge yew bushes outside the Gardener's Cottage.

Today Haddon Hall, which has been described as 'the most perfect medieval manor house in England', reflects a sense of history that can only come from remaining in the same family for over 400 years. Whether the story that Dorothy Vernon escaped from the Long Gallery in 1558, down her eponymous stairs and over the packhorse bridge to elope with her lover, John Manners, is true or merely a piece of Victorian melodrama is open to question, but the story is perfectly in keeping with the romance of the place.

Owing to its remarkably untouched state of preservation, Haddon is much in demand as a film and TV set. The house and grounds have played host to no less than three versions of *Jane Eyre* and other screen credits include *The Princess Bride*, *Elizabeth*, *Pride & Prejudice* and *The Other Boleyn Girl*.

▼ Haddon Hall, rose garden

But it's not just the house that commands your attention –
it's the gardens too. When the ninth Duke of Rutland restored
Haddon in 1920s, he cleared the terrace of giant yews and
sycamores, as well as ivy on the walls. Pairs of clipped yew
trees are again a feature of this garden which, in the spring,
glows with more than 60 varieties of daffodil, polyanthus and
wallflower. As summer approaches, the roses take over: first
the climbers, then the floribundas and the hybrid teas in the
formal beds. Haddon also boasts a collection of clematis, with
'Mrs Cholmondeley' showing large, blue blooms in early
summer beside the upper door.

▼ The garden of Haddon Hall

▶ Hadfield MAP REF 277 D3

The unlikely claim to fame for Hadfield, a small village a mile west of Glossop (see page 155), is that it doubled as the bizarrely eccentric Royston Vasey, with its notorious 'local shop for local people', in the darkly humorous BBC TV series *The League of Gentlemen*, screened between 1999 and 2002, and in the 2005 film of the same name.

Hadfield village is an eccentric mixture of old and new, where the oldest building is the Stuart Old Hall in The Square, which bears a date stone of 1646 over its door. A number of textile mills were built in Hadfield during the Industrial Revolution, but all are now gone. The village was part of the enormous estate of the Duke of Norfolk, and the Victorian Roman Catholic Church of St Charles was built by Baron Howard of Glossop in 1868. Various members of the Howard family are buried inside the church.

Standing at the western entrance to Longdendale (see page 203), one of the major trans-Pennine routes now followed by the constant, thunderous stream of traffic on the A628, Hadfield is also the western terminus of the Longdendale Trail. This in turn is part of the Trans-Pennine Trail, a walking, riding and cycling leisure route which follows the line of the former Great Central's Woodhead railway line.

▶ Hardwick Hall

see highlight panel overleaf

▶ Hartington MAP REF 273 E2

Hartington, standing at the northern entrance to Dove Dale, wears the air of a prosperous market town, although it is nearly 800 years since its market charter was first granted and many years since a market was last held in its spacious town square.

The classical three-arched facade of the Town Hall, built in 1836, adds to this urban impression, and The Square is ringed by ancient inns and elegant 18th- and 19th- century stone cottages.

At the heart of The Square is the village duck pond, or mere, which sits like a pearl in a circlet of duck-cropped lawn. Nearby is Ye Olde Cheese Shoppe, selling the superb local Dove Dale Blue, a tasty substitute for the Stilton which used to be made in the village's famous former cheese factory, which is now being redeveloped for housing. Just a stone's-throw away are tea rooms, shops, a pottery and two old coaching

Hardwick Hall MAP REF 275 F2

nationaltrust.org.uk

Doe Lea, S44 5QJ | 01246 850430

Check online for opening times for the Hall; park, garden, shop & restaurant open all year daily 9–6

By any standards, Elizabeth, Countess of Shrewsbury – known as 'Bess of Hardwick' – was a remarkable and very shrewd woman. She came from a fairly modest social background and proceeded to outlive her four husbands, each one richer and higher up the social scale than the one before. With all her wealth, Bess had a penchant for building great houses, including the original Tudor Chatsworth (see page 109). But it is Hardwick Hall – built on an airy hilltop overlooking the Doe Lea valley and the buzz of the M1 between Chesterfield and Mansfield – which is perhaps her most lasting legacy. It was the last house she built, incredibly, begun when she was 70 years old, after the death of her fourth husband, the Earl of Shrewsbury, in 1590.

With architect Robert Smythson, Bess created an impressive mansion with enormous windows and six great towers surmounted by her ornately fashioned monogram –

'ES'. Such was the expanse of then highly expensive glass, the house was known locally as 'Hardwick Hall – more glass than wall'.

One of the first English houses to have the Great Hall built on an axis through the centre of the house, instead of at right angles to the entrance, it consists of three main storeys. A grand stone staircase leads to the state rooms on the second floor. The hall was designed specifically to house the collection of tapestries that still line its walls, and the Long Gallery, running the length of the east front, is hung with family portraits.

When Bess died in 1608 Hardwick passed to her grandson William Cavendish, who bought his brother's share in Chatsworth and made that the principal family seat. Thus, like Haddon Hall (see page 165), Hardwick Hall was left quite unaltered by succeeding generations.

As well as being a splendid example of its age, Hardwick has some particularly important works of embroidery; some worked by Bess herself and others by Mary, Queen of Scots, who was confined here for a time. The sumptuous embroidery of the bedhead in the state bedroom is an outstanding example. It's also worth taking tour round the garden, which has pretty parkland walks.

inns, which act as further reminders from the days when Hartington was a significant market town. The Charles Cotton Hotel is a reminder of one of Hartington's most famous sons, co-author with Izaak Walton of *The Compleat Angler*, (1653) who lived at nearby Beresford Hall (of which only an ornate Fishing Lodge remains) in Beresford Dale.

Another famous visitor to Hartington in the past was Prince Charles Edward Stuart (Bonnie Prince Charlie) on his ill-fated march on London in 1745. He is alleged to have stayed at the lovely 17th-century mansion of Hartington Hall, southeast of the village centre, which is now surely one of the most palatial youth hostels in the country. Hartington Hall was built by Robert Bateman in 1611, and is a typical Derbyshire three-gabled, stone-mullioned, H-plan manor house, converted to a youth hostel in 1934.

The hilltop church of St Giles is one of the most interesting in the Peak, with a two-storey porch, transepts and aisles dating mainly from the 13th and 14th centuries. The massive and dignified battlemented Perpendicular west tower stands watch over the village below. It's at the centre of one of the biggest parishes in the country, divided into four quarters – Town, Upper, Nether and Middle.

Three miles to the north in Hartington Upper Quarter are the mysterious mounds and banks of Pilsbury Castle, a Norman motte-and-bailey castle watching over the remote upper reaches of the Dove. A later historical landmark to the east of the village is the signal box on the former Ashbourne–Buxton Railway, which closed in 1967. It is now a fondly looked-for feature on the Tissington Trail walking and riding route.

EAT AND DRINK

Beresford Tea Room
Market Place, Hartington,
SK17 0AL | 01298 84418
This tea room is also the village post office. As ever, local produce and local baking is to the fore; try some of the local Dove Dale Blue (maybe on a chilli oatcake). In the winter months, the hotpot is particularly welcoming. Light meals are available throughout the year.

The Jug & Glass Inn
jugandglass.biz
Ashbourne Rd, Hartington,
SK17 0BA | 01298 84848
An ideal base for hiking the trails of Derbyshire's Peak District, strolling through the streets of Ashbourne and Bakewell, or visiting famous sights such as Chatsworth. Ales include Church End, and Whim from nearby Hartington, while the menu lists all the comfort food you could wish for. Superb views complete the picture.

▶ Hassop MAP REF 278 B6

It always comes as a bit of a shock to stumble across what seems to be a little Grecian or Roman temple stranded in the heart of the Peak District. The reason for the presence of the Classical Revival building of the Roman Catholic Church of All Saints at Hassop lies just across the road at Hassop Hall.

This elegant early 17th-century house was the family seat of the staunchly Catholic Eyre family, quite a rarity in this land of Nonconformism. The church, with its Etruscan temple front and Tuscan pilasters at the rear, was built in 1816 and contains under its coved and coffered ceiling a wonderful painting of the Crucifixion by Lodovico Carracci, and a fine monument to its founder, Thomas Eyre, who died in 1833.

Hassop Hall, now an exclusive hotel and restaurant, is a fine, three-storeyed country house standing within its own landscaped park. Inside there are black marble chimney pieces by White Watson of nearby Ashford in the Water (see page 66) and some excellent early 19th-century plasterwork.

Just below the hall on the road to Bakewell stands The Dower House, an imposing late 17th-century three-gabled house which used to be the village post office but which has now been converted into luxury flats. The Old Eyre Arms is a popular hostelry on the road to Calver, which is clad in Virginia creeper, vividly scarlet in the autumn.

EAT AND DRINK
The Old Eyre Arms
eyrearms.com
Hassop, DE45 1NS
01629 640390

In a village-edge location between the formality of Chatsworth's vast estate, bold gritstone edges and the memorable wooded limestone dales of Derbyshire's River Wye, this comfortably unchanging, creeper-clad old inn ticks all the right boxes for beers and food too. Real ales from Peak Ales and Bradfield breweries couldn't be more local, while all meals are prepared in-house and include a range of tasty dishes such as casseroles, fish dishes and vegetarian options.

Oak beams, comfortable furnishings and log fires provide a warm welcome and will almost certainly take the chill off after a long ramble.

▼ The Old Eyre Arms pub, Hassop

▶ Hathersage MAP REF 278 C5

Whether or not there ever was a real Little John, Robin Hood's faithful lieutenant, hardly seems to matter; most visitors to Hathersage want to believe that it really is his grave they see between two stunted yews in the churchyard of Hathersage's hilltop parish church of St Michael.

The grave close to the south porch has been excavated several times without producing any bones, though there is a story that a huge thighbone was unearthed here in 1784. In fact the half-hidden stones at the head and foot of the grave were probably set up as the village 'perch' (as in 'rod, pole and perch'), the standard measure used to mark out land in the days of open-field or strip farming.

The church has a battlemented 15th-century Perpendicular tower with a graceful spire but dates mainly from the 14th century. The east window, with its stained glass by Thomas Kempe, was taken from the church at Derwent when it was submerged under the rising waters of the Ladybower Reservoir, further up the valley. The brasses to the Eyre family in Hathersage church are among the finest in the Peak, and deserving of special mention is that of Robert Eyre, who died in 1459, complete in his plate armour, and another Robert Eyre, of around 1500.

Hathersage (the name means 'heather edge') stands on a south-facing shoulder beneath Stanage Edge, a three-mile

▼ The Vicarage at Hathersage

▶ The grave of Little John

long curtain of rock famous for its rock climbs on the abrasive gritstone. It was the abrasiveness of that gritstone which was the basis of Hathersage's first industry. Making the millstones was a local speciality in the 18th century and the were hewn directly from the rock faces of Stanage, where many can still be found abandoned in the bracken and heather. The circular stones were trundled down in pairs to the village by placing a wooden axle between them.

Then came the Industrial Revolution and five mills were built in the village to make pins and needles. The mills had a short life, as unfortunately did the men who ground the needle-points and had to breathe in the choking dust.

The most interesting buildings in Hathersage are along the main road and off School Lane. Past 15th-century Hathersage Hall and Farm, and up the narrow Church Bank, it is possible to walk around Bank Top, a green knoll overlooking the alder-lined Hood Brook and valley. To the south stands Bell House and The Bell Room, once an inn and barn beside the village green and stocks, to the west stands the Vicarage, and to the east is Camp Green, the ramparts of a possible 9th-century stockade. Just outside the village on the Bakewell road is David Mellor's award-winning circular Cutlery Factory, Design Museum, Café and Country Shop, built on the site of the former village gas holder.

Charlotte Brontë often came to Hathersage to stay with her friend Ellen Nussey at the Vicarage, and is thought to have based the town 'Morton' in *Jane Eyre* on the village. North Lees Hall (private), a fine embattled Tudor tower house a mile and a half northeast of the village, beneath Stanage Edge, is thought to have been Charlotte's model for Thornfield Hall, Mr Rochester's home. It is now let as a holiday home by the Vivat Trust. In fact, North Lees Hall is one of seven Eyre halls around Hathersage, all thought to have been built by Robert Eyre for his sons and all within sight of one another.

▲ The Derwent Valley from Stanage Edge

Stanage Edge above the village divides the featureless moorland of the Hallam and Burbage Moors from the beautiful verdant valley of the River Derwent. Prehistoric pathways, Roman roads and packhorse trails criss-cross the moors and converge below the confluence of the Derwent and the Noe, making it popular with walkers.

VISIT THE MUSEUM

David Mellor Cutlery Factory, Design Museum, Country Shop and Café

davidmellordesign.com
The Round Building, Hathersage, S32 1BA | 01433 650220 | Free guided tours of factory Sat–Sun 3pm
The factory is round because it was rather ingeniously built on the foundations of the former village gas holder. It was the brainchild of the late David Mellor, a key figure in British design with an international reputation as a designer and manufacturer, particularly famous for his innovative cutlery designs. The Factory is on the road to Bakewell, where you can also see examples of Mellor's street furniture. All the cutlery is manufactured in the modern factory. The Round Building, designed by Sir Michael Hopkins, won many architectural awards when it was built in 1990.

lights of a set of working David Mellor-designed traffic lights here. Seating 42, the cafe faces Michael Hopkins' award-winning Round Building (see page 176), and in summer the doors open to provide extra seating on the relaxing terrace. Designed by David Mellor's son Corin, the cafe is a fine example of informal modern dining style, equipped with the best of David Mellor's tableware and cutlery.
The cafe serves delicious lunches mainly using local produce, as well as specialist teas, coffee and an irresistible range of home-made cakes. The menu changes daily according to the season.

GET ACTIVE
Rock Lea Activity Centre
iain.co.uk
Station Road, Hathersage, S32 1DD
01433 650345
Caving, potholing, rock climbing, orienteering, abseiling, mountain biking and water sports, all supervised and organised by thoroughly qualified instructors.

EAT AND DRINK
David Mellor Cutlery Factory, Design Museum Café
davidmellordesign.com
The Round Building, S32 1BA
01433 650220 | Design Museum, shop and cafe open Mon–Sat 10–5, Sun 11–5
You can enjoy your lunch while sitting under the changing red, red-and-amber and green

The George Hotel ⊛⊛
george-hotel.net
Main Road, S32 1BB
01433 650436
The 500-year-old stone-built hotel looks like a little castle, with its turreted frontage and mullioned windows. Its interiors have been carefully planned to do nothing to obscure the impression of dignified venerability, the hefty stones of the walls offset by wooden floors and simple furniture in the smartly attired dining room. The George has created a name for itself over the last 15 years. The hard-working kitchen makes many of the foundation elements of the menu in-house, including breads, pasta and preserves. Most of the rest is sourced from trusted Peak District suppliers.

The Plough Inn ◉
theploughinn-hathersage.co.uk
Leadmill Bridge, S32 1BA
01433 650319
The 16th-century Plough stands in nine acres by the River Derwent where the 18th-century, three-arched Leadmill Bridge carries the Derwent Valley Heritage Way over the rapids that disturb the otherwise gently flowing waters. Inside, smart red tartan carpets work well with the open fires and wooden beams of the bar, which serves hand-pulled Adnams, Black Sheep and Timothy Taylor ales. An extensive British menu features locally sourced starters and the best part of 20 main courses, as well as traditional pub grub too. The Plough's well-stocked cellar combines a fine choice of Old and New World wines.

The Scotsman's Pack Country Inn
scotsmanspack.com
School Lane, S32 1BZ
01433 650253
Set in the beautiful Hope Valley on one of the old packhorse trails used by Scottish 'packmen', this traditional inn is a short walk from Hathersage church and Little John's Grave. Weather permitting, head outside onto the sunny patio, next to the trout stream. The pub offers a good choice of hearty daily specials perhaps best washed down with a pint of Jennings Cumberland. This is a perfect base for walking and touring the Peak District.

▶ Hayfield MAP REF 277 D4

Hayfield, a now-peaceful former industrial village, is probably best known as the western gateway to Kinder Scout, the highest hill in the Peak. Kinder exerts its unseen yet overpowering influence on almost everything about the place, and it was famously the starting point of the Mass Trespass on Kinder in 1932 (see page 191), which gave us the right to roam we enjoy today.

The picturesque name and rural setting belies Hayfield's industrial past. The village once hummed and rattled to the sounds of cotton and paper mills, calico printing and dye works. But it seems it has also always resounded to marching feet and cries of protest. In 1830, 100 years before the Kinder protest, 1,000 mill workers gathered to demand a living wage, but were dispersed by hussars. Eleven men appeared at Derby Assizes as a result, but the cotton industry was in terminal decline and all the anger was in vain.

Today Hayfield is a quiet village, catering for tourists of all kinds but particularly for those grim-faced, booted and rucksacked experienced walkers heading for the heights of Kinder. The village is split into two by the A624 Buxton–Glossop road, and the western side is now largely made up of suburban houses for people working in nearby Manchester.

It has plenty of little cafes and restaurants with quaint and inventive names. One of the most revealing places to while away a few minutes is by the bridge, next to the courtyard of the Royal Hotel, which looks out over the River Sett, from the war memorial to the jumble of cottages and sloping roofs at the back of Church Street.

Nearby the fine Georgian church of St Matthew gives a hint of the former prosperity of the village. Rebuilt in 1818 in the style popular at the time, the chancel was added in 1894. Inside, the gallery on three sides is supported by thin cast-iron columns and there are rows of box pews. The churchyard was the scene of two 'resurrections' within three years of each other during the 18th century. In 1745, several witnesses attested to seeing hundreds of bodies rise out of their graves and ascend into heaven. Three years later, there was a disastrous flood which ripped through the churchyard and disinterred many bodies, which were swept away downstream.

Hayfield was the venue for two annual cattle and sheep fairs in the past, but all that remains now is the Hayfield Sheepdog Trials and Country Fair, held every September at Spray House Farm. Hayfield also holds a popular Jazz Festival.

One of Hayfield's most famous sons was the actor Arthur Lowe, Captain Mainwaring in TV's *Dad's Army*. His father was a member of the village cricket team, and he regularly brought members of the cast to play the village team on the delightfully situated village cricket ground on the Kinder Road. The recent (2013) gritty ITV drama series *The Village*, starring John Simm and Maxine Peake, used Hayfield as its eponymous setting. The 'farm' of the impoverished Middleton family was actually a barn at Highfield Farm at Upper Booth in Edale.

The bulk of Hayfield's visitors are the serious walkers who head east out of the village, through the valley of the Kinder River and past the Kinder Reservoir to the brooding, russet expanse of the Kinder plateau. Families and other easy-going ramblers head west along the Sett Valley Trail towards New Mills. The car park at the start of this three-mile trail, separated from the main village by the A624, was once the railway station, and the trail follows the course of the single-track line.

In its heyday thousands of visitors, including many of the 1932 trespassers, arrived here from Manchester via the New Mills branch line. For them, Hayfield marked the end of their everyday lives in grimy mill towns and the start of the countryside and the freedom of the hills.

GET OUTDOORS

Etherow Country Park

stockport.gov.uk

George Street, Compstall, Stockport, SK6 5JD | 0161 217 6111

Etherow Country Park lies at the heart of the Etherow/Goyt Valley and was one of Britain's first country parks. It is a fascinating area of woodland and riverside walks that is a rich haven for wildlife. Managed by Stockport Borough Council, it covers 240 acres and is a mix of natural habitats and industrial heritage visited by thousands each year.

CYCLE THE SETT VALLEY TRAIL

A two-and-a-half-mile trail between the former stations at New Mills and Hayfield.

EAT AND DRINK

The Royal Hotel

theroyalathayfield.com

Market Street, SK22 2EP

01663 742721

Up in the High Peak, below the windswept plateau of Kinder Scout, the hotel dates from 1755. Its period charm still very evident, one place to relax with a pint of Thwaites Original or Happy Valley Kinder Falldown is the oak-panelled, log-fired bar. Others are the Cricket Room, popular with the local cricket team, whose ground is next door, and the Ramblers Bar which has hiking boots strung along the beams. The bar menu keeps things simple with hearty mains and a sandwich menu, and there's a bistro menu at the weekends.

▶ Holmfirth   MAP REF 277 E1

A little gem of a town, Holmfirth is crammed into the valley of the River Holme, where the Norman Earl Warren first built a corn mill on the northern edge of the Peak, under the frowning heights of Black Hill. For several centuries the lower valley was left to nature, and the hilltop towns of Cartworth, Upper and Netherthong and Wooldale prospered, combining farming with weaving. There are fine stone farmhouses and cottages on the upper slopes of the valley, now often absorbed into the outskirts of the newer town, which tell the tale of former prosperity. With the expansion of the cotton mills in the mid-19th century, tiers of three-storey terraced weavers' cottages sprang up lower and lower into the valley, and eventually cotton mills crowded the banks of the River Holme.

The town grew rapidly with the textile trade, creating a tight-knit community in the valley bottom in a maze of ginnels, alleyways and narrow lanes. The river, which runs through its middle, has flooded on many occasions, the most devastating flood was in 1852 when, after a period of heavy rain, Bilberry Reservoir burst its banks. The resulting torrent of water destroyed the centre of Holmfirth and claimed 81 lives. A public

▲ Holmfirth

subscription fund was started to help the survivors rebuild the town, and the traumatic events are marked by a monument situated near the bus station.

Holmfirth should be explored at a gentle pace, because most of the streets are steep. From Victoria Bridge in the middle of the town it is possible to wander up Penny Lane, round the back of the church where the surrounding hills peep out between chimney pots and sooty walls, and down cobbled lanes worn shiny and smooth by a million clogs.

Most visitors come to Holmfirth because for nearly 40 years it was the home of the BBC television series *Last of the Summer Wine* – the longest-running TV comedy in the world, which was broadcast in more than 25 countries. You might still half expect to bump into Clegg, Compo, Foggy or Nora Batty as you wander round the narrow ginnels and alleyways, and there are reminders everywhere you go, from Nora Batty's Steps (complete with a pair of Compo's wellies) next to the Wrinkled Stocking Tea Room, Sid's Café and the *Last of the Summer Wine* minibus tours.

But Holmfirth was famous for producing comic characters half a century earlier, when plump ladies and gents depicted on the saucy seaside postcards were published by the local firm of Bamforths. Postcards became a serious business for the family firm just after World War I. Before that, it had already pioneered lantern slides and the motion picture industry, but was eventually upstaged by the big dollars and somewhat kinder climate of Hollywood.

10 top film sets

▶ **Haddon Hall** (featured in *Jane Eyre, Elizabeth, The Other Boleyn Girl*), page 165

▶ **Chatsworth** (*Pride and Prejudice, The Duchess*), page 109

▶ **Lyme Park** (*Pride and Prejudice*), page 206

▶ **Stanage Edge** (*Jane Eyre, Wuthering Heights*), page 176

▶ **Holmfirth** (*Last of the Summer Wine*), page 180

▶ **Hayfield** (*The Village*), page 178

▶ **Crich, Fritchley and Longnor** (*Peak Practice*), pages page 126 & 204

▶ **Hadfield**, near Glossop (*The League of Gentlemen*), page 169

▶ **Upper Derwent Valley** (*The Dam Busters*), page 136

▶ **Thor's Cave** (*The Lair of the White Worm*), page 217

▲ Holmfirth

SEE BEHIND THE SCENES
Last of the Summer Wine Exhibition
summerwine-holmfirth.co.uk
Scarfold, HD9 2JS
01484 766897
It's an odd feeling as you walk up the famous steps and then through the familiar-looking door and into Compo's house. Here you will find not only his disreputable sleeping garments hanging up, but other fascinating props, including a rather large inflatable lady. The main display room is a real treasure trove of *Summer Wine* memories, appealing not only to dedicated *Summer Wine* fans but to just about anyone, and all age groups. The Wrinkled Stocking Tea Rooms is adjacent to Compo and Nora Batty's houses.

EAT AND DRINK
Farmer's Arms
farmersarmsholmfirth.co.uk
2–4 Liphill Bank Road, HD9 2LR
01484 683713
A small village pub run with pride, the Farmers Arms sits in typical *Last of the Summer Wine* country. There is a welcome emphasis on real ales, with an annual beer festival every autumn and regular beers, including Timothy Taylor Landlord,

Greene King IPA and Bradfield Farmers Blonde. The menu appeals too; settle by the log fire and enjoy fresh dishes. Pop in on a Wednesday night and have a go at the quiz.

The Wrinkled Stocking Tea Room

holmfirthtearoom.co.uk
Huddersfield Road, HD9 2JS
01484 681408
Cool pastel walls and crisp check tablecloths – just what Nora Batty would expect! Located at those famous steps at Compo's house, indulge in home-baked pastries and cakes and a cup of good Yorkshire tea. Sid's Café (01484 689610) is a short stroll away, near the church.

▶ The Wrinkled Stocking Tea Room

▶ PLACES NEARBY
Standedge Tunnel
canalrivertrust.org.uk
Standedge Tunnel and Visitor Centre,
Tunnel End, Waters Road, Marsden,
HD7 6NQ | 01484 844298
See website for details of boat trips
& self-powered passages

Take a boat trip into the heart of the Pennines at the Standedge Tunnel on the Huddersfield Narrow Canal at Marsden. The Huddersfield Narrow has all the records: it is the highest (643 feet above sea level), longest (3.25 miles) and deepest (636 feet) underground at its deepest point.

At the Visitor Centre at Tunnel End, Marsden, you can have a go at 'legging' through a tunnel, just like the old canal navigators did, and see how the canal was excavated under the Pennines over 17 years from 1794, at the height of 'Canal Mania'. But the trip on a glass-roofed guided narrow boat which takes you actually into the mouth of the Standedge Tunnel is a real step back in time, as you sit back and wonder at the incredible work which went into this amazing feat of 18th-century engineering.

▶ Hope   MAP REF 278 B5

It still seems strange that it was the small village of Hope which gave its name to the six-mile-long Hope Valley, between the Derwent Valley and the much larger and more prestigious township of Castleton (see page 98) at the valley head. But Hope was a more important place in medieval times, and at the time of the Domesday Book boasted both a priest and a church (a rare distinction for Derbyshire), 30 villagers, four smallholders and a mill. Hope was also an important centre of the Royal Forest of the Peak, the hunting preserve of medieval kings and princes, which was administered from nearby Castleton. Two 13th-century cross slabs in the church are thought to carry the hunting horn symbols of Royal Forest officials, or 'woodruffes'.

Also in the churchyard of St Peter's is a fine, although headless, Saxon preaching cross, with interlacing

knotwork thought to date from the ninth century. The church itself dates mainly from the 14th century, and has a fine, though stumpy, broach spire. The chancel, with good stained glass by Kempe, was rebuilt in 1882, but it incorporates a piscina and sedilia of the early 14th century. The font is all that remains from the original Norman church mentioned in the Domesday Book.

The Hope Valley is the main access route from the Derwent Valley through to Castleton and Edale (see page 143), so the B6001 road through the village is often busy. Hope lies at the confluence of the Noe and the Peakshole Water, which emerges from the bowels of the earth two miles away at Castleton. Hope railway station, on the scenic Hope Valley line, lies half a mile out of the village, and is a perfect starting point for a walk up Win Hill, at 1,516 feet (462m) one of the best viewpoints in the whole of the Peak. Lose Hill, the dark twin of Win Hill and another fine viewpoint, lies due west on the opposite side of the Noe.

South of Hope stands the tall chimney of the huge Lafarge Hope Valley cement works, undeniably a blot on the skyline and difficult to reconcile within a national park, except that it was there before the park was founded in 1951 and is an important source of local employment. Most of the shale and limestone is excavated on site, and taken out by train.

▼ Hope Valley

Perhaps tourists of the future will come specially to see it, just as today's visitors explore old lead workings and derelict mills. Other landscape features are dwarfed in the presence of this monolith, which marks the dividing line between the gritstone and limestone. The bright green fields to the south are enclosed in an intricate mesh of grey limestone walls.

EAT AND DRINK

Losehill House Hotel & Spa ◉◉

losehillhouse.co.uk

Lose Hill Lane, Edale Road, S33 6AF | 01433 621219

Losehill House, built in 1914 in the Arts and Crafts style, is in a secluded spot in the Peak District National Park and has stunning views. These views are also appreciated from the Orangery Restaurant, a light-filled, comfortable room with a contemporary look. The kitchen rounds up Peak District produce and uses it to good effect in its modern, creative style, adding intriguing elements to many dishes.

The Old Hall Hotel

oldhallhotelhope.com

Market Place, Hope, S33 6RH

01433 620160

For generations Hope Hall, as this early 16th-century building was once called, was the Balguy family seat. In 1730 it became an inn, The Cross Daggers, then in 1876 it was renamed The Hall Hotel. In the 18th century a cattle market was held here; today, on bank holidays, the Hope Valley Beer and Cider Festival draws the crowds. There's a hearty main menu as well as lighter bites at lunchtime.

Cafe Adventure

cafeadventure.co.uk

Edale Road, Hope, S33 6ZF

01433 623313

This cosy little cafe is a good place to rest after a day's hiking or cycling – and dogs are welcome too. Sandwiches, salads, hot food, as well as cakes and pastries are served and there's a kids' menu. Produce is sourced locally where possible. There's also a small gift shop to take a look at.

▷ **Ilam** MAP REF 273 E4

The River Manifold, which passes to the south of the National Trust village of Ilam, has that unnerving habit of several other rivers passing through limestone country – it often disappears in summer. On the Ordnance Survey maps the river can be traced by a thin blue line, flowing south from Longnor to meet the Dove a mile below Ilam. But the Manifold has a secret life in dry periods, abruptly disappearing and flowing underground from Wettonmill to resurface at the aptly named Boil Holes in the grounds of Ilam Hall.

Ilam, built above the confluence of the two famous rivers, has always been an important settlement, although never very large. Originally it belonged to Burton Abbey, but after the Reformation the estate was broken up among three families; the Ports of Ilam Hall, the Meverells of Throwley and the Hurts of Castern. Of these, the Meverells no longer exist and Throwley Hall is a romantic ruin higher up the valley; the Ports sold Ilam to Jesse Watts Russell in the early 19th century, and the Hurts still live at secluded Castern Hall.

Watts Russell, who made his fortune as a shipping magnate, swept away most of old Ilam and rebuilt a slightly incongruous model village, the buildings of which are all in the *cottage ornee* style and have the look of so many Swiss cuckoo clocks, with their tile-hung and barge-boarded gables. The ornate 30-foot mock-Eleanor Cross in the centre of the village was raised by Watts Russell in memory of his first wife. It was recently tastefully restored by villagers.

Ilam Hall was rebuilt on a grand, battlemented Gothic scale, but only a quarter of it remains and it is now used as a youth hostel. The lovely parkland that surrounds it is open to the public. Close by is the German-looking saddle-backed towered church, totally rebuilt by Watts Russell, with the interior dominated by an over-the-top monument by Francis Chantry to

▼ Ilam Hall

Watts Russell's father-in-law, David Watts. Fortunately, he left undisturbed the evocative shrine to the late-Saxon hermit St Bertelin, or St Bertram. There are two weathered fragments from Saxon crosses in the churchyard.

The Ilam estate passed to the care of the National Trust in 1934 and is a popular destination for day visitors, partly because of its pleasant walks and partly because it is close to Dove Dale and has literary associations – with James Boswell, Charles Cotton and Izaak Walton.

GET OUTDOORS
Ilam Park
nationaltrust.org.uk
DE6 2AZ | 01335 350503
Open all year dawn to dusk
Ilam Park makes an ideal base for exploring the southern White Peak, along with Dove Dale and the Manifold Valley, including Ecton Mine. The estate comprises beautiful woodland and parkland on the banks of the River Manifold, and the Manifold Tearooms (see below) serves a wide range of delicious homemade food, drinks and cakes. If it's nice, you can sit outside on the picnic benches.

EAT AND DRINK
Manifold Tearooms
Ilam Hall, DE6 2AZ
01335 350245
The stable block to the Hall is a National Trust tea room with an emphasis on vegetarian and organic foods. Enjoy a cup of tea and a cake or try one of the larger meals. The local cheeses are also good.

The Yew Tree Inn
yewtreeinncauldon.com
Cauldon, Waterhouses, ST10 3EJ
01538 309876
Antiques, furniture and bric-a-brac fill the warren of rooms behind the lattice windows of this magical old pub. You'll find real ales, though food is limited to pies, baps and sandwiches. Don't let the quarry dust put you off – this one is a real winner.

◀ Ilam church

Kinder Scout MAP REF 277 E4

Kinder Scout, at 2,088 feet (636m) the highest point of the Peak District, is as much a spirit as a mountain. You'll find that ramblers either love it or hate it – there's just no room for compromise on Kinder. Its modest height – it only just makes the British qualification of 2,000 feet for a mountain – belies the seriousness of its nature. People die or are seriously injured every year because they underestimate Kinder, which lies on the same latitude as Labrador or Siberia.

The botanist/rambler John Hillaby perhaps came up with the best description of the five-square-mile plateau of chocolate-brown peat groughs (drainage channels) and hags (banks) in his *Journey through Britain* (1968): 'The top of Kinder Scout looks as if it's entirely covered in the droppings of dinosaurs.' Hillaby also described Kinder as 'land at the end of its tether' because all life had been grazed, drained, burnt or eroded out, leaving only the acid peat and a few gritstone boulders behind.

▼ Kinder Scout

All that has changed in recent years, however. Kinder is greening up and showing vegetation which hasn't been seen there for years. Since the National Trust acquired Kinder Scout in 1982, it has embarked on an extensive moorland restoration programme, assisted by the Moors for the Future Partnership of the National Park. In the first 20 years of its ownership, the Trust removed no less than 38,000 so-called bandit sheep from the mountain. And in 2010, the summit plateau of Kinder was fenced off by a temporary 12-mile-long barrier designed to keep sheep – not ramblers – out, because it was finally admitted that over-grazing was the major cause of the erosion. Groughs have been dammed to 're-wet' the moor and encourage the growth of newly-planted sphagnum moss, from which the peat is created.

The most impressive feature of Kinder, apart from the weird collection of animalistic tors around its edges at places like The Woolpacks, is the 100-foot-high Kinder Downfall, the highest waterfall in the Peak, on its western edge overlooking the Kinder Reservoir. It is famous for blowing back uphill when a strong, westerly wind funnels up the Kinder valley, so you can get wet from above and beneath if you happen to be walking past it at the time.

Kinder Scout, crossed by Tom Stephenson's monumental Pennine Way and the scene of the famous Mass Trespass in

▼ Kinder Scout

1932, remains probably the most iconic and walked upon mountain in Britain. Long may it remain so.

Forgive us our trespassers
The Mass Trespass on Kinder Scout in 1932 has been described by Lord Roy Hattersley as the most effective example of direct action in Britain's history. It was certainly the most significant event in the century-old battle for the Right to Roam on Britain's mountains and moors, a right now enshrined in the 2000 Countryside and Rights of Way (CROW) Act.

The events of Sunday 24 April 1932 have long since entered the realms of rambling mythology. Turned off by gamekeepers on Bleaklow a few weeks before and frustrated by the lack of progress made by the official ramblers' federations towards the Right to Roam, members of the Communist-inspired Lancashire branch of the British Workers' Sport Federation decided they would make a public mass trespass on Kinder Scout, the highest point in the Peak District.

Avoiding a strong police presence in Hayfield, about 400 ramblers set off from Bowden Bridge quarry, east of the

▲ Mass Trespass commemorative plaque at Bowden Bridge

village, for Kinder Scout, where they were addressed by their leader, Benny Rothman. About halfway up William Clough, the trespassers turned off the right of way and scrambled up towards the Kinder plateau to come face-to-face with a small group of gamekeepers. In the ensuing scuffle, one keeper was slightly hurt, but the ramblers pressed on to the plateau. Here they were greeted by a group of Sheffield-based trespassers who had set off that morning crossing Kinder from Edale. After exchanging congratulations, the two groups joyously retraced their steps, the Sheffield trespassers back to Edale and the Manchester contingent to Hayfield (see page 178). As they returned to Hayfield, six ramblers were arrested by police accompanied by keepers, and taken to the Hayfield lock-up on Dungeon Brow. The day after the trespass, Rothman and five other ramblers were charged at New Mills Police Court with unlawful assembly and breach of the peace. All six subsequently pleaded not guilty and were remanded to be tried at Derby Assizes in July. Five of the six were found guilty and were jailed for between two and six months.

The arrest and subsequent imprisonment of the trespassers unleashed a huge wave of public sympathy, which ironically united the ramblers' cause. A few weeks later in 1932 10,000 ramblers – the largest number in history – assembled for an access rally in the Winnats Pass, near Castleton, and the pressure for access continued to grow.

But it was to be another 17 years before the National Parks and Access to the Countryside Act was pased by the post-war Labour Government in 1949. This legislation set up the mechanism for the creation of National Parks, and the process for the negotiation of access agreements to open country. The Peak District was the first to be designated, and almost immediately negotiated access agreements with landowners for the former 'battlefields' of the 1930s on Kinder Scout and Bleaklow. The CROW Act eventually followed in 2000.

In 2002, at the 70th anniversary celebration event of the Kinder Trespass at Bowden Bridge, Andrew, the late 11th Duke of Devonshire, memorably made a moving apology for his grandfather's and the other landowners' 'great wrong' in 1932.

◀ Sheep on Kinder Scout

▲ Kinder Downfall

▶ **PLACES NEARBY**

Edale (see page 143) marks
the southern start of the
Pennine Way, and the
experienced team in the
Moorland Centre (see page
146) will help out with weather
advice, maps and guidebooks.
The centre is also headquarters
of the Moors for the Future
Partnership, providing a
national focus for moorland
research. Head along the
Pennine Way in the other
direction and you'll come to the
Snake Pass (see page 240).

7 modern wonders of the Peak

▶ **Kinder Downfall**, Kinder Scout

▶ **Alport Castles**, Bleaklow

▶ **Lud's Church**, Staffordshire Moorlands

▶ **Peter's Stone**, Wardlow

▶ **Thor's Cave**, Manifold Valley

▶ **Resurgence of River Lathkill** from Lathkill Head Cave

▶ **Dove Dale**

▶ **Langsett** MAP REF 278 B2

The northeast corner of the Peak is probably the least visited sweep of country for 50 miles around. Driving south from Holmfirth or west from Penistone takes you across open moorland and peaty plateau, with what seems the whole of Yorkshire spread out below in the cerulean haze.

There are very few villages to catch your immediate attention, but the upper valleys of the Little Don or Porter (one of the few British rivers with two names), which rise on the same watershed as the Derwent on Howden Moor, are full of interest. The Porter has been dammed in several places above Stocksbridge, and there are good access points to the reservoirs and riverside and high up onto the moors.

Langsett village provides the best starting point for an exploration of the Don and Porter and its string of reservoir pearls. Before Sheffield Corporation bought up the valley for water catchment this area was farmland, with some of the finest medieval cruck-framed farmhouses and barns in the country. Many of the buildings survive today, some still as dwellings but few as working farms.

One of these is Langsett Barn, which bears a date stone of 1621 and is now the village hall and National Park Ranger briefing station. It is worth a visit both for information and displays about the park and to see the solid functional beauty of the barn's ancient cruck construction.

Heading out from the car park it is possible to explore the woodlands and pine-lined shoreline of Langsett Reservoir or walk along the dam wall, past the crenellated valve tower (said to have been modelled on the keep of Lancaster Castle), to the old stone-built hamlet of Upper Midhope.

Above Langsett Reservoir, the Brook House Bridge gives access to the ancient trackway known as the Cut Gate, an old drovers' road which started at Derwent and led all the way to Penistone. The track climbs south over Midhope Moor, which is uncompromising high ground inhabited mostly by mountain hares, grouse and short-eared owls, littered with ancient flints and overlooked by the heights of Featherbed Moss and Margery Hill. This is the territory of the well-equipped and experienced walker, and is not a good place to get caught out in bad weather.

▶ Lathkill Dale MAP REF 274 B2

It's hard to believe, but although Lathkill Dale is now a haven of beauty, wildlife and serenity, it was once a hub of industry, ringing with the sounds of explosions, rumbling wagons and the constant hum of voices.

For centuries, the dale was at the centre of the White Peak lead rush, and many of the valley sides were exploited for their precious veins of lead ore (galena). But nature is a great healer, and the shafts, tunnels, drainage channels and spoil heaps have been absorbed into the natural landscape to such an extent that today they add a contrasting note which actually seems to enhance its natural beauty. Most of the lead was exhausted by the 18th century, but in the 1840s there was an ambitious attempt to drain the deepest mines by building a steam engine, powered by a huge waterwheel fed by the Mandale aqueduct. Today, the columns of the aqueduct and the ivy-covered ruins of the Mandale Mine Engine

▼ The Old Mill, Lathkill Dale

5 top dales

▶ **Dove Dale:** probably the most famous and easily the most popular of the Peak District dales, threaded by Izaak Walton's 'Princess of Rivers', page 139

▶ **Wolfscote Dale and Beresford Dale:** northern extensions of Dove Dale, with features Frank i' the Rocks caves and Pike Pool

▶ **Lathkill Dale:** Jewel in the crown of the Derbyshire Dales National Nature Reserve, with abundant wildlife and ivy-clad remains of industry, page 195

▶ **Manifold Valley:** Just as spectacular, with features like Thor's Cave and Beeston Tor, as its neighbour Dove Dale, but much less busy and more accessible by the broad, level Manifold Track, page 217

▶ **Chee Dale:** Threaded by both the River Wye and the Monsal Trail: highlights include Chee Tor and the Monsal Trail tunnels, page 229

▲ The River Lathkill

House emerge from the ash woods like Mayan temples deep in the rainforest. The truncated stone pillars of an aqueduct which carried water away from the mine and worked a waterwheel can also still be seen in the depths of the dale, and there are also various adits and shafts running off from the daleside path.

The River Lathkill, which runs east from the village of Monyash (see page 231) to join the River Bradford at Alport and eventually reach the Wye below Haddon Hall (see page 165), is one of the purest rivers in England, because it runs for the whole of its three-mile length over limestone. Like other limestone rivers, in summer and times of drought the Lathkill disappears underground for long periods. But when the

crystal-clear water is flowing, its purity means it is particularly rich in wildlife, such as native brown trout, dippers, kingfishers and the nationally rare water vole and white-clawed crayfish. Among the Lathkill's other rarities is the pink-flowered shrub mezereon; some of the finest stands of the deep-blue flowered Jacob's Ladder in the country are found in the rocky, upper reaches of the dale.

Unlike the pasture and silage fields of the plateau above, the grasslands in the upper part of the dale are ablaze with wild flowers in summer. The rabbit-cropped south-facing slopes sparkle with rockrose and trefoil, which attract blue and northern argus butterflies and burnet and forester moths. In the winter or in particularly wet periods, the Lathkill bursts from Lathkill Head Cave between the tributary Ricklow and Cales Dales in an impressive torrent.

Further down the Lathkill, following the well-worn footpath towards Over Haddon, the open grassland gives way to scrub and eventually to deep ash woodland that, in the early summer, casts a translucent shade and is full of songbirds. Access to Lathkill Dale is from Monyash or Over Haddon (see page 234).

▶ Leek   MAP REF 272 C3

Leek is the capital of the Staffordshire Moorlands, and as every Staffordshire person likes to tell you, the best bits of Derbyshire are actually in Staffordshire. Unlike most of the other towns circling the Peak District, Leek is not overshadowed by the hills and makes no extravagant claims to be an adventure centre. All around are green valleys and rolling pastures, full of dairy cattle and sheep. To the south lies the Churnet Valley, with visitor attractions, such as the Churnet Valley Railway and the old Cheddleton Flint Mill. To the southwest is Stoke-on-Trent with its fine pottery heritage. But to the east the foothills rise inexorably towards the serrated skyline of The Roaches (see page 237), Ramshaw Rocks and Hen Cloud, with bleak moorlands behind.

The heart of old Leek, easily missed on a fleeting visit, is the cobblestoned Market Place. At one end of it stands the 17th-century Butter Cross, a link with the town's dairying tradition. The cross was removed from its original location, at the lower side of the square towards Sheep Market, nearly 200 years ago and has since been restored. An attractive working watermill stands at the edge of the town as a monument with an adjacent museum devoted to James Brindley, the 18th-century so-called father of Britain's canals, who lived here during his childhood and early years.

Brindley was actually born at Wormhill, near Tideswell, but his family moved to Leek in 1726 when he was 10 years old. He was apprenticed to a millwright at Sutton, near Macclesfield, when he was 17 and was soon solving all sorts of engineering problems. Most of his ideas worked, and he was nicknamed 'Schemer'. Wealth and notoriety followed, but in his later years he became famous for his canal designs, particularly the Trent and Mersey and its Harecastle Tunnel. He died from pneumonia in 1772.

Textiles transformed Leek from a medieval market town into an industrial centre, and silk making was the speciality, which meant that many of the early mills were small and clean, with better working conditions than those endured in the cotton mills of the Peak District. Textiles from Leek were hugely supported by William Morris, founder of the Victorian Arts and

Crafts movement. Most of the mill buildings are now put to other uses, but the wealth generated by silk is recalled in the many imposing buildings commissioned from the Victorian architects William and Larner Sugden.

A few miles north of the town, the River Churnet has been dammed to form Tittesworth Reservoir (see page 252), with facilities including a visitor centre, woodland walks, car parks and a bird hide overlooking the shallow northern corner. Further upstream, a tributary of the Churnet was dammed to create Rudyard Lake, to supply water for the Trent and Mersey Canal. Allegedly, Rudyard Kipling's parents honeymooned here, and that's how he got his name.

VISIT A MUSEUM
Brindley's Mill & Museum
brindleymill.net
Mill Street, ST13 8FA
01538 483741 (local tourist office)
Open Apr–Sep weekends & BHs 2–5
This mid-18th-century working corn mill celebrates the work and genius of James Brindley, millwright and canal engineer who is renowned as the pioneer of the canal system. Dating from 1752, the mill has been restored from dereliction by the Brindley Mill Preservation Trust, and is the only known corn mill attributable as the work of Brindley. The mill also houses a museum with displays illustrating the life and work of Brindley and the history of milling, while still preserving the atmosphere of a working corn mill.

TAKE OFF
Peak Hang Gliding Centre
peakhanggliding.co.uk
8 Whitfield Street, ST13 5PH
07000 426445
Learn to hang-glide at this centre that's been established since 1974.

EAT AND DRINK
Roaches Tea Rooms
roachestearooms.co.uk
Paddock Farm, Upper Hulme
ST13 8TY | 01538 300345
The friendly folk at Paddock Farm cater for walkers and climbers, and this is a very homely place in which to indulge in that local delicacy, the Staffordshire oatcake (a dream with bacon and cheese). If that doesn't appeal, you can try the cream teas, calorific treats or maybe just a mug of tea or coffee, enjoying the remarkable scenery out over The Roaches.

Three Horseshoes Country Inn & Spa ⊛⊛
threeshoesinn.co.uk
Buxton Road, Blackshaw Moor
ST13 8TW | 01538 300296
The stone-built inn overlooked by lowering gritstone outcrops in the southern stretches of the Peak District does a good job of covering many bases. It's a country pub, a smart rural hotel and a chic brasserie and grill all in the one package. The original oak beams in the

brasserie and grill are offset by contemporary styling, with an open-to-view kitchen augmenting the dynamic atmosphere. An enticing menu includes the odd Southeast Asian dish among more traditional offerings.

▷ **PLACES NEARBY**

Blackbrook Zoological Park

Winkhill, near Leek, ST13 7QR
01538 308880 | Call for opening times

A visit to the Blackbrook Zoological Park is a great family day out, and a good chance to get up close and personal to some of the most endearing and rare animals in the world. A wealth of attractions includes the Pink Paradise; Flights of Fantasy in the Tropical House; The Warty Pig Walk, with endangered warty pigs; the Lemur Lodge; Pelican Cove; and Swan Lake; not to mention the ever popular World of Penguins.

Cheddleton Flint Mill

cheddletonflintmill.com
Leek Road, Cheddleton, ST13 7HL
Call 0161 408 5083 for opening times

Cheddleton Flint Mill is a fine example of a watermill built to grind flint for the pottery industry. The site features two watermills, a small museum, a period cottage, the canal and other exhibits. The Cheddleton Flint Mill Preservation Trust was formed in 1967 to preserve the unique mill complex and provide educational information concerning the historical development of pottery raw materials. In 1972 the Trust widened its objectives to encompass more of Britain's Industrial Heritage and became the Cheddleton Flint Mill Industrial Heritage Trust.

Churnet Valley Railway

churnet-valley-railway.co.uk
Cheddleton Station, Cheddleton, ST13 7EE | 01538 750755
See website for times & events

The Churnet Valley Railway takes you back to the classic days of railway travel on a 10.5 mile rural line that passes through beautiful countryside, known as Staffordshire's 'Little Switzerland'. The line passes through Kingsley and Froghall, Consall, Cheddleton and Leekbrook, the picturesque stations offer lots of interest with a complete range of visitor facilities, and there's plenty more to see and enjoy along the way. In addition to the return journey along the valley, there's contrasting moorland scenery on the 16-mile round trip along the Cauldon branch.

Kingsley Bird & Falconry Centre

kingsleyfalconry.co.uk
Sprink Lane, Kingsley, ST10 2BX
01538 754784 | See website for times & events

Formerly known as the Churnet Valley Wildlife Park, the Kingsley Bird and Falconry Centre is situated in the beautiful Churnet Valley, with breathtaking views over the surrounding countryside. It provides a unique habitat where visitors can marvel at the sight of spectacular birds of prey from all around the world. A wide variety of owls, hawks, falcons and eagles can be seen in the bird park, and you can take a one-hour guided tour accompanied by expert staff. A special experience is the one-to-one half-day visit which take you into the bird enclosures and behind the scenes to gain a greater understanding of the birds and how the park is run. You can also take a falconry flying experience, and learn how birds of prey were used for hunting.

Rudyard Lake
rudyardlake.com
ST13 8XB | 01538 306280
This lake was created to feed the canal system of the West Midlands more than 200 years ago. Today, the two-and-a-

half-mile lake is a lovely day out, offering boat hire, sailing and coarse angling. It also is a good spot for a walk and to keep an eye out for wildlife.

Rudyard Lake Steam Railway
rlsr.org
Rudyard Station, Rudyard Road, nr Leek, ST13 8PF | 01538 306704
See website for times & events
The Rudyard Lake Steam Railway is one of the UK's finest heritage steam railways, providing a trip along Rudyard Lake and a great family day out. It uses narrow-gauge steam engines, which are equivalent to about half the size of a normal narrow-gauge railway, with 10.25-inch gauge tracks. Trains have covered coaches and run in all weathers.

The lake was developed by the North Staffordshire Railway for the workers of the Midlands and Northwest. It was recently named as the third most romantic spot in the UK.

The Limestone Way MAP REF 274 C2

Waymarked with the head of the Derbyshire ram, the Limestone Way is a delightful 46-mile walk through the limestone plateau of the White Peak. Despite the hilly nature of the terrain, the walk is not over-taxing, and can easily be accomplished in three days.

There are many fine views and constantly changing scenery along the route, and also constant reminders of Derbyshire's lead mining industry of the 18th and 19th centuries, and of its agricultural past, with a network of pearly white drystone walls dominating much of the landscape.

The route starts from Castleton in the Hope Valley (see page 98) and finishes at Rocester in Staffordshire. It passes through the heart of the Derbyshire dales and visits some interesting hamlets and villages along the way. From Castleton, the route goes through Peak Forest, Miller's Dale, Flagg, Monyash, Youlgreave, Winster, Matlock, Bonsall, Parwich, Tissington and Thorpe, before crossing the Dove into Staffordshire. It then passes through Marten Hill, Lower Ellastone and finishes back in the Dove Valley at Rocester.

▶ Litton   MAP REF 278 B6

Clustered around its long village green with an ancient cross and stocks at one end, Litton, a small village 1,000 feet up on the limestone plateau, is very much a typical White Peak village. The enclosing range of solidly stone-built cottages mainly date from the 17th and 18th centuries, and is as pretty as a picture, and as a result, much-photographed. The Red Lion is a popular hostelry at the centre of the village.

Much of Litton's prosperity was built on the traditional White Peak dual industries of lead mining and farming, of which only farming now remains as an important employer of local labour. The combined School, Church and Library was built by Canon Samuel Andrews, vicar of nearby Tideswell (see page 248), in 1865, and the more modern church was built in 1929. Litton hosts a popular well dressing in June each year.

Down in the dale is Litton Mill, a grim-looking early cotton mill, built in 1782 and now converted to holiday and residential accommodation. This was the scene, if the propagandist 1828 *Memoirs of Robert Blincoe* are to be believed, of some of the worst examples of child exploitation in the 19th century, perpetrated by the owner, Ellis Needham. Whatever the truth, the *Memoirs* were a potent catalyst towards long-overdue factory reforms.

One of Litton's less infamous sons was William Bagshawe, the so-called 'Apostle of the Peak', who was an outstanding Nonconformist preacher in this land of Nonconformism, and is buried at Chapel-en-le-Frith (see page 106).

EAT AND DRINK

Red Lion Inn

theredlionlitton.co.uk
Litton, SK17 8QU | 01298 871458
New owners are at the helm of this tiny pub in a terrace of green-side, stone-built cottages, which has served locals and visitors for two centuries. The warren of hobbit-sized rooms ooze character, shadows cast by log fires flit across the low beams, village chit-chat and happy ramblers returning from nearby limestone gorges add to the atmosphere, while beers from local microbreweries and a hearty menu completes the picture. Due to space, children aged under six can't be accommodated inside the pub.

▶ Longdendale MAP REF 277 D3

Follow in Alfred Wainwright's footsteps as you trudge along the Pennine Way from the atmospheric isolation of Bleaklow (see page 83), and you'll next drop into Longdendale. It's a picturesque valley stamped more firmly with man's hand than many others which you'll encounter in the Peak – the additional infrastructure, of varying degrees of sensitivity, includes a series of five reservoirs, a railway line, the constantly crowded and busy main A628 road, and a string of high-voltage power lines – but one which still cuts a dramatic cleft through some of the most desolate wildernesses of the Peak.

The valley was formed by the River Etherow, a tributary of the Mersey. Over a century ago the river was dammed to create a string of reservoirs, at the time, the largest man-made expanse of water in the world. From the west, these are Bottoms, Valehouse, Rhodeswood, Torside and Woodhead, and as well as supplying good clean Pennine water to Manchester, they add a softening agent to the wild scene, altering the character of the place so that it can sometimes look like an oasis in a desert. On Torside Reservoir white sailing dinghies now pirouette and scud, and the former Great Central railway line linking Sheffield and Manchester, which threads through

▼ The Longdendale Valley

the valley, has been converted to the Longdendale Trail, a pleasant walking and riding route which is now part of the Trans-Pennine Trail.

The building of the three-mile-long Woodhead tunnels under the moors at the eastern end of the valley was costly in terms of loss of life, and the graveyard of lonely Woodhead Chapel, set on a shoulder above the banks of the reservoir, contains the last resting place of navvies and their families who died of cholera while the second railway tunnel was being built in 1849.

The little former mill town of Tintwistle (pronounced 'Tinsel') lies at the western end of the valley, and has some attractive weavers' cottages. Crowden in Longdendale – brusquely dismissed by Wainwright as 'Manchester-in-the-country' in his *Pennine Way Companion*, though on what basis it's hard to know – above the Torside Reservoir, has a popular youth hostel on the Pennine Way and is a welcome sight to walkers after the rigours of Bleaklow to the south (see page 83) or Black Hill to the north. Apart from a few isolated farms there are no other settlements in the valley. Despite its fine scenery, Longdendale, in the shadow of the moors, often suffers from a wild and woolly climate, and the Woodhead road is one of the first to close and the last to reopen when winter snows arrive.

CYCLE THE LONGDENDALE TRAIL

This is a fantastic six-mile multi-user trail between Hadfield and the Woodhead Tunnels.

▶ Longnor   MAP REF 273 E2

The fate of little Longnor was sealed by the demise of the turnpikes and the lack of a railway link; its worthy ambition to be a proper market town withered away. It stands now in no man's land, on a ridge between the Manifold and the Dove, but at a pivotal point in the Peak District, in the very heart of the country. Around it lie strip fields dating back to medieval times; just to the north lies Derbyshire and the limestone country, while to the west are the darker gritstone hills of Staffordshire.

The Manifold at Longnor is no more than a babbling brook, but the valley is broad, with meadows and sandstone barns. Yellowhammers and whitethroats sing from the thorn bushes, and swallows swoop for insects over the reed-grass. Longnor presides over the long, straight road like a drowsy cat over a barn floor. The village is pretty and compact, with a little square and a Victorian market hall, now a craft centre and coffee shop.

▲ View near Longnor

A wooden notice above the entrance still carries the tariff of ancient market tolls.

The village found fame as the original set for *Peak Practice*, the long-running TV soap based on a Peakland veterinary practice.

EAT AND DRINK

Longnor Craft Centre and Coffee Shop

longnorcrafts.co.uk
Longnor Market Hall, SK17 0NT
01298 83587

This enterprising little cafe serves a variety of home-baked produce including Staffordshire oatcakes. The little Victorian Market Hall is also home to locally made art and crafts, all for sale.

Cobbles Tea and Coffee Shop

cobblescafe.co.uk
Market Square, Longnor SK17 0NU
01298 83166

Open seven days a week, this lovely little tea shop serves breakfasts, light lunches, sandwiches and cream teas.

▶ Lyme Park MAP REF 276 C5

nationaltrust.org.uk

Disley, Stockport, SK12 2NR | 01663 762023 | Park open all year;
see website for detailed opening times

Lyme Park, on the western edge of the Peak District, is a smoke-blackened mirror image of Chatsworth. It's a fine example of the Palladian style, the work of the Italian architect Giacomo Leoni in the 1720s, and famously featured as 'Pemberley' in the 1995 BBC TV adaptation of *Pride and Prejudice*. Darcy, played by Colin Firth, took his famous dip in the lake in front of the house.

Lyme, set in a rural idyll of gardens, parkland and moorland, yet only a stone's throw from metropolitan Stockport, was the home of the Legh family for 600 years. The interior, a mix of Elizabethan and later rooms, houses some remarkable Mortlake tapestries, the Lyme Caxton Missal prayer book and a nationally important collection of clocks.

If you prefer outdoor attractions to the splendours of the house, you'll enjoy the wildfowl on the lake and the deer on the moorland. The 1,300-acre park has excellent short walks and viewpoints. If you're lucky, the walk up to the 18th-century turreted former hunting lodge, known as The Cage, may reward you with a view of the Peak's largest herd of red deer, running freely alongside their smaller fallow cousins. Children can let off steam in the Crow Wood Playscape with its giant slide, badger den and rope walks.

EAT AND DRINK

The Timber Yard Coffee Shop

nationaltrust.org.uk

The Timber Yard, Lyme Park,
SK12 2NR | 01663 762023

In the shadow of Lyme Hall, this unpretentious and welcoming place offers plenty of delicious hot and cold snacks, soups and a range of cakes. There's a more extensive restaurant in Lyme Hall itself.

▶ Macclesfield MAP REF 276 B6

Specialising in silk was the salvation but ironically also the downfall of the Cheshire town of Macclesfield. Originating as a market town serving the surrounding rich Cheshire farming countryside, Macclesfield first became known for buttons, then for all kinds of silk products. By the mid-19th century, the town was literally bursting at the seams, with 56 silk 'throwsters' (producing the thread or thrown silk) and 86 businesses creating silk fabric or finished goods.

Despite this success, or perhaps because of it, the workforce lived in wretched conditions, with an appalling level of infant mortality, and with nowhere to go when the industry hit one of its frequent declines.

Silk mills, chapels and banks – solid square buildings of blackened stone – are still scattered throughout the town today. Among them is the huge Sunday school on Roe Street, which is now a heritage centre with a silk museum and shop. Near the old market cross, behind St Michael's Church and its beautiful soot-blackened chapel of 1501, lies a narrow garden

▲ Trentabank Reservoir

terrace known as Sparrow Park (officially, these are the Broadhurst Memorial Gardens).

This is a pivot of the old town; a place to stop and ponder its rich and chequered history. Below the gardens there is a steep bank, down which run the famous and picturesque '108 Steps'. There is a view through the shrubs of the railway station and over the hinterland of the town, to the green foothills on the western face of the Peak.

On the farmland of the foothills, above Sutton Lane Ends and a growing patchwork of housing estates, lie the two Langley reservoirs. They were built in the mid-19th century to provide clean water for Macclesfield, as a response to the rampant infant mortality and disease among the mill workers. But the young Charles Tunnicliffe, the famous country artist and wood engraver, knew them in more peaceful times as a haunt of sandpiper and moorhens. Head further into the hills and you'll find the Ridgegate and Trentabank Reservoirs, the

▲ The former silk mill, Macclesfield

winter resort of pochard and goldeneye and the home to
Cheshire's largest heronry. Then comes the conifer blanket of
Macclesfield Forest, once part of a vast royal hunting forest but
now offering bike and walking trails.

Close to Trentabank is the wooden log cabin-style Forest
Visitor Centre, from which there are many walks and drives for
exploring the area.

At the eastern edge of the forest lies the tiny Chapel of St
Stephen, where a rush-bearing ceremony is held each August,
recalling the days when abundant rushes were a common, and
renewable, floor covering.

At the highest southern access point there is a path that
leads onto open moorland and up to Shutlingsloe, a
distinctive ridged 1,660-foot (506m) summit known as the
'Matterhorn of Cheshire', and the scene of the dramatic
denouement of local author Alan Garner's children's fantasy
novel, *The Weirdstone of Brisingamen*.

VISIT THE MUSEUMS
The Old Sunday School
silkmacclesfield.org.uk
Heritage Centre, Roe St, SK11 6UT
01625 613210 | Open Mar–Nov
daily 10–4; call or check website for
winter opening times
The story of silk in Macclesfield,
told through a colourful
audio-visual programme,
exhibitions, textiles, garments,
models and room settings. The
Silk Museum is part of the
Heritage centre, a restored
Georgian Sunday school, which
runs a full programme of
musical and artistic events
throughout the year.

Silk Industry Museum & Paradise Mill
silkmacclesfield.org.uk
Park Lane, SK11 6TJ | 01625 612045
Open all year, Mon–Sat 10–4,
BHs 12–4
A working silk mill until 1981,
the museum now has restored
hand looms. Knowledgeable
guides, many of them former
silk mill workers, illustrate the
silk production process with the
help of demonstrations from
weavers. Exhibitions and room
settings give an impression of
working conditions at the mill
during the 1930s. The adjacent
Silk Industry Museum focuses
on design and manufacturing
processes.

West Park Museum
silkmacclesfield.org.uk
Prestbury Road, SK10 3BJ
01625 613210
Open Mar–Nov Tue–Sun 1.30–4.30,
Dec–Feb Wed–Sun 1–4

You'll be transported back to
the land of the ancient
Egyptians at Macclesfield's
purpose-built West Park
Museum. Travel down the
Nile with Victorian explorer
Marianne Brocklehurst,
daughter of Macclesfield mill
owner Charles Brocklehurst,
and see the treasures she
collected from her explorations
in the 19th century. Alongside
this renowned collection is a
local history display, including a
selection of works by local
bird and countryside artist
Charles Tunnicliffe.

VISIT...
Macclesfield Forest Visitor Centre
peakdistrict.gov.uk
Forest Road, Macclesfield Forest
SK11 0NE | 01260 252832
Managed by the Peak District
National Park and the place to
find out more about the flora
and fauna of the forest.

GO ROUND A GARDEN
Hare Hill
nationaltrust.org.uk
Over Alderley, Stockport,
SK10 4PY | 01625 584412
Check website or call for detailed
opening times
The beautiful parkland at Hare
Hill features a tranquil walled
garden with a pergola, and two
wire sculptures commissioned
by the last owner of Hare Hill.
There are woodland paths and
ponds, and, in late spring, a
brilliant display of more than 70
varieties of rhododendrons and
azaleas. The grounds were

originally developed as the setting for a Georgian mansion. The surrounding parkland has an attractive permitted path to nearby Alderley Edge.

PLAY A ROUND
Macclesfield Golf Club
maccgolfclub.co.uk
The Hollins, SK11 7EA
01625 423227 | Open Mon–Tue, Fri & Sun except BHs
Hillside heathland course situated on the edge of the Pennines with excellent views across the Cheshire Plain. The signature hole is the 410-yard 3rd, which drops to a plateau green situated above a babbling brook. The 7th hole is aptly named Seven Shires as seven counties can be seen on a clear day, as well as the Welsh mountains.

Prestbury Golf Club
prestburygolfclub.com
Macclesfield Road, SK10 4BJ
01625 828241
Mon, Thu–Fri except BHs
Undulating parkland with many plateau greens. The 9th hole has a challenging uphill three-tier green and the 17th is over a valley. The club has been host to county and inter-county championships, including Open qualifying events.

Shrigley Hall Hotel, Golf & Country Club
thehotelcollection.co.uk
Shrigley Park, Pott Shrigley, SK10 5SB | 01625 575757
Open daily all year

Parkland course set in a 262-acre estate with breathtaking views of the Peak District and Cheshire Plains. Designed by Donald Steel, this championship standard course provides a real challenge.

The Tytherington Club
thetytheringtonclub.com
Dorchester Way, Tytherington, SK10 2JP | 01625 506000
Open daily all year
Modern championship course in a beautiful, mature parkland setting with eight water features and over 100 bunkers. Testing holes, notably the signature 12th hole (par 5), played from an elevated tee with adjacent snaking ditch and a lake guarding the green.

EAT AND DRINK
The Alderley Restaurant ⊚⊚⊚
alderleyedgehotel.com
Macclesfield Road SK9 7BJ
01625 583033
Chef Sean Sutton conjures up exciting modern British food brimming with locally sourced ingredients and a trio of multi-course tasting menus. The conservatory restaurant hogs pole position for views over lush grounds and gardens, offering a splendid retro setting and crisp napery on well-spaced tables, while well-informed and amiable staff keep the wheels turning smoothly. There's also a more relaxed brasserie with a separate menu, serving British classics with a twist.

The Coffee Tavern

Shrigley Road, Pott Shrigley,
Bollington, SK10 5SE

01625 576370

A firm favourite with walkers,
cyclists and diners, here you
can enjoy anything from a pot of
tea and a cake or a light snack
to a three-course meal.

The Swan Inn

Macclesfield Road, Kettleshulme,
Whaley Bridge, SK23 7QU

01663 732943

Huddled in the shadow of the
craggy Windgather Rocks in the
Cheshire Peak District, the
Swan is an atmospheric
15th-century village inn. The
new dining room offers an
eclectic and international menu
as well as an extensive seafood
menu. Local craft ales such as
Thornbridge keep ramblers and
locals very contented, especially
at the pub's beer festival on the
first weekend in September.

▶ PLACES NEARBY

Capesthorne Hall

capesthorne.com

SK11 9JY | 01625 861221

Open Apr–Oct Sun & Mon; Park
& Garden 12–5; Hall 1.30–4
(last entry 3.30)

Capesthorne has been the
home of the Bromley-Davenport
family since the Domesday
Book. The present house dates
from 1719 and was designed by
the Smiths of Warwick. It was
subsequently altered by Edward
Blore in 1837, and after a fire in
1861 was rebuilt by Anthony
Salvin. Capesthorne contains a
great variety of sculptures,
paintings and other collections.
There are also lakeside gardens
and an ice house. Events run
throughout the year.

Gawsworth Hall

gawsworthhall.com

SK11 9RN | 01260 223456

Open Jul–Aug daily 2–5; see website
for other opening times

This Tudor black-and-white
manor house was the
birthplace of Mary Fitton –
thought by some to be the 'Dark
Lady' of Shakespeare's sonnets.
The house is a treat of
timberwork, paintings and suits
of armour while the grounds
are a rare example of an
Elizabethan pleasure garden,
include a tilting ground. Open-
air theatre and craft fairs run
here during the summer.

Tegg's Nose and the Gritstone Trail

cheshireeast.gov.uk

Buxton Old Road, Macclesfield,
SK11 0AP | 01625 374833

The best introduction to the
Cheshire part of the Peak
landscape is from Tegg's
Nose Country Park, along
Buxton Old Road to the east of
Macclesfield. There are views
from the Windy Way car park
across the Cheshire Plain and
walks along a network of
tracks and pathways, by the
old quarry or down through
woodland to the reservoirs
above Langley. It is possible at
this point to join the Gritstone
Trail, a waymarked footpath
running the length of Cheshire
from Lyme Park to Mow Cop.

▶ Magpie Mine   MAP REF 274 B1

Undoubtedly the most impressive of the remains of the once-great lead mining industry in the Peak are the evocative ruins of Magpie Mine, whose silhouetted chimneys and walls are a notable landmark high on the limestone plateau near Sheldon.

Magpie Mine was first worked in 1740 and then more or less continuously for the next 200 years, and although now silent, the buildings and some of the machinery have been carefully preserved by the Peak District Mines Historical Society. The site, a scheduled ancient monument, shows the various stages of its development, from the earliest, almost ecclesiastical, stone buildings through to the black, corrugated iron sheds and steel headgear which date from the last unsuccessful attempt to revive the mine in the 1950s.

Lead mining was always a dangerous business. There was a constant threat from rock falls, flooding and poisonous gases, as well as bitter disputes between different miners. Magpie was just one of several mines exploiting interlinked lead veins, which sometimes led to violence. In 1833, rival miners lit fires to smoke out their competitors, resulting in the deaths of three men. All of the accused were later acquitted.

Public footpaths run across the site of Magpie Mine and it's free to look around. What's particularly refreshing is that the site is not overrun with modern interpretation boards or waymarked trails, nor are there lots of fences or prohibitive notices. But do beware of sudden drops and don't touch any of the old machinery. At weekends, there's often someone at the adjacent PDMHS's field study centre, the former mine manager's office, on hand to answer questions or provide information.

▶ Magpie Mine

▶ Mam Tor MAP REF 277 E5

With its spectacular views and close proximity to the road and
Mam Nick car park just outside Castleton, it's hardly surprising
that Mam Tor is the best known and most popular of the Peak
District's hillforts. This popularity and ease of access has
resulted in the National Trust having to pave the footpath and a
large area around the airy, 1,695-foot (517m) summit in order
to prevent further serious erosion.

Known as the Shivering Mountain because of the instability
of the shale layers on its east face, Mam Tor is home to one of
the highest and largest hillforts in the Pennines (it covers
16 acres), and is one of the few to be excavated. In the mid-
1960s Manchester University chose Mam Tor as a training site
for its archaeology students, producing a wealth of information.

▼ Mam Tor

What can be seen today are the ramparts of a heavily fortified Late Bronze Age–early Iron Age settlement. The single rampart, with an outer ditch and another bank, can still be traced round the hillside until it meets the sheer, crumbling east face, which it is now thought formed part of the original defences. There were two entrances to the settlement, one leading to the path from Hollins Cross and the other down to Mam Nick. Mam Tor was probably a partially defended site with a timber palisade that was later replaced with stone.

Two Bronze Age barrows were discovered on the summit, the highest of which the National Trust has encapsulated in stone to make sure it is preserved. There was also an earlier settlement enclosed by the ramparts, and several circular houses or huts had been built on terraced platforms on the upper slopes of the hill. The pottery and other artefacts uncovered are of a style often found in house platforms of this

type and date from the Late Bronze Age. Radiocarbon dating of charcoal found in the huts put them somewhere between 1700 and 1000 BC.

Archaeologists have suggested that the fort could have been built as a shelter for pastoralists using the hills for summer grazing, but it may also have had a strategic military purpose. Depending on when it was actually built, it could have seen action during intertribal struggles of the native Brigantes, and may also have been used as a defensive position against the Romans.

Like most settlements from this far back in time, Mam Tor will probably never reveal all its secrets, but it's enough just to try to imagine the effort that went into building such an enormous fortification with nothing but primitive tools.

Standing on the summit and looking across to the brooding Kinder Plateau to the north, down to Castleton (see page 98) and the beautiful Hope Valley to the south, and along the Great Ridge to Hollin's Cross and Lose Hill, is to enjoy one of the finest views in the Peak. It was named as one of England's Top Ten viewpoints by the columnist and former National Trust chairman, Sir Simon Jenkins.

7 ancient wonders of the Peak

▶ **St Ann's Well**, Buxton, page 92

▶ **Ebbing & Flowing Well**, Tideswell or Barmoor Clough, page 248

▶ **Peak Cavern**, Castleton, page 104

▶ **Poole's Cavern**, Buxton, page 96

▶ **Mam Tor**, Castleton, page 214

▶ **Eldon Hole**, Peak Forest, page 236

▶ **Chatsworth House**, page 109

▶ Manifold Valley MAP REF 273 E3

The Manifold Valley, whose river rises within a mile of the Dove on Axe Edge, has managed to escape all the Victorian hype and carnival atmosphere of its over-populous neighbour.

But the Manifold heads south through equally superb limestone country, twisting and turning and passing some amazing geological features. These include the copper-rich Ecton Hill, which made the fifth Duke of Devonshire enough money to build The Crescent at Buxton (see page 88) in the 18th century; the awesome Thor's Cave, a gaping void in a 300-foot crag, the home of prehistoric man which, along

◀ Mam Tor rising above Castleton

with nearby Ossom's and Elderbush Caves, has revealed bones and flints from the Stone and Bronze Ages; and bustling Beeston Tor, with its treasure-yielding caves. It eventually joins the Dove in the prim model village of Ilam (see page 186).

Warslow (see page 254) and Wetton villages, on the 1,000-foot contour on opposite sides of the valley, are the main access points for the most dramatic section of the Manifold. A steep side road north of Warslow, off the B5053, drops down to Ecton, and the most beautiful section of the valley begins.

It runs southwards along a thin strip of level meadow, with steep, flower-studded, almost alpine-looking grassland on either side. The road, and what is now the Manifold Track, follows the route of the ill-fated Leek and Manifold Valley Light Railway, which opened in 1904 but survived for only 30 years. If its odd Indian-style engines with their primrose yellow carriages were still running today, the line would undoubtedly make a fortune as a heritage line.

Close to Wettonmill the Manifold usually disappears in summer down swallet holes, travelling the rest of the way to Ilam underground. Meanwhile its tributary, the Hamps, heads southwards and the Manifold Track stays with the old railway line along the Hamps to the large village of Waterhouses.

Many of the domed limestone hills hereabouts are called Lows, which means they are capped by burial mounds, and it is very easy on these dry 'karst' hillsides to imagine yourself in another, older world.

GET OUTDOORS

Cyclists and ramblers following the Manifold Track are passing through some of the finest ash woods anywhere in Europe. Clothing the gorge-sides in their feathery foliage, the woodlands provide a home for a remarkable range of wildlife; more than 240 plant and 150 insect types are present, together with dozens of bird species drawn by this natural bounty. Summer evenings find bats skimming the river's languid pools and fragrant meadows for bugs and moths.

EXPLORE BY BIKE

Brown End Farm Cycle Hire
manifoldcycling-brownendfarm.co.uk
Brown End Farm, ST10 3JR
01538 308313

Manifold Valley Cycle Hire
visitpeakdistrict.com
Old Station Car Park, Earlsway, ST10 3EG | 01538 308609
Mountain bikes, tandems etc.

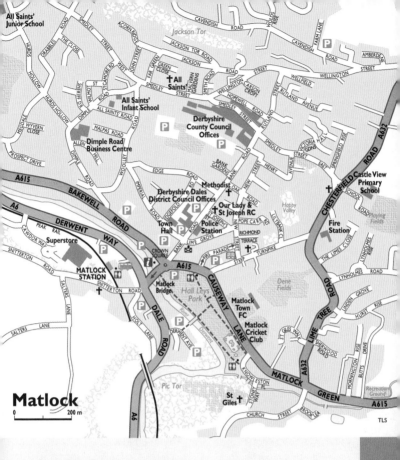

Matlock MAP REF 275 D2

When you look at it, it's highly appropriate that Derbyshire County Council should have its headquarters in the busy little township of Matlock, south of Bakewell on the A6. The name of the place comes from the Old English *Meslach* and probably means 'the oak where the moot was held'. It would seem that local government has been administrated from this place on the River Derwent ('the river of oaks') for over 900 years. John Smedley's huge Hydro, where Derbyshire County Council now meets, still lords it over the town from the Matlock Bank hillside where it was built in 1853. It is an amazing building with terraced gardens and a central domed tower, and looks more like a seaside hotel than local government offices.

Smedley was the man who founded modern Matlock, promoting it as a centre for the then-fashionable cure of hydrotherapy, which involved all kinds of showers and other bathing contraptions and the appliance of copious amounts of spring water at various temperatures. In the early 20th century there were 20 hydros on Matlock Bank alone.

Patients reached the Hydro up the very steep Bank Road and Rutland Street by cable-hauled tramcars, said to be the steepest tramway on a public road in the world. The Matlock trams became quite a famous tourist attraction and ran safely for 34 years until the lines were taken up in 1927.

Nearby is All Saints Church, built in 1883, which has a beautiful William Morris and Company east window by Burne-Jones, dating from 1905. Smedley also built the fairy-tale but now ruined Riber Castle, which overlooks the town in most views from its prominent hilltop to the south.

Matlock Station, which still links to Derby and the East Midland main line, is now the home of Peak Rail, which has long-term plans to reopen the former Midland line through the Peak District all the way to Buxton. At present, it only reaches the outskirts of Rowsley, but runs regular steam trains at weekends and a Santa Special at Christmas.

TAKE A TRAIN RIDE
Peak Rail – Matlock Station
peakrail.co.uk
Matlock, DE4 3NA | 01629 580381
See website for timetable & events
Experience the thrill of steam on the Peak Rail preserved railway, which operates over four miles between Matlock and Rowsley, and is open to the public throughout the year. The line was part of the old Midland Railway's route between Manchester Central and London St Pancras, which was closed in 1968. Most of the rest is now the Monsal Trail walking and riding route.

The northern terminus at Rowsley Station is on the site of the former LMS/BR locomotive depot. Facilities include an exhibition showing how the line was rebuilt by volunteers.

PLAY A ROUND
Matlock Golf Club
matlockgolfclub.co.uk
Chesterfield Road, Matlock Moor,
DE4 5LZ | 01629 582191
Open daily all year
Matlock is a moorland course with fine views across the Peak District.

EAT AND DRINK
The Red Lion
65 Matlock Green, DE4 3BT
01629 584888
This friendly, family-run free house makes a good base for exploring local attractions like Chatsworth House, Carsington Water and Dove Dale. Walks in the local countryside help to work up an appetite for bar lunches, or great tasting home-cooked dishes in the restaurant. On Sunday there's a popular carvery with freshly cooked gammon, beef and turkey. In the winter months, open fires burn in the lounge and games room, and there's a boules area in the beer garden for warmer days. Some of the ales from the bar were brewed on the Chatsworth Estate.

Stones Restaurant ◉◉
stones-restaurant.co.uk
1c Dale Road, DE4 3LT
01629 56061

Stones may be an intimate basement venue, but it has the best of both worlds on fine days thanks to a tiled sun terrace perched above the River Derwent. Fully refurbished after a fire, there's a new conservatory to go with a brasserie-style decor that works a mix of subtle earthy tones, wooden floors and designer fabric to match the Mediterranean-style menu of contemporary British dishes.

▶ **PLACES NEARBY**

Riber Castle
Riber Road, DE45 5JU

An eye-catcher for miles around, John Smedley's famous embattled castle, built in 1862, is now a roofless shell and recently it was estimated that the place had a life expectancy of only about 30 years. But planning permission has since been granted for the creation of a number of apartments inside and outside its crumbling walls.

Although Smedley built his castle merely as a romantic talking point for visitors to his Hydro in Matlock, after the death of his widow it became a preparatory school until being deserted in 1929. It became a government food store during the war, then the home of the Riber Castle Wildlife Park, where rare and endangered species were kept, occasionally being returned to the wild.

Although Riber Castle is always visible from Matlock, the small hilltop hamlet of Riber is quite difficult to get to, and has to be approached via Tansley or Cromford. East of the castle stand two charming 17th-century mullioned and gabled houses, Riber Hall, now an exclusive restaurant, and Riber Manor House, which has a date stone of 1633.

Lea Gardens
leagarden.co.uk
Long Lane, Lea, Matlock, DE4 5GH
01629 534380
Open in season daily 10–5

Lea Gardens is famous for its springtime displays of rhododendrons and azaleas. Covering approximately 3.5 acres, the gardens are in a woodland area, with access paths which allow visitors to see the 500 or more varieties of rhododendrons and other plants. The gardens are open to the public for viewing and plant sales, and there is also a cafe.

Matlock Farm Park
matlockfarmpark.co.uk
Jaggers Lane, Two Dales, DE4 5LH
01246 590200 | Open Jan to mid-Dec daily 10–4.30 (to 5.30 summer weekends); mid to end Dec daily 10–4

Matlock Farm Park is set on a 600-acre working farm, and has a varied selection of animals, including llamas, goats, turkeys, peacocks, cattle and sheep. The rabbits are always a favourite with children, as are the playgrounds and go-carts.

Matlock Bath   MAP REF 274 C3

Matlock Bath is the beach resort of the Peak District – just without the beach. It's a popular destination for motorcyclists, and on summer weekends, bikers can be seen sunning themselves and admiring each other's gleaming machines along the South Parade by the river. Add in the wealth of fish 'n' chip shops, museums, gift shops and theme parks, and Matlock Bath is the entertainment capital of the Peak.

There's nothing new in this. The town has been a tourist destination since the health-giving properties of its warm springs were first discovered in the late 17th century. The original attraction may have been the lime and salt-rich solutions from the springs which coat anything they come into contact with in a rock known as tufa, as demonstrated in The Wishing Well near the Pavilion.

Matlock Bath is squeezed into the bottom of the steep-sided Derwent Gorge, with the great 300-foot (90m) limestone shield of High Tor overshadowing everything. This crag is a popular destination for serious rock-climbers, who can often be seen hanging precariously off the smooth, blank white wall of rock.

On the other side of the river, the wooded slopes of the Heights of Abraham (named after General Wolfe's famous Quebec battle in 1759) can be reached much more easily, but just as spectacularly, by the Cable Cars (see page 225), which swing up from the Whistlestop Centre of the Derbyshire Wildlife Trust, to the Victoria Tower which marks the summit.

The Great Rutland and Masson Caverns are former lead mines which have been opened up so that visitors can enjoy the underground caves which riddle the Heights of Abraham. The Royal Cave and Temple Mine are former fluorspar workings which are also open to visitors, near the fascinating Peak District Lead

▶ Matlock Bath

Matlock Bath

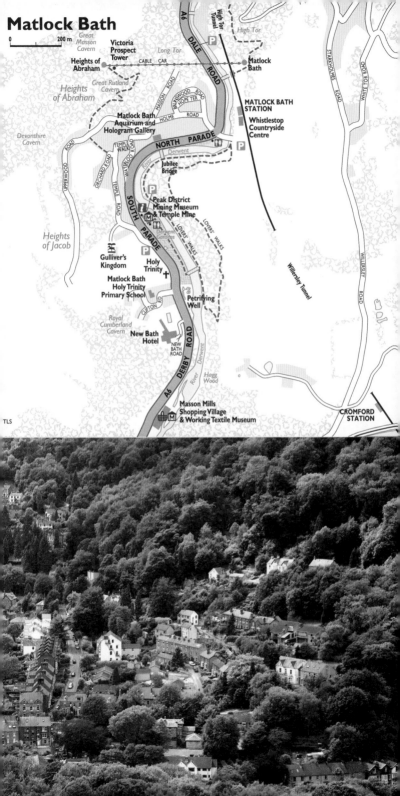

0   200 m

Great Masson Cavern

Victoria Prospect Tower

Heights of Abraham

Long Tor

CABLE CAR

Matlock Bath

Great Rutland Cavern

Heights of Abraham

Devonshire Cavern

Matlock Bath Aquarium and Hologram Gallery

MATLOCK BATH STATION

Whistlestop Countryside Centre

MASSON ROAD

BRAMSWOOD ROAD

HOPE TER.

HOLME ROAD

DALE ROAD

High Tor Tunnel

High Tor

A6

STARKHOLMES ROAD

OLD TOR ROAD

WHITE TOR ROAD

NORTH PARADE

Derwent

TEMPLE WALK

River Derwent

Jubilee Bridge

UPPERWOOD

ORCHARD ROAD

WALKER STREET

TEMPLE ROAD

SOUTH PARADE

Peak District Mining Museum & Temple Mine

Derwent Gardens

LOVERS' WALKS

LOVERS' WALKS

Heights of Jacob

Gulliver's Kingdom

Holy Trinity

Matlock Bath Holy Trinity Primary School

CLIFTON ROAD

Petrifying Well

Willersley Tunnel

Willersley Tunnel

WILLERSLEY ROAD

Royal Cumberland Cavern

New Bath Hotel

NEW BATH ROAD

DERBY ROAD

A6

River Derwent

Hagg Wood

Masson Mills Shopping Village & Working Textile Museum

CROMFORD STATION

TLS

Mining Museum, which is housed in the pink-painted Pavilion, originally built in 1885 for the spa trade. The major exhibit in the museum is the large water-pressure engine, rescued from a local lead mine and dated 1819. There are also replica shafts and tunnels for children to climb and crawl through, among a host of other interesting exhibits. The elegant spire of Holy Trinity church, built in 1842, dates from the period of Matlock Bath's prominence as a spa. But the most beautiful piece of ecclesiastical architecture is the recently restored little hillside Chapel of St John the Baptist on Cliff Road high above the village. This was built in 1897 to a design by Sir Guy Dawber as a chapel-of-ease, and its medieval-looking turrets and oriel windows are matched inside by a rood screen, reredos, and exuberantly-painted walls, all in the Arts and Crafts style.

The coming of the railway to Matlock Bath in 1849 gave a great boost to its emerging tourist industry, and the line still connects to the main line at Derby, 15 miles away.

VISIT A MUSEUM
Peak District Lead Mining Museum
peakdistrictleadminingmuseum. co.uk
The Pavilion, DE4 3NR | 01629 583834 | Open all year, daily Apr–Oct daily 10–5, Nov–Mar 11–3
A large display explains the history of the Derbyshire lead industry from Roman times to the present day. The geology of the area, mining and smelting processes, the quarrying and the people who worked in the industry, are illustrated by a series of static and moving exhibits. The museum also features an early 19th-century water pressure pumping engine, and the kids will particularly enjoy scaling a replica lead mine shaft.

ENTERTAIN THE FAMILY
The Heights of Abraham Cable Cars, Caverns & Hilltop Park
see highlight panel opposite

Gulliver's Kingdom
gulliversfun.co.uk
Temple Walk, DE4 3PG
01629 580540 | See website for opening times
As many parents will know to their cost, finding days out for young and older children alike can be a tricky task. But the Gulliver's Kingdom theme park at Matlock Bath claims to be unique in that it is specially designed for families with children aged between the years of two and 13. There's a wide range of rides and attractions – from the Western World and pirates play area, and Toyland with rides for the under 5s to the log flume and Drop Tower and the SpyZone. Its location some 300 feet above the valley on a steep hillside makes for a different theme park experience, adding an extra dimension to the thrills of the rides, especially the rather scary log flume.

▶ The Heights of Abraham Cable Cars, Caverns & Hilltop Park

MAP REF 274 C3

heightsofabraham.com

Matlock Bath, DE4 3NT | 01629 582365

Open 7–22 Feb and 21 Mar–1 Nov daily 10–4.30, 23 Feb–15 Mar weekends only 10–4.30

The Heights of Abraham, now a unique hilltop country park, is reached using the famous cable cars. Once at the summit you can join exciting underground tours of two spectacular show caverns. Above ground there are play areas, picnic spots, exhibitions, shops, cafe and summit bar all with stunning views across the surrounding Peak District. Recent attractions are the Heath and Heaven and Fossil Factory exhibitions, plus brand new, state-of-the-art lighting in the Great Masson Cavern, which reveals its magnitude as never before.

10 top rainy day destinations

GET INDUSTRIAL
Temple Mine
peakdistrictleadminingmuseum.co.uk
The Pavilion, DE4 3NR
01629 583834 | Open Apr–Oct daily timed visits at 12 and 2, Nov–Mar, timed visits at 12 and 2 weekends only

This typical Peak District mine was worked from the early 1920s until the mid-1950s for fluorspar and associated minerals. Here you will be shown examples of the methods used by the old miners, giving you a unique insight into the primitive and often dangerous working conditions they had to endure while underground.

MEET THE SEALIFE
Matlock Bath Aquarium and Hologram Gallery
matlockbathaquarium.co.uk
110 North Parade, DE4 3NS
01629 583624 | Open Easter–Oct daily 10–5.30, Nov–Easter 10–5
The Matlock Bath Aquarium is much more than just a collection of over 50 species of fish. It is also the site of the only remaining petrifying well in Matlock Bath, and has one of the largest public displays of holograms in Europe. There is also a wonderful collection of gemstones and fossils from around the world, and you can take a trip down memory lane in the 'Past Times in Matlock Bath' exhibition.

▶ Middleton (by Wirksworth) MAP REF 274 C3

Mining and quarrying have been important aspects of the local economy in this part of Derbyshire for hundreds of years, and the enormous Hopton Wood Quarries, south of the village, are still producing limestone.

So it was entirely appropriate that the National Stone Centre should be set up in a disused quarry south of Middleton adjacent to the High Peak Trail, formerly the Cromford and High Peak Railway. The site covers 50 acres, about half of which is now designated as a Site of Special Scientific Interest, and contains no less than six former quarries, four lime kilns and over 120 disused lead mine shafts. The centre tells the important story of stone in the Peak District landscape – from fossils to quarrying – and visitors can even pan for gems in one of the many 'hands-on' exhibits.

Close by is the Middleton Top Engine House on the High Peak Trail, which was used to haul waggons up the 1:8 gradient of the Middleton Incline. The steam engine used to haul the waggons has been restored and is often 'in steam' at weekends in the summer.

The village of Middleton has a number of good old stone cottages, especially around the Jail Yard, which is a reminder that Middleton was a place of correction for miscreant lead miners in the past. The Holy Trinity church was built in 1844 but is somewhat overshadowed by the Congregational Chapel which was built by a Matlock Bath minister to serve the needs of Middleton's large number of lead miners.

The author DH Lawrence spent a year at the small house known as Mountain Cottage, overlooking the Via Gellia (see Bonsall, page 84). It is thought that the village of 'Woodlinkin' in his short story *The Virgin and the Gypsy*, written in 1926, was based on Middleton by Wirksworth. It was made into a film using local locations including Lathkill Dale in 1970.

VISIT THE MUSEUM

National Stone Centre

nationalstonecentre.org.uk
Porter Lane, Middleton by Wirksworth, DE4 4LS
01629 824833 | Open Apr–Sep daily 10–5, Oct–Mar 10–4

It seems fitting that the National Stone Centre should be located here, close to the Derwent Valley Mills World Heritage Site, where rocks and geology are never far from the surface. Exhibitions tell the story of stone, with guided walks and gem panning. Half of the site is now a Site of Special Scientific Interest (SSSI). Courses and workshops on drystone wall conservation are also available. The site is free to enter.

TAKE A TRAIN RIDE

Steeple Grange Light Railway

steeplegrange.co.uk
Middleton, DE4 4LS, park at National Stone Centre
01246 235497

See website for timetable & events

Established in 1985, the Steeple Grange Light Railway is an 18-inch gauge line near Middleton by Wirksworth, built on the trackbed of a branch of the old Cromford and High Peak Railway, now the High Peak Trail. Motive power is provided by ex-industrial diesel, battery-electric and petrol locomotives, and passengers are carried in an old National Coal Board manrider. Visitors can enjoy a unique 20-minute train ride (every 10 minutes) through dramatic limestone scenery, hear about why and how the railway was built, investigate some of the vintage locomotives and rolling stock, discover fossils and wild flowers, and see work under way on the proposed extensions towards Middleton and the National Stone Centre.

EXPLORE BY BIKE
Middleton Top Visitor Centre
Middleton by Wirksworth, DE4 4LS
01629 823204
Cycle hire.

▶ Monsal Head   MAP REF 274 B1

Monsal Head, just outside the village of Little Longstone, is one of the most accessible and popular viewpoints in the Peak District National Park. The view from outside the strangely alpine-looking Monsal Head Hotel looks out over the graceful, five-arched Monsal Head Viaduct, built in 1860 as part of the Midland Line, north into Upper Dale and west down Monsal Dale, with the impressive Iron Age hillfort-topped headland of Fin Cop dominating the scene.

The building of the Midland Line through Monsal Dale in the 1860s was the cause of one of the Victorian critic and conservationist John Ruskin's most famous outbursts. In his *Fors Clavigera*, he fumed:

▼ Monsal Head viaduct

There was a rocky valley between Buxton and Bakewell, once upon a time, divine as the Vale of Tempe... You enterprised a Railroad through the valley – you blasted its rocks away, heaped thousands of tons of shale into its lovely stream. The valley is gone, and the Gods with it; and now, every fool in Buxton can be at Bakewell in half an hour, and every fool in Bakewell at Buxton.

Now, of course, the viaduct is a listed structure and very much part of the Monsal Head scene, forming part of the National Park's Monsal Trail walking, cycling and riding route. The tunnels between here and **Chee Dale** have recently been reopened by the Park authority, so you can enjoy views of the River Wye not seen since the railway closed in the 1960s. There are plans for the restoration of a steam railway to the line, so the ghost of Ruskin may still rise to haunt the developers...

SEE THE VILLAGE
Little Longstone
The tiny hamlet of Little Longstone is perhaps best known today for its tiny but welcoming 16th-century Packhorse Inn, much beloved of walkers on the Monsal Trail. But the Victorian rustic-Gothic Church of England chapel standing in a field at the western end of the village has many admirers, and the 17th-century Manor House standing behind its yew hedges in the centre of the hamlet was the home of the Longsdon family for 28 generations.

EAT AND DRINK
The Monsal Head Hotel
monsalhead.com
Monsal Head, DE45 1NL
01629 640250
Located close to Chatsworth House and the viaduct, the Monsal Head Hotel has a rustic ambience with a flagstone floor, seating in horse stalls and a log fire – the perfect place to enjoy a range of cask ales from microbreweries. The same menu, which uses lots of local produce, is offered in the bar and the airy and spacious Longstones restaurant.

The Packhorse Inn

packhorselongstone.co.uk
Main Street, Little Longstone,
DE45 1NN | 01629 640471

Situated just off the Monsal Trail, this tiny pub is surrounded by some of the most striking scenery the Peak has to offer. Settle down by the open fire or linger with a glass of real ale and tasty food.

▶ **PLACES NEARBY**

Great Longstone

In common with many other Peak villages, Great Longstone suffers from a distinct lack of parking space. Driving through the linear village on the road up to Monsal Head, you are usually faced with just one lane open to traffic, due to the number of

5 top viewpoints

▶ **Monsal Head:** views of Monsal Dale and Monsal Head Viaduct, page 228

▶ **Holme Moss:** extensive views north over *Last of the Summer Wine* country

▶ **Mam Tor:** at the head of the Hope Valley, with views north to Kinder Scout and south over Castleton and the White Peak, page 214

▶ **Barrel Inn, Bretton:** sweeping views over a pint across the White Peak plateau

▶ **Surprise View, Hathersage:** the length of the Hope Valley is revealed from a bend in the A625 Sheffield–Hathersage road

cars parked outside the many 18th-century cottages. The village is centred on its sloping village green and war memorial cross, around which carol services are conducted at Christmas. Yet another lead mining centre, Longstone's wealth was based on the lead ore (galena) won by generations of miners from nearby Longstone Edge, which until very recently was still being quarried for fluorspar – a mineral the lead miners rejected as waste.

At the top of the village street behind a high brick wall is the handsome Georgian manor house of Longstone Hall (private), built in 1747. The Crispin Inn, almost opposite the Hall, is a reminder of another of Longstone's traditional trades, that of boot and shoemaking (Crispin is the patron saint of shoemakers). St Giles' church is originally medieval, dating from the 13th century, but was restored in 1873.

EAT AND DRINK

The White Lion

whiteliongreatlongstone.co.uk
Main Street, Great Longstone,
DE45 1TA | 01629 640252

Whether arriving on foot, two wheels, or four legs, visitors to this pub are sure to recuperate from their exertions. Sitting under the mass of Longstone Edge, Greg and Libby Robinson's gastro-pub has a peaceful outside patio and a dog-welcoming snug bar. There's also a kids' menu.

▶ Monyash   MAP REF 273 E1

The name of Monyash means exactly what it (almost) says. The Old English name literally means 'many ash trees'. But the village, standing high and dry on the White Peak limestone plateau, was founded because of the presence of its 'meres' – ponds which owe their existence to a bed of impervious clay which held the precious water. Only Fere Mere, on the road towards Buxton, now remains, and the site of Jack Mere has been converted to a car park.

This small, unpretentious village at the head of beautiful Lathkill Dale (see page 195), part of the Derbyshire Dales National Nature Reserve, was granted a charter to hold a weekly market as long ago as 1340. The stump of the ancient Market Cross remains on the spacious village green opposite the 17th-century Bull's Head public house, but the market went long ago.

Monyash has a pleasing collection of typical White Peak cottages, originally built for the lead-mining and farming community. As with many White Peak villages, lead mining was formerly a keystone of the local economy, and the village was the site of its own Barmote Court, which administered the industry. The area now depends mainly on farming and tourism.

The church of St Leonard dates from the 12th century, and is one of the prettiest in the Peak. The elegant spire rises from a solid, battlemented and unbuttressed tower and the spacious interior has wide north and south transepts. Among its treasures is an enormous iron-bound Parish Chest, which may date as far back as the 13th century.

Monyash became a centre of the Quaker movement in the late 18th century, when its importance for the lead mining industry was at its height. In contradiction to Monyash, One Ash Grange, above the deep ravine of Lathkill Dale, was originally a penitentiary for recalcitrant monks and later the home of John Gratton, a prominent Quaker preacher. At Ricklow, at the head of Lathkill Dale, a flourishing 'marble' quarry existed in Victorian times. The marble was in fact a highly polished, fossil-filled limestone.

EAT AND DRINK

The Bull's Head
thebullsheadmonyash.co.uk
Church Street, DE45 1JH
01629 812372
Traditionalists were relieved when the popular Bull's Head at Monyash reverted to its ancient name a few years ago, after being somewhat unfortunately dubbed 'The Hobbit' by a misguided, Tolkien-influenced former owner. The Bull's Head is

situated at the very heart of the village, adjoining the village green, with its ancient market cross. The well-stocked bar serves real ales including Tetley, Burton and one guest beer, such as Black Sheep Special and Hartington. There are two separate dining areas, so you are able to enjoy the extensive lunchtime and evening menu throughout.

The Old Smithy

oldsmithymonyash.co.uk
Church Street, DE45 1JH
01629 810190

Set beside the village green and ancient cross, the Old Smithy provides supremely well for walkers and visitors to this delightful village. Renowned for its all-day breakfast, the traditional cream teas and pastries are also draws.

▶ New Mills MAP REF 276 C4

The former industrial township of New Mills, at the junction of the River Sett with the Goyt got its name from the cotton mills which sprang up here in the later years of the 19th century. Until it became a single parish under the name of New Mills in 1884, there were a series of small hamlets known as Ollersett, Beard, Thornsett and Whittle. Ollersett Hall, at Low Leighton, is a gabled and mullioned 17th-century manor house.

Some of the 'new' mills which gave the town its name are still left today, most standing vacant and vainly looking for a new use. But New Mills is nonetheless a lively and enterprising community today. The soaring stone viaducts and bridges which span the picturesque and surprisingly deep gorge of the Goyt as it passes through the town are a constant reminder of the industrial past, but recent improvements to what is now known as the Torrs Riverside Park have greatly enhanced the scenic beauty of this unexpectedly spectacular spot. The construction in 2000 of the award-winning – though slightly scary and highly vertiginous – £500,000 Millennium Walkway across one of the massive Victorian railway retaining walls over the rushing waters of the Goyt is the crowning glory of The Torrs. The Torrs was also the site of an innovative Hydro Archimedes Screw providing electrical power to the town in 2008. The proximity of the former railway line now known as the Sett Valley Trail, which runs from here to Hayfield (see page 178), provides another great recreational opportunity for both townsfolk and visitors.

St George's church was built in 1831 in the Early English style and St James the Less, with its attached Almshouses, in 1880 by Swinden Barber as a memorial to the local philanthropist James Ingham. But this is mainly Nonconformist country, and it is the chapels, such as the Congregational

Providence Chapel in Mellor Road (1823) and the Methodist Chapel in St George Road (1810), which answered most of the spiritual needs of the millworkers. Their more temporal needs have been answered by the Bull's Head public house in the High Street since the 18th century.

VISIT THE HERITAGE CENTRE
New Mills Heritage Centre
newmillstowncouncil.org.uk/heritage.php
Rook Mill Lane, SK22 3BN
01663 746904 | Open Tue–Sun 10.30–4
Free to enter, the heritage centre contains a museum telling the history of New Mills, from the original formation of the Torrs gorges through to its development as a mining town. There's also an information centre and a shop.

GET OUTDOORS
Just outside the town are Goytside Meadows Nature Reserve – pastures and meadowland, filled with flowers – and Mousley Bottom Nature Reserve, with woodland, ponds and reed beds.

PLAY A ROUND
New Mills Golf Club
newmillsgolfclub.co.uk
Shaw Marsh, SK22 4QE
01663 743485 | Open daily all year
Moorland course with panoramic views of the Kinder Plateau and the Cheshire Plain, and first-class greens.

EAT AND DRINK
Pack Horse Inn
packhorseinn.co.uk
Mellor Road, SK22 4QQ
01663 742365

High above New Mills, the Pack Horse Inn has fantastic views to the great moorland plateau of Kinder. It's a lovely stone-built place with a growing reputation for good wholesome food and an eclectic choice of hand-pulled real ales – the pub has been CAMRA-listed for more than 10 years.

The Pride of the Peaks
59 Market Street, New Mills, SK22 4AA | 07974 519222
The Pride of the Peaks is a very popular traditional, family-run pub, serving breakfasts, bar snacks and main meals, from 9am to 2pm seven days a week. It is situated in the heart of the bustling town of New Mills, close to local attractions such as the spectacular Millennium Walkway, the Torrs Riverside Park and the Sett Valley trail.

▶ PLACES NEARBY
In the hills to the north of New Mills is the tiny, picturesque gritstone hamlet of **Rowarth**, sheltering beneath Lantern Pike. **North of Rowarth**, on the summit of Cown Edge are a pair of round pillars known as Robin Hood's Picking Rods. No one is sure exactly when or what they were built for, but tradition claims they were used by the legendary outlaw for bending and stringing his bows.

▶ **Over Haddon**   MAP REF 274 B1

Although Over Haddon is over a mile from Haddon Hall (see page 165), it gets its name from being the higher of two medieval Haddons. The lower, or Nether, Haddon is a deserted village of which only humps and bumps remain on the hillside above the Duke of Rutland's manor overlooking the Wye. Over Haddon is a typical White Peak village of sturdy stone-built, mainly 18th-century cottages, which stands on the brink of Lathkill Dale, surely one of the loveliest of the Peak District dales (see page 195). It was made the first National Nature Reserve in the Peak District in 1972, and now forms the nucleus of the Derbyshire Dales National Nature Reserve.

The town was formerly a centre of the lead mining industry, and there are many reminders of those days in the surrounding fields, and even among the trees in the protected depths of Lathkill Dale. The Lathkill is one of Derbyshire's disappearing rivers, and in high summer it can often run dry as the water seeps through the limestone. It is also one of the cleanest and purest rivers in the country, unusually running for the whole of its length across limestone.

Over Haddon was the scene in 1854 of a Derbyshire Klondike and mini-Gold Rush after what was thought to be gold was discovered in a lead mine at Manor Farm. A company was formed to extract the ore, and there were even plans to build a railway to Over Haddon from Bakewell two miles away to transport the precious metal away. However, it was eventually discovered that the 'gold' was nothing more than iron pyrites, also known as 'fool's gold', and the enterprise came to nothing.

The village pub, the Lathkil (strangely spelt with only one 'l') Hotel, has a good reputation for bar meals and welcomes walkers. Conksbury Bridge, to the southeast of the village, crosses the Lathkill by a narrow, low-arched medieval bridge. A hillfort, possibly dating from the Iron Age, has recently been discovered above the dale near here.

SADDLE UP
Haddon House Riding Stables
tychetwo.co.uk/edwin
Over Haddon, DE45 1HZ
01629 813723
There are miles of ancient bridleways in and around Bakewell, and you can enjoy many of them by hiring a horse from the Haddon House Riding Stables at Over Haddon.

EAT AND DRINK
The Lathkil Hotel
lathkil.co.uk
School Lane, Over Haddon,
DE45 1JE | 01629 812501
This long-established inn was built to serve lead miners. Today's guests are mainly walkers, who tuck into a mix of simple bar meals and beers from Peak District breweries.

▶ Peak Forest MAP REF 277 E5

Peak Forest is a windswept village high on the White Peak plateau on the A623 between Stoney Middleton and Chapel-en-le-Frith (see page 106), and a quirk of ecclesiastical law led to once being known as 'the Gretna Green of the Peak'.

The highly unusual dedication of the church of King Charles the Martyr gives a clue to its extra-parochial powers, for the original church was built in 1657 by the wife of the second Earl of Devonshire during the time of the Commonwealth's ban on church building. It thus fell outside the law, and the priest, as 'Principal Officer and Judge in Spiritualities in the Peculiar Court of Peak Forest', was able to conduct marriages without question and at any time. The strange situation continued until early in the 19th century, earning successive incumbents considerable sums of money. Couples can still be married in the church without banns being read, providing that one of the couple has lived in the village for 15 days prior to the ceremony.

The village gets its name because it once stood at the centre of the medieval Royal Forest of the Peak, not a wooded wilderness in the present sense of the word but a 40-square-mile hunting preserve. The Royal Forest of the Peak was a strictly protected habitat of deer, wild boar and wolves which were hunted by kings and princes staying at nearby Peveril Castle at Castleton until the relaxation of the Forest Laws in 1250. In the 16th century, the area surrounding the village was emparked, and managed by a ranger who lived at a house called the Chamber of the Peak, on the site of the present 18th-century Chamber Farm.

Swainmotes, or forest courts, settled any disputes. It was the foresters' task to care for the deer, by controlling grazing, by preventing walls from being built and by keeping people out. The deer increased fourfold, but this was only a temporary triumph. Around 1655 the land was allocated to the Dukes of Devonshire and was officially deforested, though the last of the trees had already been felled to provide pit props for the coal mines on Combs Moss. Scrub and heath took over the countryside until the turn of the 19th century.

Considering its colourful past, Peak Forest is a modest little place. The present village of stone-built houses and farms grew up around a church built by the Dowager Duchess of Devonshire when the land was first acquired. The present, quite imposing, Victorian church was built on the site of the old chapel in 1878. The Venetian-style window and porch of the old church were reused in the village Reading Room.

A post office and pub (The Devonshire Arms, of course) cater for any secular needs.

EAT AND DRINK

The Devonshire Arms

Hernstone Lane, Peak Forest
SK17 8EJ | 01298 23875

The Devonshire Arms in the centre of the village of Peak Forest is a traditional 17th-century coaching inn on the A623 road between Stoney Middleton and Chapel-en-le-Frith. It is now a free house, and includes a dining area where homemade dishes and traditional favourites are served.

▶ PLACES NEARBY

Eldon Hole

About a mile north of the village on the slopes of Eldon Hill is Eldon Hole, one of the traditional 'Seven Wonders of the Peak' and the biggest open pothole in the Peak District. Long thought to be bottomless and an entrance to hell, it was descended for the first time by John Lloyd in 1770 and found to be only 245 feet deep. There are apocryphal tales of a goose being lowered into the awesome void in Tudor times, only to emerge three days later at Peak Cavern in Castleton, with its feathers apparently singed by the fires of hell. Today, the tree-fringed entrance to Eldon Hole is strictly the preserve of expert potholers and cavers.

▶ The Roaches   MAP REF 272 C2

There are few real peaks in the Peak District, but perhaps
the most striking and unexpected are The Roaches, Hen Cloud
and Ramshaw Rocks, when approached on the A53 Buxton
road out of Leek. The 18th-century traveller Dr Plot described
them perfectly:

> *Here are also vast Rocks which surprise with Admiration...*
> *They are of so great a Height and afford such stupendous*
> *Prospects that one could hardly believe they were anywhere to*
> *be found but in Picture.*

The jagged and serrated skyline is formed of gritstone
outcrops, just like those in the northern and eastern Moors, but
here they were more heavily contorted, leading to a landscape
of misfit valleys, steep slopes and outstanding rock faces
rather than moorland plateaux.

The Roaches ridge runs northwest to southeast from
Roach End to Five Clouds, with the outlier of Hen Cloud
standing like some stranded, inland Rock of Gibraltar at its
southern terminus. The sheer and sometimes overhanging

crags face the setting sun,
and are a popular destination
for rock climbers. Many of the
most fearsome routes, such
as The Sloth (so-named
because the climber spends
much time hanging upside
down from his fingertips),
were put up by the Mancunian
pair Joe Brown and Don
Whillans, and the climbers'
hut beneath the crags
formerly known as Rock Hall
is named after Whillans.

For the less athletic, a
footpath follows the crest of
the ridge, linking with Back
Forest and creating a four-
mile ridge walk with superb
views. Heather clothes the
upper hills, bracken and
woodland the slopes. The
area was famous as the home
of a colony of red-necked

◀ The Roaches

wallabies, a Tasmanian oddity that escaped from a private zoo at Swythamley Hall in the 1930s and formed a wild breeding population for a few years.

The spiky outline of Ramshaw Rocks is probably the most well-known outlier of the Roaches, towering above the roadside on the A53. It has a famous face-like formation known as the Winking Man.

▶ Rowsley MAP REF 274 C1

These days the village of Rowsley is most notable as a gateway to the Peak District National Park on the A6, and home to the Peak Shopping Village and mall.

But the site where the shopping mall stands today was formerly an important railway station (the station block, designed by Joseph Paxton, is still there) for nearby Haddon Hall (see page 165), with marshalling yards and a large dairy to supply London with dairy products via the milk train. The Midland Line closed in 1968, and now only Peak Rail steam trains run from here to Matlock.

Nearby is the fine Peacock Hotel, with the bird which is the badge of the ruling Manners family proudly displayed over the pedimented doorway. Originally built in 1652 as a dower or manor house for John Stevenson, agent to the Manners family at nearby Haddon, the Peacock today is a refined restaurant and exclusive resort of anglers fishing on the Rivers Wye and Derwent. The name of the nearby Grouse and Claret pub refers

▼ The 1849 station building, now in the Peak Shopping Village

to a fishing fly, rather than the game bird and the red wine, and is another reference to the piscatorial pursuits of many of Rowsley's visitors. The pub, originally known as the Station Hotel, was built after the railway came to the village in 1849.

Caudwell's Mill, an old water powered turbine-driven corn mill, is just across the road. The 19th century mill is now an interesting craft centre which still produces flour. Visitors can visit the mill and stroll along the paths beside the mill race and alongside the Wye.

There are actually two Rowsleys – Great and Little. The main village is on the A6 Matlock–Bakewell road and the minor one on the side road to Chatsworth.

St Katherine's church only dates from 1855 – until that date, the villagers of Rowsley had to attend either Bakewell or Beeley churches. Inside there is the marble tomb and effigy of Lady Catherine Manners who died in 1859, and her child, and a Saxon cross head dating from the ninth century, which was rescued from the bed of the River Wye.

GET INDUSTRIAL
Caudwell's Mill
caudwellsmill.co.uk
Rowsley, DE4 2EB | 01629 734374
Open daily 10–5
Caudwell's Mill is a beautifully preserved Victorian corn mill, thought to be the only water-powered turbine roller flour mill in the country still in operation. There are four floors of fascinating machinery to be inspected, and the visitor can come away with freshly ground flour from the mill. The mill's stableyard is now a craft centre, with working demonstrations and a restaurant.

TAKE A TRAIN RIDE
Peak Rail
peakrail.co.uk
Train from Matlock (see page 220)
The steam and diesel engines on the Peak Rail preserved railway, which runs for four miles along the Derwent Valley between the former Rowsley South Station and Platform Two at Matlock Station. The line was part of the old Midland Railway line between Manchester and London, which fell under the Beeching axe in 1968.

▶ Glass-blowing, Caudwell's Mill

Regular steam trains run at weekends and there is a Santa Special at Christmas. There are long-term plans to reopen the line through the Peak District all the way to Buxton.

The northern terminus at Rowsley is situated on the site of the former LMS/BR locomotive depot. Facilities include free car parking, a large buffet providing a selection of hot and cold light refreshments, a gift shop selling a wide range of books, DVDs, memorabilia and souvenirs, and an exhibition showing the history of the rebuilding of the railway by volunteers. During the summer there is also a picnic area where the kids can play with outdoor games, while parents can relax with a cup of tea or ice cream from the snack bar.

EAT AND DRINK

The Country Parlour

Caudwell's Mill, Rowsley, DE4 2EB

01629 733185

The tea rooms, squeezed between the River Derwent and the mill race, serve scones, cakes and pastries baked on site, many using flour from Caudwell's Mill itself. Rest easy in old chapel seats and pews, before a trip to the mill.

The Peacock at Rowsley ⊛⊛⊛

thepeacockatrowsley.com

DE4 2EB | 01629 733518

The Peacock at Rowsley is famed for its seven miles of fly-fishing on the adjacent Rivers Wye and Derwent, and anglers come from all over the world to fish for the wild rainbow trout and a unique strain of brown trout. Owned by the Rutlands of nearby Haddon Hall, the hotel has been styled by award-winning designer India Mahdavi and the main dining room looks out on the well-tended gardens. Dan Smith, the head chef, worked with Tom Aikens in London before returning to Derbyshire. He has prepared and designed the menus for the award-winning restaurant and bar using, wherever possible, locally sourced ingredients.

▶ ## The Snake Pass   MAP REF 277 E3

Winter weather warnings on television and radio have made the Snake Pass infamous. Even if the winter sun is shining across the rest of the Pennines, the Snake Pass, which takes the A57 between Sheffield and Glossop, may well be closed because of severe blizzards and the threat of avalanches from overhanging cornices. It is decidedly not a good place to be stuck in a car.

The road from the Ladybower Reservoir and the Woodlands Valley strikes northwest, sheltered on a shoulder of the River Ashop, but after Lady Clough it has nowhere to hide and crosses a windswept desert at the 1,680 feet (512m) summit of the pass. The wildernesses of Bleaklow (see page 83) and

Kinder Scout – the highest ground in the Peak – lie to the north and south. In places the peat has been stripped away to reveal outcrops of weathered rock, which is exactly how the glaciers left the place after the Ice Age. There are no trees, no barns nor walls.

Of course, the remote wilderness of the Snake – taking its name not from the winding nature of the road, as some people seem to think, but from the snake on the coat of arms of local landowners the Dukes of Devonshire – is irresistible to many, and in fine weather, with the sun shining on the heather, it can be magical. The upper Woodlands Valley is pretty, dotted with old farms and birch-lined cloughs. Most of the Peak District has been designated as an Environmentally Sensitive Area, which means that farmers get special payments for agreeing to manage the land with conservation as a priority. In the case of the high moors, the most important thing is the stocking rate – fewer sheep are now overwintered on the heather, and this should benefit the flora and fauna.

A tributary of the Ashop runs north to Alport Dale and Alport Castles, which are not castles at all but an impressive natural landslipping of rock – said to be Britain's biggest – from Birchinlee Pasture above. It is accessible by a bridleway and makes a good walk from the Snake. The barn at Alport Castles Farm is used on the first Sunday in July each year for a Lovefeast service. These 'love feasts' originated during the 18th-century religious revival spearheaded by the Wesley brothers. They converted multitudes of workers, from mines and mills, farms and factories, to a pattern of religious life which inspired them to build a number of 'wayside Bethels' in remote places like Alport.

Back along the Snake Pass there are two or three last farms and cottages before you reach the lonely Snake Pass Inn. At the top of Lady Clough, on the highest and most featureless ground, The Snake is crossed by the Pennine Way, close to the paved trackway of ancient Doctor's Gate which may originally have been a Roman road and leads down into Old Glossop. It is said to have been named after Dr John Talbot of Glossop, who paid for its paving. Travellers have been venturing across these moors for thousands of years, but seldom without a shiver of apprehension.

EAT AND DRINK
The Snake Pass Inn
thesnakepassinn.co.uk
Snake Rd, Bamford, S33 0BJ
01433 651480

The Snake Pass Inn was built by the Duke of Devonshire in 1821 as Lady Clough House, when the original medieval track was transformed into a turnpike road. If any visitor should need a reminder about how remote this hostelry is, there is a milestone outside the inn that records that it is 21 miles to Manchester and 17 miles to Sheffield – and there's nothing much in between. The low stone-built inn is an ideal place to stop for refreshment, and good, home-made food is served most days of the week. The Snake also offers a range of overnight accommodation.

▶ Stanton in Peak   MAP REF 274 C2

The single village street climbs steeply up the western flank of Stanton Moor, an isolated 1,000-foot (300m) high gritstone outlier in the heart of White Peak limestone country, and one of the richest prehistoric sites in Derbyshire.

Stanton village has some fine 17th- and 18th-century stone cottages, and an inn with the strange name of the Flying Childers – which commemorates a successful racehorse trained by Sir Hugh Childers and owned by the 4th Duke of Devonshire. Holly House, opposite the pub, still has eight of its 14 windows blocked, which was done to avoid the Window Tax of 1697. The initials 'WPT' over the doorways of some cottages stands for William Paul Thornhill of Stanton Hall (private), home to generations of Thornhills. The house, behind a high stone wall, has a late 18th-century front backed by a 17th-century rear. The parish church of Holy Trinity dates from 1839 and is unusually aligned from south to north. There is a bronze Italian Holy Water stoop dated 1596 from the workshops of Bellini.

The parish of Stanton also includes the hamlets of Stanton Lees, Pilhough and Congreave, which mainly consist of small farms. Birchover Lane, running south of Stanton, follows the western edge of Stanton Moor (see below). Parking places give access to pathways through birch scrub and over heather and bilberry to the Bronze Age landscape.

GO BACK IN TIME
Stanton Moor

Over 70 Bronze Age burial mounds have been identified among the heather and birches of the moor, which prompted the historian H J Massingham to remark that it was 'as thick with tumuli as a plumduff with raisins'. Among several other ritual monuments on the moor, the most important being the Nine Ladies Stone Circle and King Stone. The story goes that the stones are a fiddler and nine maidens who were turned to stone for dancing on Sunday, a typical example of prehistoric culture being Christianised. There are several gritstone quarries, some still active, around the edge of the moor, together with some strange natural formations such as the Andle Stone and the Cork Stone. The Earl Grey Tower is a prominent local landmark on the moor's eastern edge and was erected by the Thornhill family, prominent local landowners, to honour the man responsible for the passing of the Reform Bill in 1832.

EAT AND DRINK

The Flying Childers Inn

flyingchilders.com
Main Road, DE4 2LW
01629 636333

Named after a champion racehorse owned by the 4th Duke of Devonshire. Little log fires warm the cosy, beamed interior, where settles and magpie-furniture fit an absolute treat. The lunchtime-only menu is small but perfectly formed; home-made soups, casseroles, filled cobs, toasties and hearty ploughman's, all with locally sourced ingredients. Local real ales, a beer garden and a great welcome for canine companions, too.

5 top edges

▶ **Stanage Edge:** described by the British Mountaineering Council as 'the Queen of Grit', this three-mile long escarpment has fine views and 850 climbing routes, page 176

▶ **Froggatt Edge:** overlooking the beautiful wooded valleys of Grindleford and Padley, page 154

▶ **Curbar Edge and Baslow Edge:** looks down on the valley of the River Derwent and the villages of Curbar and Calver, page 133

▶ **The Roaches:** the last western escarpment of the Pennines, haunt of peregrine falcons and generations of intrepid rock climbers, page 237

▶ **Derwent Edge:** wild and remote, frowning down on the valley of the Upper Derwent, and punctuated by weird and wonderful rock formations such as the Salt Cellar and the Coach and Horses, page 24

▼ Nine Ladies Stone Circle

▶ Stoney Middleton MAP REF 278 C6

Stoney by name and stony by nature, Stoney Middleton is squeezed into the narrow defile of Middleton Dale and hemmed in by forbidding cliffs of limestone and the dusty quarry faces at the western end of the village. It has a long history going back to Roman times. Stoney was on the main highway between the forts at Navio (Brough) and Chesterfield, and although there is no proof of Roman usage, the restored so-called Roman Baths in The Nook still has the warm springs which may well have attracted the passing legionnaires. Two wells are still dressed every summer.

Later the village became a centre for lead mining and lime burning, and old engravings show the dale clear of trees with smoke billowing up from the lime kilns.

St Martin's church, hidden away off the main street, is one of the most unusual in Derbyshire. An octagonal church, with a lantern roof on piers, was added to the original low, 15th-century Perpendicular tower in 1759. It seems a strange mixture of styles, but it still manages to create a charming impression, with the congregation worshipping 'in the round'.

Just to the east of the church is Stoney Middleton Hall, the 17th-century Jacobean former home of Lord Denman, Lord Chief Justice in 1832. Denman was a great Victorian reformer who advocated the abolition of slavery and who was the first national chairman of the Women's Institute. He also famously defended Queen Caroline at her trial, when King George VI tried to obtain a divorce by proving her guilty of adultery.

Back on the Main Road, the octagonal Toll House of 1840 now serves as the village 'chippy'. Further along this busy artery is the cliff known as Lover's Leap, a favoured destination for rock climbers. It gets its name from the leap of village girl Hannah Badderley in 1762. Jilted by her lover, she decided to end it all by jumping from the cliff high above the village street. It's said she was saved by her billowing petticoats, which acted as a parachute and deposited her harmlessly on the ground beneath.

▶ Sudbury MAP REF 274 B6

Neat, red-brick Sudbury on the southern edge of the Peak has a strong claim to be one of the prettiest villages in Derbyshire, and, as is often the case, it owes its perfection to the fact that until fairly recently it was to all intents and purposes a feudal village. The 'big house' in Sudbury's case was the matchless Jacobean perfection of Sudbury Hall, the home of the powerful Vernon family.

Hidden from view behind the great house stands the parish church of All Saints. Rather over-restored, it's an originally 14th-century building, with a low tower and many memorials to the Vernons, the earliest of which is the alabaster effigies of John and Mary Vernon (the builders of the Hall). There is some fine Victorian stained glass in the east window.

The rest of the village of Sudbury consists of one long street of mainly 17th-century red-brick and pantiled cottages with the distinguished Vernon Arms, built by George Vernon in 1671, at the end. The village was mercifully bypassed by the A50 Derby–Stoke trunk road in 1972, saving it from the worst of the ravages of heavy traffic congestion. HM Open Prison, Sudbury, is to the north of the village near Oaks Green, on a site which was originally an American Army hospital during World War II.

TAKE IN SOME HISTORY

Sudbury Hall and the NT Museum of Childhood

nationaltrust.org.uk
Sudbury, DE6 5HT | 01283 585305
See website for opening times

Sudbury Hall was begun by Mary Vernon in 1613 and completed by her son George between 1670 and 1695. The grand facade by William Wilson has more than a touch of the Baroque which was fashionable at the end of the 17th century, borne out by the hipped roof, balustrade and cupola. Inside, the house has many elegant rooms with plasterwork by Bradbury and Pettifer, painted ceilings by Laguerre and wonderful carved woodwork by Edward Pierce and Grinling Gibbons. The magnificent Long Gallery, reached by a superb carved staircase, fills the whole of the south front of the house. Sudbury Hall was the home of Queen Adelaide, widow of William IV, for three years after his death.

The house is now the home of the National Trust's Museum of Childhood, a fascinating insight into how Victorian and Edwardian children worked and played, complete with a genuine Victorian schoolroom, and Betty Cadbury's collection of toys and dolls. In the grounds is a lovely lake and a strange, castellated Eye Catcher gatehouse folly, built around 1800.

▶ Taddington MAP REF 273 E1

Taddington is a typical one-street, White Peak village, standing in a little depression at over 1,000 feet above the sea. From Humphrey Gate above the village, fine sweeping views can be enjoyed down Taddington Dale to flat-topped Fin Cop and across to the neighbouring hamlet of Priestcliffe.

The close-knit village regained its rural quiet after the construction of the A6 bypass just after the war. Before that it was on the main road between Bakewell and Buxton, as an iron milestone preserved in the main street recalls. In those days the Queen's Arms at the eastern end of the village catered for much passing traffic. The Waterloo Hotel, which is at the other end of the village on the A6, is also a popular hostelry.

The most important building in Taddington is St Michael's church, dominated by its slender spire. Dating from the early 14th century, it has an elegant four-bay arcade and tall chancel lighted by flat-headed windows like those at Tideswell. The church was extensively restored in 1891 and contains a fine brass to Richard Blackwall, his wife and children, which is dated 1505.

GO BACK IN TIME
Five Wells Chambered Tomb

Above the village and to the west, on the crest of the windswept escarpment of Taddington Moor, is the important Five Wells Neolithic chambered tomb, the highest such monument in the country, dating from around 4500 to 2000 BC. The great limestone slabs of the tomb command a fine view across country to the north, and were originally covered with soil and entered by two low passageways. Current thinking is that the bones of the ancestors buried in these tombs were periodically taken out and used in some ritual ceremonies.

▸ **Taxal** MAP REF 277 D5

One of the fascinating series of memorials which hold most of the interest in the chiefly 19th-century St James' church at Taxal is an inscription to Michael Heathcote 'Gentleman of the Pantry and Yeoman of the Mouth to his late Majesty King George II'. Heathcote's duties as 'Yeoman of the Mouth' apparently included tasting the king's food before he ate it as a guard against possible poisoning attempts. Heathcote lived to the ripe old ages of 75 years old, so presumably nobody tried to poison the king during his time as official food-taster.

There are many other memorials in the church to the Jodrells – a famous Cheshire family now chiefly remembered in many pub names and the nearby Jodrell Bank radio telescope. The earliest is to William Jauderell 'the Archer' who died in 1375, and his son Roger Jaudrell who fought at Agincourt and died in 1425.

Taxal is a tiny, cul-de-sac village overlooking the lovely Goyt Valley (see page 156) on the border with Cheshire, of which it was a part until local government boundary changes of 1936. The 17th-century stone-built inn has the unusual name of The Bells of Taxal, and overlooking the village to the west are Windgather Rocks, an outcrop of gritstone which is a favoured training ground of beginner rock climbers.

Thorpe MAP REF 274 B4

Although Ashbourne (see page 59) calls itself 'the Gateway to Dove Dale', the tiny limestone village of Thorpe really has a much stronger claim to the title. It stands at the foot of the impressive Thorpe Cloud, the cone-shaped, rocky 942-foot (287m) eastern portal of the famous dale, and near the junction of two of the Peak's prettiest rivers, the River Dove and the River Manifold.

Thorpe is the starting point for many superb walks into the heart of these lovely dales, with the route through Lin Dale to Dove Dale's famous Stepping Stones probably the best known.

Thorpe gets its name from the old Scandinavian for an outlying farm or hamlet, and after 1,000 years, it still has that quality – a remarkable example of the continuity of the Peak District landscape. Being the nearest settlement to Dove Dale, Thorpe has been in demand for tourist accommodation since the earliest days that 'romantic' scenery became fashionable. Nearest to the village is the large Peveril of the Peak Hotel, while at the entrance to the dale, the Izaak Walton Hotel, which recently (2013) went into administration, recalled the man who first popularised the dale as a place for fishing.

The quaint church of St Leonard has a stocky little Norman tower and other Norman work inside, together with a fine altar rail which dates from the Elizabethan period.

EAT AND DRINK

Peveril of the Peak Hotel

Wintercroft Lane, Dove Dale,
DE6 2AW | 01335 350396
This quiet countryside retreat located in beautiful Peak District scenery is close to the many wonders of Dove Dale (see page 139) and offers plenty of creature comforts – no wonder it is so popular. It takes its name from one of Sir Walter Scott's heroic novels, which was actually set further north at Peveril Castle in Castleton. Not far from the historic market town of Ashbourne, The Peveril of the Peak is set in 11 acres of grounds among some of the finest scenery in the White Peak. It is very popular with walking groups, and some walks even start in the grounds of the hotel itself.

▶ Tideswell MAP REF 277 E6

The cynical Daniel Defoe, searching for the famous 'Seven Wonders of the Peak' in 1726, was not impressed by the ebbing and flowing well he viewed in a garden in Manchester Road in Tideswell. This may have been because he was looking at the wrong well (the original 'Wonder' was probably at Barmoor Clough, near Chapel-en-le-Frith), but in any case the water no longer ebbs and flows like the tide, and Tideswell got its name from a Saxon chieftain called Tidi.

This is not to say that wells were not important in the village; it lies at the 1,000-foot contour on the limestone plateau, set in a dry bowl amid a grey cobwebbing of walls and wind-scorched fields. Tideswell is renowned for the quality of its well-dressing ceremony, which starts the Wakes Week on the Saturday nearest St John the Baptist's Day (24 June). The week's festivities are concluded with a traditional torchlight procession and a unique Morris Dance.

In the 14th century, Tideswell was a thriving place, confident in the future of the wool trade and lead mining. The cathedral-like parish church, dedicated to St John the Baptist and often described as the Cathedral of the Peak, reflects this optimism. It was built in just 75 years and was of classic cruciform shape, of Decorated and Perpendicular styles, spacious and with superb fittings. Many of the modern wood carvings are by the local family of the Hunstones, and there is the best collection of brasses in the Peak, the most notable of which is to Bishop Robert Pursglove, a noted local benefactor and the founder of Tideswell's Royal Grammar School in 1560.

▼ Tideswell Church

That Tideswell dwindled to a village was in some ways a stroke of luck, particularly as the glorious church was bypassed by rich patrons and Victorian restorers, and stands today in splendid unaltered isolation. Around the church, the largest in the area, run lawns and railings separating it from the more prosaic buildings at the heart of the village.

Two of Tideswell's renowned musical forefathers are also buried in the church. They are 'the Minstrel of the Peak', William Newton, who died in 1830, and Samuel Slack, who died in 1822. Slack, whose name bore no relation to his vocal chords, was famous for two things: singing for George III and for stopping a bull dead in its tracks by bellowing at it. His voice, apparently, could be heard a mile away.

EAT AND DRINK

The George

georgeinntideswell.co.uk
Commercial Road, SK17 8NU
01298 871382
Set in the shadow of St John the Baptist's church (known locally as the Cathedral of the Peak), this stone-built coaching inn offers a simple, unfussy menu focusing on traditional pub fare – lunchtime sandwiches and full meals such as mushroom and Stilton crumble followed by traditional rag pudding with gravy, and sticky toffee pudding for dessert. There's also a good selection from the grill, ranging from steaks to a fish medley or Cajun chicken.

▶ **PLACES NEARBY**

Wheston

The great glory of Wheston, a hamlet near Tideswell, is its almost complete 15th-century Village Cross, one of the most perfect in the Peak and a scheduled ancient monument. It stands 12 feet high inside a walled enclosure surrounded by trees, and features a cusped head and a rather primitive carving of the Crucifixion and the Virgin Mary. A local tradition is to float a cross made of grass blades on the water and make a wish. Wheston Hall (private) is a Georgian manor house which probably stands on the site of a much older house.

▶ **Tissington** MAP REF 274 B3

Tissington is perhaps a bit too beautiful for its own good, especially when visited on summer Sundays. But it is always a gift to any photographer. The classic approach is off the A515, through a gateway and over a cattle grid, then along a drive lined with lime trees. The original avenue of venerable pollards and tall standards has recently been felled, but there are rows of young trees set further back to take their place.

Into the village itself, past a walled yew and the first of several wells, the limestone cottages are set back behind wide

▲ Tissington

grass verges and shaded by elegant beeches. There is a village green, with the stream running through it, a duck pond complete with ducks, a squat, hilltop Norman church and a grand Jacobean Hall. The overwhelming impression of Tissington is of its perfect blend of old stone houses, trees and water. Every wall seems to be draped in flowers and creepers. This is, and has been for centuries, an idyllic, well-managed estate village.

Tissington Hall, low and wide with mullioned windows and tall chimneys, has been the home of the FitzHerbert family since the reign of the first Elizabeth. Set behind a low wall and a gate of fine wrought ironwork by Robert Bakewell, it is open to the public (phone for details).

WATCH A LOCAL CEREMONY
Well dressings
The most famous and picturesque of all the Peak District traditions, well dressing, probably has its roots in pagan ceremonies to placate water spirits, but the Christian version has its origins at Tissington, where the five wells ran with pure water through the years of the Black Death. The villagers believed they owed their lives to the water, and dressed the tops of the wells as a sign of thanksgiving. Well dressing involves pressing flower petals, cones, seeds and fruits onto a clay base to create a picture, often of a biblical or local scene. Well dressings take place throughout the late spring and summer.

TAKE IN SOME HISTORY
Tissington Hall
tissingtonhall.co.uk
Tissington, DE6 1RA | 01335 352200 | Open selected days only; see website for more information
Tissington Hall is a Grade II listed, early 17th-century

Jacobean mansion which overlooks the village green at Tissington. It has been the home of the FitzHerbert family for over 400 years. The former moated manor was replaced with the new mansion in 1609 by Francis FitzHerbert.

Tissington Hall is one of a small group of Derbyshire mansions in which, unusually, a central hall runs through the house from front to back. The Hall is open to the public at specified times – check the website for details.

SADDLE UP
Tissington Trekking Centre
tissingtontrekkingcentre.co.uk
Tissington Wood Farm, DE6 1RD
01335 350276 | Open Apr–Oct

WALK THE TISSINGTON TRAIL
The famous Tissington Trail runs for 13 miles from Parsley Hay to Ashbourne, along the old railway line that closed in 1963. You will find that the trail is particularly suitable for families and cyclists; it is possible to hire bikes at either Parsley Hay or Ashbourne, or bring your own and leave your car at the car park, on the site of the old railway station.

EAT AND DRINK
Bassett Wood Farm
bassettwood.co.uk
Tissington, DE6 1RD
01335 350254
This friendly, welcoming and informal tea room set in a

▶ Well dressing at Tissington

working farmhouse is always heady with the rich aroma of home-baking. Look out for local jams, honey and dairy produce and indulge in tasty ice creams.

▶ PLACES NEARBY
Ballidon
Five miles north of Ashbourne and overshadowed by a gigantic limestone quarry, this tiny hamlet is in fact all that remains of a disappeared medieval village, as the numerous earthworks, lynchets and evidence of ridge and furrow cultivation in its fields indicate. The only building still left is the tiny chapel of All Saints, isolated in a field surrounded by the former crofts and tofts of the shrunken village. Originally Norman in construction, the chapel (usually locked) has been much restored over the years.

At the end of the minor road which passes right through the quarry is **Roystone Grange**, the

site of a monastic farm which was systematically excavated by Sheffield University over many years to reveal a continuous occupation going back to Roman and even prehistoric times. The Roystone Grange Archaeological Trail interprets the finds via an easy, four-mile walk. Nearby, across the High Peak Trail, is the Neolithic **Minninglow** chambered tomb, one of the highest in the country, standing within a halo of windswept beeches.

Parwich

Parwich is a pretty limestone village on the southern edge of the White Peak which spreads around its green and village pond (or mere) – once the village sheepwash – above the Bradbourne Brook. It is dominated by Parwich Hall (private), a commanding 18th-century five-bay house with beautiful terraced gardens on the hill above the village.

St Peter's church was rebuilt in the late 19th century but still contains much Norman work, including a fine tympanum over the west doorway, showing the Lamb of God with a cross, a wolf, a stag trampling on a serpent, and other strange animals, which was discovered under the plaster. The original Norman chancel arch, with beak heads and grotesques, is now in the tower.

▶ Tittesworth Reservoir MAP REF 272 C2

Tittesworth Reservoir shines like a liquid eye when viewed from the heights of the nearby Roaches escarpment. The dam and reservoir were built in 1858 to collect water from the River Churnet and provide a reliable water supply to Leek's thriving textile and cloth-dying industry.

By 1963 work to increase its size had been completed and local farmland was flooded to create a reservoir capable of supplying drinking water to Stoke-on-Trent and surrounding areas. With a capacity of 6.5 billion gallons, when full it can supply 10 million gallons of water every day.

The land around the reservoir provides a habitat for a wide variety of wildlife and many creatures can be seen in the course of a walk around it. Look out for brown hares in the fields near the car park. Look also for holes in the banks along the River Churnet, where it enters the reservoir. They may be the entrance to water vole burrows and home to a vole like Ratty in Kenneth Grahame's *The Wind in the Willows*.

Europe's smallest bat, the pipistrelle, can be seen at dusk near the restored pond near Churnet Bay, flying at an incredible speed, twisting and turning as they dive to gobble up caddis flies, moths and gnats. Bird life around the reservoir is also abundant and there are two hides from which visitors can observe it in comfort. Look out particularly for the skylarks that nest in the meadows around Tittesworth. At various times of the year you might also spot barnacle geese, great crested grebes, pied flycatchers, kingfishers, cormorants and even a rare osprey that has visited here several times in recent years.

GET OUTDOORS

Tittesworth Water Visitor Centre

stwater.co.uk

Meerbook, Leek, ST13 8SW

01538 300188

The Roaches form a spectacular backdrop to Severn Trent's Tittesworth Water Visitor Centre, on the shores of the reservoir. The centre includes an interactive exhibition, restaurant, shop, play area and water-saving garden. The River Churnet enters the reservoir just by the visitor centre, where there is a picnic area and bird-watching hides and trails. The reservoir has a wide range of wildlife. Note that fishing is not allowed at the reservoir.

▶ **Tunstead**
see **Wormhill & Tunstead**, page 264

▼ Tittesworth Reservoir

▶ Wardlow MAP REF 278 B6

The dome-like detached limestone rock known as Peter's Stone, at the northern end of Cressbrook Dale just to the west of Wardlow, looks like an Arizonian butte transported to the Peak. But is has a more gruesome tale to tell, because it marks the site of Derbyshire's last public gibbeting in 1815. The unfortunate victim was 21-year-old Anthony Lingard, who had been convicted of the murder of Hannah Oliver, the toll-keeper at Wardlow Mires on the main Chesterfield to Chapel-en-le-Frith road (now the A623).

William Newton, the famed 'Minstrel of the Peak' (see Tideswell, page 248) was so appalled by the inhumanity of the gibbet that he wrote a poem about it which was to play a large part in the campaign which eventually led to the abolishing of the barbarous punishment.

Wardlow itself is a typical one-street limestone village, high on the White Peak plateau. It takes its name from the rounded 1,214-foot hill known as Wardlow Hay Cop to the south, which is topped by the inevitable tumuli. The name is thought to mean 'lookout hill', and it would certainly make a fine place to watch out for approaching enemies. The little Victorian Gothic church of the Good Shepherd in the main street was built in 1872, and look out for the Victorian letterbox, mounted in the wall near Manor Farm.

EAT AND DRINK
Three Stags' Heads
Wardlow, SK17 8RW
01298 872268
A remarkable survivor, this unspoilt and rustic 17th-century Pennine longhouse stands in renowned walking country and features a stone-flagged bar and huge range fire. The bar counter, a 1940s addition, sells Abbeydale beers, including the heady Black Lurcher and Brimstone bitter, and several real ciders. Hearty food is also served in the dining room. Note the restricted opening hours, which allow owners Geoff and Pat Fuller time to make pottery, which you can buy. Sorry, it's not a pub for children.

▶ Warslow MAP REF 273 E2

Warslow, in the very heart of the Staffordshire moorlands, doesn't make many concessions to tourism, and wears a utilitarian, workaday look. The village has some pleasant 18th- and 19th-century cottages, and a welcoming pub called the Greyhound, a 250-year-old former coaching inn, once known as the Greyhound and Hare. The village hall provides seasonal afternoon refreshments.

Warslow is an estate village of the Harper Crewe family, of Calke Abbey, south of Derby, and lies at the very foot of the gritstone moors, which can be reached by taking the side road to the northwest. Warslow Hall, a mile and a half outside the village on the road to Longnor, was built as a shooting lodge by Sir George Crewe, the village's main benefactor.

Dominating the village is the Victorian parish church of St Lawrence, which was built by Sir George in 1820. The church has an unusually wide chancel built in 1908, with stained-glass windows by the noted Pre-Raphaelite William Morris.

EAT AND DRINK
The Greyhound Inn
Leek Road, SK17 0JN
01298 687017
It's generally a sign of a good pub when it offers regular events, such as quizzes and themed food nights. The Greyhound at Warslow, which dates back to 1750, offers all these things, and occupies a peaceful setting in which to enjoy a meal or a drink. The high-quality food is home-prepared by the head chef, and the Greyhound also offers fine cask real ales and a range of other top-line beers and ciders from the bar. It is an ideal base from which to explore the Staffordshire Moorlands, and is popular with tourists wishing to enjoy the many walks the area has to offer. Dogs are welcome in the bar.

▶ Whaley Bridge MAP REF 277 D5

This bustling little town grew up with dust on its face and Goyt water in its veins. Coal and textiles formerly provided the most gainful work – but both have now gone. These days there is hardly a whisper of past industry and employment is more varied, with many residents commuting to nearby Manchester or Stockport every day. Passers-by call in on their way to the Goyt Valley (see page 156) or to visit the Peak Forest Canal.

In the centre of the town, the main buildings of interest are the early 19th-century Jodrell Arms Hotel near the Railway Station, the Wesleyan Chapel (rebuilt in 1867) and the Methodist Sunday School of 1821. The canal basin in the town is an engaging spot, but the true glory of the waterway is at nearby Buxworth (see page 107), half a mile to the east, where the canal and tramroad interchange has been restored.

The Roosdyche is a natural feature on the hillside which runs up from the Goyt Valley towards Eccles Pike to the east of the town. It is a strange, shallow, steep-sided valley about three-quarters of a mile long. Long thought to be a racecourse for Roman chariots, it is now believed to be a sub-glacial drainage channel dating from the last Ice Age.

South of the town is Toddbrook Reservoir, built to feed the Peak Forest Canal, and tiny Taxal village (see page 246), clustered around its 19th-century church.

▶ The White Peak   MAP REF 273 E2

The White Peak represents the bare, whitened skeleton of the Peak District, and its oldest rocks. It takes its name from the limestone area of the central and southern Peak District, and to distinguish and contrast it from the gritstone Dark Peak (see page 133) that encloses it to the north, west and east.

The White Peak limestone plateau stretches from the tourist honeypot of Dove Dale in the south to the great Mam Tor–Lose Hill ridge in the north. It is bounded to the east by the broad shale valley of the River Derwent, and to the west by the dramatic outcrops of The Roaches and the Cat and Fiddle Moors above Buxton.

▼ Monsal Dale in the White Peak

The plateau, which seldom goes below 1,000 feet above the sea, is dissected by many steep-sided and usually roadless dales, carved through the limestone by Ice Age meltwaters around 10,000 years ago. These famous Peak District dales – such as Lathkill Dale (see page 195), Monsal Dale, Miller's Dale and Middleton Dale – usually run from west to east, although Dove Dale (see page 139) and the Manifold Valley (see page 217) are the exceptions, running north–south. Perhaps the most famous is Dove Dale, cut by the River Dove through a landscape of bizarre rock pinnacles and caves steeped in mythology. The River Manifold, too, cuts a dramatic gorge, flanked by limestone crags and mysterious, dark chasms.

Up on the plateau, which is enmeshed in a spider's web of drystone walls, you'll find many pretty villages, such as Tissington (see page 249), Hartington (see page 169), Monyash (see page 231), Parwich (see page 252) and Ashford in the Water (see page 66) – fine places to take afternoon tea or relax in a friendly pub.

The White Peak is threaded by the 46-mile Limestone Way (see page 201), a long-distance footpath which links Castleton (see page 98) and Rocester in Staffordshire.

▶ Wildboarclough MAP REF 272 C1

Wildboarclough, anciently known as Crag, used to boast the largest and most imposing village post office in the country. But the elegant, three-storey 19th-century building in warm pink gritstone which was built as the administration building of the Crag Silk Mill is now a private house.

This quiet rural backwater sheltering under the south-western slopes of Shutlingsloe was once an outpost of the nearby Macclesfield silk industry, and boasted three mills, employing more than 600 people. Crag Mill was the most important, however, and made carpets which were sent to the Great Exhibition of 1851. James Brindley, later of canal-building fame, installed the machinery at the silk mill while he was an apprentice. Other mills in the village specialised in bleaching, printing and dyeing first cotton, then later carpets.

Along the valley today you'll find that most traces of the village's industrial heritage are gone, and have been replaced by shrub-covered foundations, grassy trackways and mossy walls. The Clough Brook stream boasts waterfalls and deep pools and is the territory of dippers and grey wagtails, while the surrounding area is famous for its early spring displays of rhododendrons, which cloak the stone-walled lanes.

The little dormer-windowed Edwardian Gothic red sandstone parish church of St Saviour was built by local landowner, the 16th Earl of Derby as a memorial for the safe return of his sons from the South African War. Earl Frederick Arthur Stanley had more reason than most for his thankfulness, because no fewer than five of his eight sons had served in the Boer War, his eldest son and heir being the aide-de-camp to Field Marshal Lord Frederick Roberts, Commander in Chief and one of the most successful generals of the Victorian era.

GO FISHING
Danebridge Fisheries
danebridgefisheries.com
Wincle, SK11 0QE
01260 227293
Fly-fishing.

EAT AND DRINK
Brookside Café
Wildboarclough, SK11 0BB
01260 227632
Popular with ramblers and cyclists, the Brookside has been offering sustenance for more than 40 years. Expect great home-cooking, from afternoon teas to wholesome meals, and all served amid some very stunning countryside.

The Crag Inn
Wildboarclough, SK11 0BD
01260 227239
The cosy Crag Inn at Wildboarclough boasts open fires, a selection of real ales and traditional food, including a popular Sunday carvery.

The Ship Inn

Barlow Hill, SK11 0QE

01260 227217

The adjoining villages of Danebridge and Wincle straddle the River Dane, which here in the western Peak District National Park divides Cheshire from Staffordshire. The park's moors, lush woodland and drystone-walled pastures are a favourite with walkers, many of whom beat a path to this 17th-century, pink-hued pub with a flagstoned taproom serving J W Lees' Manchester-brewed Coronation Street ale. New owners maintain the interesting and regularly changing menu. There are splendid views from the beer garden.

▶ **PLACES NEARBY**

Blaze Farm

blazefarm.com

Wildboarclough, SK11 0BL

01260 227229 | Open Tue–Sun 10–5.30 all year

A successfully diversified farm specialising in the making of delicious ice cream. You can sample creamy 'Hilly Billy' ice cream in a vast range of unusual flavours, made from the farm's own milk. Choose from Double Dutch Chocolate, Ginger, Irish Cream, Pistachio and Almond, Turkish Delight and White Chocolate Mountain, to mention just a few. You'll also find a friendly tea room, farm trail suitable for all ages and a paint-a-pot studio to keep the children amused.

▶ Winster MAP REF 274 C2

Winster is one of the Peak's most complete 18th-century villages, and like Bakewell (see page 71) and Hartington (see page 169), it gives an urban impression which is much more like a small town. It was not granted the right to hold a market until around the turn of the 17th century, and the grand Old Market Hall dates from the end of that century. It became the first National Trust property in Derbyshire and the Peak District in 1906, and like Bakewell's Market Hall, it originally had an open ground floor with pointed arches, to which was later added a brick upper floor and gables. The arches are now all filled with brick, and the building serves as a National Trust information centre.

Pilastered Winster Hall, almost opposite, was the 18th-century Georgian-style home of Llewellyn Jewitt, the distinguished late 19th-century Derbyshire antiquarian, and was once a hotel. The inn sign used to show the famous Winster Morris Men, one of the oldest teams in the country, who have their own dance and tunes and who remain very popular at local festivities. The great folklorist Cecil Sharp came to Winster in 1908 just to hear and see the Winster Morris Men. Another more recent Winster tradition is the

Pancake Race, run annually down the main street on Shrove Tuesday. It began as light-hearted fun, organised by the local headmaster as a diversion during wartime for the children, but has now become a more serious affair, with secret race training and stringent rules about making the batter.

The double-gabled Dower House at the western end of Winster's main street has a 17th-century date, but most of Winster's fine houses date from the 18th century heyday of the local lead mining industry. This is also reflected in the name of the Miner's Standard Inn, just outside the village at the top of West Bank, which recalls the unit of measurement of lead ore and still has some of the old lead-mining equipment on display.

The parish church of St John the Baptist has an unusual two-aisled nave which was added in 1833 and which is divided by a lofty arcade. The rather plain tower dates from 1721.

TAKE IN SOME HISTORY
Winster Market House
nationaltrust.org.uk
Winster, DE4 2DJ | 01335 350503
See website for opening times
This was the first property to be acquired by the National Trust in the Peak District in 1906 – for the princely sum of £50. The late 17th- to early 18th-century Market House was probably originally timber-framed, and the now filled-in arches were once used by street traders, while the upper storey was used to sell dairy products from the surrounding area. It is now an information centre.

▸ Wirksworth MAP REF 274 C3

Until relatively recently, the hillside market town of Wirksworth was choked with quarry dust and thundering lorries, and could be said to be growing old disgracefully. Now, thanks to the initiative of the lively local community, it is an award-winning example of a town which has reinvented itself.

The local Civic Society, Civic Trust and the Derbyshire Historic Buildings Trust among others saw that the town underwent a marvellous transformation in the 1980s, winning a Casa Nostra and several other awards for the restoration of the town centre with its steeply-sloping, cobbled Market Place.

The Market Place is the heart of Wirksworth, from where it is possible to explore the town in several directions. Up Dale End there are wickedly sloping lanes with cobbled gutters, leading past the old smithy, opposite Green Hill, a fine 17th-century gabled house built of limestone with sandstone mullioned windows. Further up the hill is Babington House (not open), of similar vintage, with a fine view over the town. It is a three-storey residence, with a sundial on the gable wall.

South from the Market Place past the Town Hall is Coldwell Street with several old inns, including The Red Lion, The Vaults (originally called The Compleat Angler, after Izaak Walton's classic anglers' bible), and The George. Down Chapel Lane is the Moot Hall (not open), the only place in England where lead-miners' Barmote Courts are still held, every April. This ancient court is one of the oldest in Britain and is used to settle lead mining disputes. The courts started in 1266, though the present building, decorated outside with sculpted representations of the miners' tools, only dates back to 1814. Inside there is a Miners' Standard Dish, dated 1513, which was used for measuring the ore, as a levy had to be paid to both the King and the Barmaster who was in charge of the court for every claim.

Hidden away behind ranks of tall houses in a cathedral-like close is St Mary's parish church, one of the most interesting in the Peak.

Wirksworth is a shining example of what can happen with a little vision and civic enthusiasm, but to its credit, it has never forgotten its industrial heritage. The lead mining industry may have disappeared many years ago to be replaced by quarrying, still of considerable local importance, but its influence lives on.

▼ Babington House, Wirksworth

The National Stone Centre (see page 227) just outside the town gives a fuller picture of this dependence on the mineral wealth of the Peak. Nearby is the old gritstone quarry of Black Rocks, a popular picnic spot and rock climbing crag, with a four-mile forest trail over Cromford Moor and access to the High Peak Trail, the former railway line that once transported stone to the Cromford Canal.

VISIT A MUSEUM
Wirksworth Heritage Centre
storyofwirksworth.co.uk
Crown Yard, Wirksworth, DE4 4ET
01629 825225 | Open 2 Apr–Sep
Wed–Sat & BHs 10.30–4.30 & Sun
1.30–4.30 (last admission 4)
The Centre has been created in an old silk and velvet mill. The three floors of the mill have interpretative displays of the town's past history as a prosperous lead-mining centre. Each floor offers many features of interest including a computer game called 'Rescue the Injured Lead Miner', a mock-up of a natural cavern, and a Quarryman's House. During the Spring Bank Holiday you can also see the famous Well Dressings. Exhibits on the top floor include one on quarrying, information about local round-the-world yachtswoman Ellen MacArthur, and local memories from World War II. There's also a small art gallery carrying local works.

SEE A LOCAL CHURCH
St Mary's Church
Church Street, Wirksworth, DE4
4DQ | 01629 824707
Among the greatest treasures in St Mary's is a Saxon coffin lid, only discovered in 1820, which must have been from the sarcophagus of a very important person. It is probably the earliest Christian monument in the Peak, and dates from around AD 800. It is embellished with vigorous carvings which show scenes from the life of Christ, including about 40 stumpy figures which show the washing of the disciples' feet, the burial of Christ, the Harrowing of Hell, and Christ's ascension, among others. There are numerous other Norman architectural fragments in the north transept of the church, as well as a Norman font.

Nearly as famous is 'T'owd Man of Bonsall a carving of a medieval lead worker, holding the tools of his trade. Elsewhere in the church are dozens of other fragments of

5 top bookshops

▸ **The Book Shop**, Market Place, Wirksworth

▸ **Country Bookstore**, Brierlow Bar, Buxton

▸ **Hassop Station Bookstore**, Hassop Road, Bakewell

▸ **Scarthin Books,** The Promenade, Cromford

▸ **Scriveners' Bookshop**, Buxton

▲ Saxon carvings in St Mary's Church

Saxon carving, sometimes in groups (a king and queen, heads of assorted creatures, odd bits of jumbled stonework), and sometimes singly (Adam with a sinuous serpent seemingly eating the apple), all adding up to a gallery of early sculpture.

Although heavily restored by Sir George Gilbert Scott in 1876, the cruciform church dates originally from the 13th and 14th centuries, with a crossing tower, transepts and aisled chancel. There are 16th-century monuments to the Blackwell and Gell families, including a fine alabaster effigy of Anthony Gell, the founder of Wirksworth's grammar school, who died in 1583, and the celebrated Parliamentarian General, Sir John Gell.

▶ PLACES NEARBY

Middleton Top Engine House
derbyshire.gov.uk/countryside Middleton Top Visitor Centre, DE4 4LS | 01629 823204 Information Centre open Easter–Aug daily 9.30–4.45, Sep–Easter weekends only; Engine House see website for details

The octagonal Middleton Top Engine House is home to a beam engine built in 1829 for the Cromford and High Peak Railway, still in its original condition. The engine's job was to haul wagons up the steep Middleton Incline, and its last trip was in 1963 after being in service for an astonishing 134 years. The visitor centre tells the story of this historic railway.

264

WIRKSWORTH

Ecclesbourne Valley Railway

e-v-r.com
Wirksworth Station, DE4 4FB
01629 823076
See website for timetable & events

The Ecclesbourne Valley Railway operates passenger services on the line between Wirksworth and Duffield mainly using heritage diesel railcars, with some steam-hauled services on the branch between Wirksworth and Ravenstor. It is operated by WyvernRail plc, a community venture founded in 1992 to rescue the line from long disuse.

▶ Wormhill & Tunstead   MAP REF 277 E6

The small hamlet of Tunstead, just west of Wormhill high in the hills above the valley of the River Wye, is famous in industrial history circles as the birthplace in 1716 of one of Britain's most renowned, though unlikely, engineering giants. James Brindley, known as the father of the canal system, was the eldest of seven children of a small farmer who moved to Leek in Staffordshire when he was ten. He never learned to read or write, but became an apprentice millwright at 17 and then a millwright in his own right in 1742.

His engineering skills brought him to the attention of Francis, Duke of Bridgewater, and it was he who employed Brindley to construct his pioneering Bridgewater Canal to transport coal between Worsley and Manchester. Brindley later constructed many more canals around Britain, and counted Josiah Wedgwood and many other 18th-century worthies among his patrons and friends. He died in 1772 at the age of 56.

Brindley is remembered by the ornate memorial erected in 1895 on the pretty, sloping village green at Wormhill, which now serves as the centrepiece for the village well dressings in August. Brindley's cottage at Tunstead, a hamlet teetering on the edge of the massive Tunstead limestone quarry, no longer exists.

Wormhill's little parish church of St Margaret has an unusual Rhenish helm-type tower, like the Saxon one at Sompting in Sussex. It was largely rebuilt in 1864 on a medieval tower. Wormhill Hall (private) is an attractive, H-shaped late 17th-century stone mansion on the approach up to the village from the Wye valley, built by the local Bagshawe family in 1697. Old Hall Farm, north of the village centre, dates from the 16th and 17th centuries, and may have been the original Manor House for Wormhill before the hall.

▶ St Margaret's Church, Wormhill

▶ Youlgreave   MAP REF 274 B2

A hard-working, linear village on the hills above Bradford Dale, Youlgreave (nicknamed 'Pommie' by locals) is one of the largest villages in the Peak District. With three long-distance paths passing through, it's a great base for walkers, as well as more general tourists.

There have been more than 60 different spellings of its name, including Jalgrave, Iolgrave, Yelgrave and even Hyolegrave, and even today, there is controversy. Locals always spell it 'Youlgrave', which is how it is pronounced, but the Ordnance Survey and various other branches of officialdom insist on inserting the extra 'e' to call it Youlgreave. The name is thought to mean 'yellow grove' or 'the grove of Geola' – a 'groove' being the old term for a lead mine, an important industry in these parts for at least 200 years, while the 'yellow' may refer to the colour of the local rocks.

The landscape around Youlgreave is pockmarked with the remains of lead mines, and none serves as a more poignant reminder of the area's industrial past than those of the former Mawstone Mine. In 1932 the mine closed down after a gas explosion killed five miners and three of the rescuers.

In common with many other of the larger Peak District villages, Youlgreave has one of the most accomplished well dressings in the Peak District, taking place at midsummer each year, when five wells (here known as 'taps') are elaborately dressed, usually with biblical scenes. Records of Youlgreave's well dressings go back to 1829, coinciding with the provision of the village's private water supply, which it still enjoys, via a conduit from the dale below. The water is gathered in a large circular stone tank called The Fountain, which stands in the middle of the village. Villagers used to pay six pence a year for the right to use the water, queueing up to collect it in buckets every morning prior to the introduction of universal plumbing. Allegedly, in springtime the pipes were often blocked by frogs. Nearby, on the opposite side of the street, is the former village Co-operative Society building, built in 1887, which once had a vital role in the social survival of the area but is now a youth hostel. Here, you can sleep in a room still labelled 'Ladies' Underwear'. Further down the village street is the Old Hall, a mullioned-windowed and gabled building which dates from 1650. Behind it and unseen from the street is Old Hall Farm which is even older, dating from 1630.

Next to the road which drops down the dale to Alport stands All Saints parish church, one of the most impressive in the

Peak. Essentially Norman and with an unusually broad nave, the most obvious feature of All Saints is its splendid 14th-century tower, chunky and stylish in the best Perpendicular tradition. Inside are sturdy columns and a 13th-century font, unique in that it has two bowls. The fine monuments in the chancel include a miniature armoured effigy of Thomas Cockayne, who died in 1488, whose head rests on a cockerel, an amusing pun on the family name. In the north wall is the early 14th-century cross-legged effigy of a bearded knight holding his heart in his hands. Other monuments in this fascinating building include a beautiful oblong panel to Robert Gylbert who died in 1492, his wife and their 17 children.

On the north wall opposite the entrance is a delightful cameo of a little stone pilgrim carrying her staff and bag. The east window and the south window in the chancel are both among Edward Burne-Jones's stained glass masterpieces, and there are others by Kempe in the north aisle and south nave. The church was restored in 1870.

One word of warning: as with many Peak District villages, the cottages in the long Church Street were constructed in the 18th or 19th centuries – before garages were commonplace – so everyone has to park outside their houses, creating a single lane thoroughfare in the main village street for much of the time. Be prepared to navigate carefully if you're driving, or use the car park on Moor Lane, about a mile from the centre.

Three bridges cross the River Bradford below Youlgreave, including a clapper bridge of stone slabs and a packhorse bridge, which is now used as a footbridge. The short walk to the confluence with the Lathkill is popular, but by turning southeast, over the main bridge and on to the Limestone Way, you can explore the fine countryside towards Birchover, past the Iron Age hillfort of Castle Hill and the Nine Stones Close Circle (four of which are still standing), to the great tumbling rock tors of Robin Hood's Stride (once known as Mock Beggars Hall), Cratcliffe Rocks and Rowtor Rocks.

EAT AND DRINK
The Farmyard Inn
farmyardinn.co.uk
Main Street, Youlgreave, DE45 1UW
01629 636221
This old farmhouse, which became an inn in 1829, looks south across Bradford Dale and its picturesque stretches of tree-hung, crystal-clear water. Warm and friendly, the bar offers two guest real ales and a good selection of wines.

▶ PLACES NEARBY
Alport
Alport, at the junction of the Rivers Lathkill and Bradford south of Bakewell, is many people's candidate for the

Peak's prettiest village. And in truth, it's a lovely little hamlet of mainly 17th- and 18th-century houses with beautiful, flower-filled gardens, clustered along the banks of the Lathkill, which cascades down through the village in a series of weirs to meet the Bradford coming down from Youlgreave.

This was the heart of lead-mining country in the 18th and 19th centuries, and the wealth won from the lead is reflected in the quality of some of the fine old houses, and the graceful 18th-century bridge. The Hillcarr Sough, started in 1766, was one of the longest soughs (underground canals draining water from lead mines, pronounced 'suffs') in the Peak. It ran for four and a half miles, from Alport to the River Derwent at Rowsley, and cost £32,000 when it was finished in 1787. Such were the profits being made from lead mining in those days, the sough is said to have paid for itself within two years.

Middleton (by Youlgreave)

Centred around the broad, almost urban, open space of The Square, this charming little village above Bradford Dale was once the home of the Fulwood family. Nothing now remains of their castle except for a mound and a few crumbling and ivy-covered ruins behind Castle Farm. Sir Christopher Fulwood supported the King during the troubled times of the Civil War, and when his home was raided by Roundheads, he hid in a rock crevice in the dale but was discovered and shot.

Lomberdale Hall, a Victorian mansion half way between Middleton and Youlgreave, was the home of William and Thomas Bateman, the leading antiquarians and pioneer archaeologists of their day. Between them they excavated most of Derbyshire and the Peak District's prehistoric burial mounds, carefully recording and collecting what they found. When Thomas Bateman died in 1861, the outstanding family collection of artefacts was transferred to the Weston Park Museum in Sheffield, where it can still be seen. Thomas Bateman's grave, ornamented with a replica Bronze Age collared burial urn, can be found behind the former Congregational Chapel (now a private house), built in 1828 by his grandfather in the centre of the village. Almost opposite is the substantial, twin-gabled Square House, formerly a public house known as the Bateman Arms.

Two miles to the west on Middleton Common lies the atmospheric **Arbor Low** henge and stone circle, the most famous and impressive prehistoric site in the Peak, sometimes dubbed 'the Stonehenge of the North' (see page 57).

▶ (Overleaf) Neolithic henge monument, Arbor Low

0 |___| 5 miles
0 |___| 10 kilometres

BRADFORD

LEEDS

A1(M)

A63

M1

A646

HALIFAX

M62

WAKEFIELD

ROCHDALE M62

HUDDERSFIELD

KIRKLEES

M66

A62

A635

A629

Holmfirth

A61

OLDHAM

BARNSLEY

A628

A616

MANCHESTER

Glossop

Howden
Reservoir

M1

Derwent
Reservoir

278–9

STOCKPORT

276–7

A57

Ladybower
Reservoir

ROTHERHAM

SHEFFIELD

A6

PEAK DISTRICT

Chapel-en-
le-Frith

A623

A6135

A537

NATIONAL

A61

Macclesfield

A537

Buxton

A619

**CHESHIRE
EAST**

A54

PARK

Bakewell

CHESTERFIELD

A53

A515

A6

DERBYSHIRE

Congleton

Matlock

Leek

Alfreton

M1

STOKE-
ON-TRENT

272–3

A52

274–5

A38

Ilkeston

NEWCASTLE-
UNDER-LYME

Ashbourne

A52

A34

A50

DERBY

A6

Stone

A51

Uttoxeter

Long
Eaton

A50

STAFFORDSHIRE

A511

BURTON UPON
TRENT

A518

STAFFORD

Blithfield
Reservoir

A515

A38

A42

M1

M6

Rugeley

CANNOCK

M6 Toll

M54

TAMWORTH

M42

LEICESTERSHIRE

WALSALL

ATLAS

HINCKLEY

NUNEATON

BIRMINGHAM

★ A-Z places listed

• Places Nearby

M6

KIDDERMINSTER

COVENTRY

RUGBY

WORCESTERSHIRE

WARWICKSHIRE

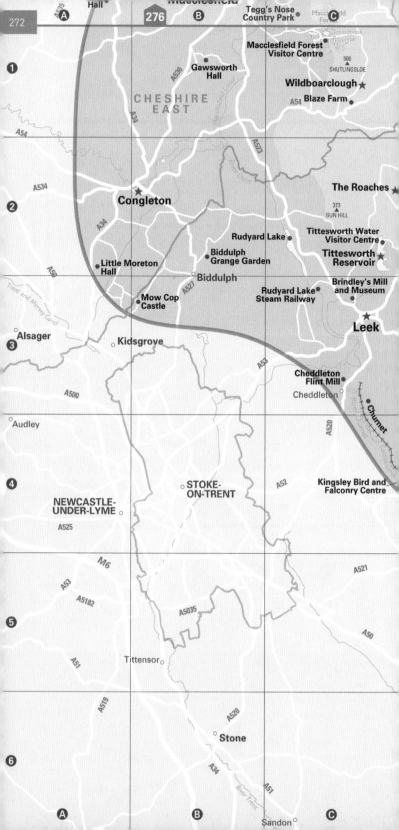

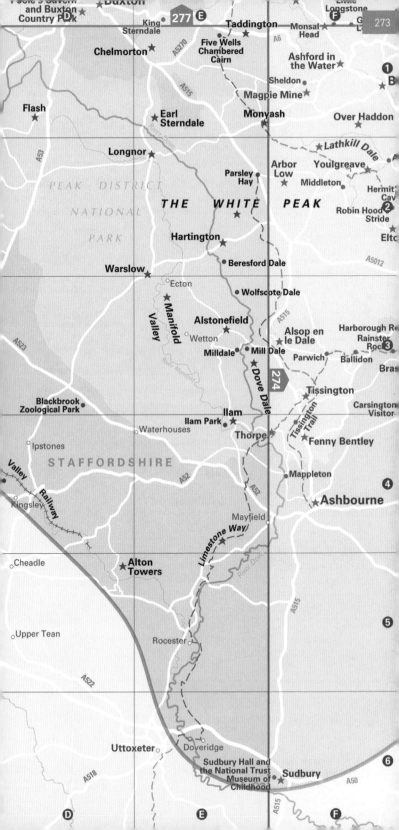

279

D   E   F

★ **CHESTERFIELD**

A619

A632

**Bolsover ● Bolsover
Castle**

1

A617

Heath

DERBYSHIRE

Glapwell

North
Wingfield

Pleasley

● **Matlock
Farm Park**

A6191

★ **Ashover**

A175

M1

★ **Hardwick
Hall**

A632

Clay
Cross

**The Herb
Garden**

A38

2

Tibshelf

★ **Matlock**

HIGHOREDISH

● **Riber
Castle**

Ogston
Reservoir

A615

A61

South
Normanton

**Kirkby in
Ashfield**

**Cromford
Mills**

Alfreton

A611

● **Lea Gardens**

3

● **High Peak Junction**

Pinxton

★ **Crich Tramway
Village**

Swanwick

Selston

**Steeple Grange
Light Railway**

★ **Crich**

**National
Stone Centre**

NOTTINGHAMSHIRE

Ripley

Codnor

A38

4

● **Belper**

Heanor

● **Eastwood**

River Derwent

A6

Kilburn

A610

A609

Awsworth

Duffield

A609

Ilkeston

A608

M1

A609

5

A6096

Stapleford

DERBY

A52

Ockbrook

Risley

Borrowash

**Long
Eaton**

6

A514

A453

A50

Shardlow

D   E   F

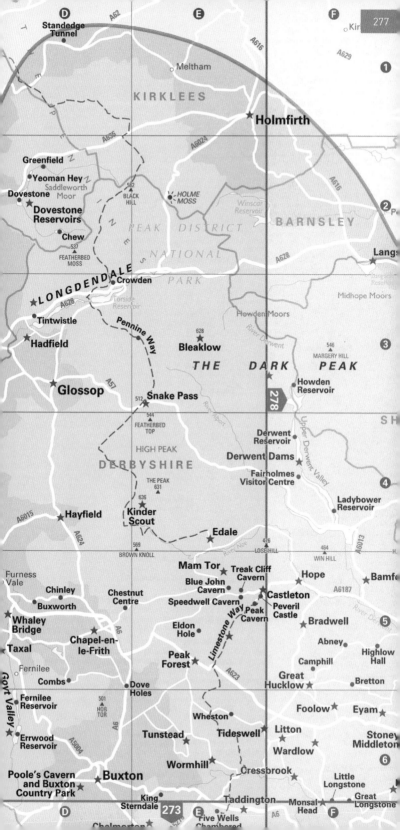

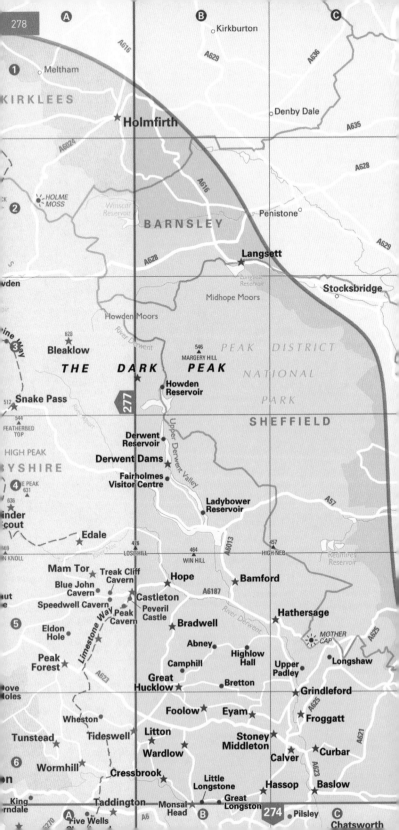

A   **B**   **C**

1

Meltham

Kirkburton

A616

A629

A636

KIRKLEES

Holmfirth

Denby Dale

A635

A6024

A616

2

HOLME MOSS

Winscar Reservoir

BARNSLEY

Penistone

A628

Langsett

Langsett Reservoir

A628

A629

wden

Midhope Moors

Stocksbridge

Howden Moors

River Derwent

628

Bleaklow

3

THE DARK PEAK

546
MARGERY HILL

PEAK DISTRICT

NATIONAL

512

Snake Pass

277

Howden Reservoir

River Alport

544
FEATHERBED TOP

PARK

SHEFFIELD

HIGH PEAK

BYSHIRE

Derwent Reservoir

Upper Derwent Valley

4

E PEAK
631

636

Derwent Dams

Fairholmes Visitor Centre

inder
cout

Ladybower Reservoir

A57

469

Edale

River Noe

476
LOSE HILL

464
WIN HILL

A6013

457
HIGH·NEB

Redmires Reservoir

N KNOLL

Mam Tor

Treak Cliff Cavern

Hope

Bamford

Blue John Cavern

Castleton

A6187

River Derwent

Hathersage

ut
e

Speedwell Cavern

Peak Cavern

Peveril Castle

MOTHER CAP

A625

5

Eldon Hole

Bradwell

Abney

Highlow Hall

Upper Padley

Longshaw

Limestone Way

Camphill

Peak Forest

A623

Bretton

Grindleford

ove
oles

Great Hucklow

A625

Wheston

Foolow

Eyam

Froggatt

Tunstead

Tideswell

Litton

A621

Stoney Middleton

Curbar

6

Wormhill

Wardlow

Calver

Cressbrook

Little Longstone

Hassop

Baslow

King
rndale

Taddington

Monsal Head

Great Longstone

274

Pilsley

A6

Five Wells

A270

Chatsworth

A   **B**   **C**

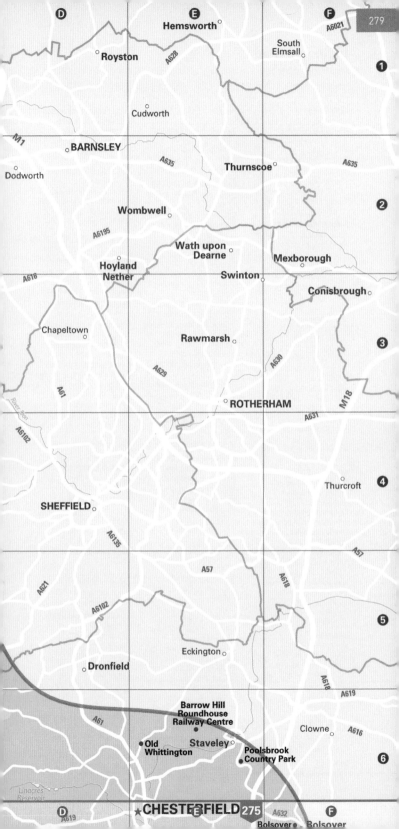

Index, themed

Page numbers in **bold** refer to main entries; page numbers in *italics* refer to town plans

Index, places

Page numbers in **bold** refer to main entries; page numbers in *italics* refer to town plans

The Automobile Association wishes to thank the following photographers and organisations for their assistance in the preparation of this book.

Abbreviations for the picture credits are as follows – (t) top; (m) middle; (b) bottom; (l) left; (r) right; (c) centre; (AA) AA World Travel Library.

4tl Courtesy of Alton Towers; 4tr AA/T Mackie; 4bl AA/A Midgley; 5bl Courtesy of Heights of Abraham; 5r AA/A Midgley; 8–9 Ed Rhodes/Alamy; 11 Steve Tucker/Alamy; 12t Courtesy of Alton Towers; 12b Courtesy of Chatsworth House Trust; 13t Courtesy of Heights of Abraham; 13mr AA/M Birkitt; 13ml Courtesy of Hardwick Hall; 13b Courtesy of Speedwell Cavern; 14t Courtesy of Haddon Hall/Ian Daisley; 14mr Courtesy of Visit Peak District/Linda Bussey; 14ml AA/T Mackie; 14b AA/T Mackie; 15 AA/T Mackie; 16 AA; 17 William Robinson Derbyshire/Alamy; 20l Albaimages/Alamy; 20r–21 AA/T Mackie; 22l AA/T Mackie; 22r–23l AA/T Mackie; 23r AA/T Mackie; 24 AA/M Birkitt; 26 AA/A Hopkins; 28 Ian Francis/Alamy; 29 Tim Hill/Alamy; 31 AA/M Birkitt; 32 WilliamRobinson Derbyshire/Alamy; 34 Steve Tucker/Alamy; 35 AA/T Mackie; 36 Courtesy of Chatsworth House Trust/D. Vintiner; 37 Courtesy of Peak Cavern/Richard Tooley; 38 AA/R Newton; 40 AA/J Tims; 42–3 AA/T Mackie; 43 AA/T Mackie; 45 AA/T Mackie; 49 AA/T Mackie; 50 Courtesy of Chatsworth House Trust; 51 Courtesy of Chatsworth House Trust; 52 AA/A Burton; 53 AA/J Tims; 54–5 AA/T Mackie; 57 AA/T Mackie; 60–1 AA/T Mackie; 61 AA/T Mackie; 64–5 Courtesy of Alton Towers/MEPICS/Martin Elliott; 66–7 Robert Harding World Imagery/Alamy; 69 AA/A Hopkins; 71 AA/T Mackie; 72 AA/P Baker; 74 AA/P Baker; 79 AA/L Whitwam; 84 AA/N Coates; 88–9 AA/P Baker; 90 AA/P Baker; 91 Robert Harding World Imagery/Alamy; 92 eye35.pix/Alamy; 93 AA/T Mackie; 95 AA/T Mackie; 96 Courtesy of Visit Peak District/Linda Bussey; 99 AA/T Mackie; 100–1 AA/M Kipling; 103 Steve Tucker/Alamy; 104 AA/A Midgley; 105 AA/M Birkitt; 109 Courtesy of Chatsworth House Trust; 110 Courtesy of Chatsworth House Trust; 111 Courtesy of Chatsworth House Trust/D. Vintiner; 112 Courtesy of Chatsworth House Trust; 114 Courtesy of Chatsworth House Trust; 117 AA/A Tryner; 123 AA/J Beazley; 124 AA/J Welsh; 127t AA/T Mackie; 127b AA/T Mackie; 128–9 AA/T Mackie; 129 AA/T Mackie; 131 AA/T Mackie; 135 AA/A Hopkins; 138–9 AA/T Mackie; 140–1 AA/P Baker; 145 Robert Harding World Imagery/Alamy; 148 AA/A Hopkins; 149 AA/A Midgley; 150 AA/A Midgley; 157 AA/M Birkitt; 158–9 AA/T Mackie; 161 AA/A Hopkins; 162 Travel England – Paul White/Alamy; 165 AA/P Baker; 166 AA/A Hopkins; 167 Courtesy of Haddon Hall/Ian Daisley; 168 AA/P Baker; 170 Courtesy of Hardwick Hall; 171 The National Trust Photolibrary/Alamy; 173 AA/T Mackie; 174 AA/A Hopkins; 175 AA/A Hopkins; 176–7 AA/N Coates; 181 AA/A Hopkins; 182–3 AA/A Hopkins; 183b AA/T Mackie; 184–5 AA/T Mackie; 187 AA/M Birkitt; 188 AA/A Tryner; 189 AA/T Mackie; 190 AA/T Mackie; 191t AA/M Birkitt; 191b AA/T Mackie; 192 AA/T Mackie; 193 AA/M Birkitt; 194–5 AA/N Coates; 196–7 AA/T Mackie; 203 AA/A Hopkins; 205 Steve Tucker/Alamy; 206 AA/M Birkitt; 208–9 AA/A Hopkins; 209t AA/J Mottershaw; 209b AA/J Mottershaw; 213 AA/M Birkitt; 214–5 Ed Rhodes/Alamy; 216 AA/M Birkitt; 222–3 AA/T Mackie; 225 AA/T Mackie; 228–9 AA/M Birkitt; 236–7 AA/A Hopkins; 238 Christopher Nicholson/Alamy; 239 AA/A Tryner; 243 AA/M Birkitt; 248 AA/T Mackie; 250 AA/T Mackie; 251 Mark Titterton/Alamy; 253 AA/C Jones; 256–7 AA/T Mackie; 261 AA/A Hopkins; 263 AA/A Hopkins; 265 John Keates/Alamy; 266 Tom Bowett/Alamy; 270 Robert Morris/Alamy Stock Photo

Series editor: Rebecca Needes
Author & updater: Roly Smith
Project editor: Sandy Draper
Designer: Liz Baldin

Proofreader: Kathryn Glendenning
Digital imaging & repro: Ian Little
Art director: James Tims

Additional writing by other AA contributors. *Lore of the Land* feature by Ruth Binney. Some content may appear in other AA books and publications.

Has something changed? Email us at travelguides@theaa.com.

YOUR TRUSTED GUIDE

The AA was founded in 1905 as a body initially intended to help motorists avoid police speed traps. As motoring became more popular, so did we, and our activities have continued to expand into a great variety of areas.

The first edition of the AA Members' Handbook appeared in 1908. Due to the difficulty many motorists were having finding reasonable meals and accommodation while on the road, the AA introduced a new scheme to include listings for 'about one thousand of the leading hotels' in the second edition in 1909. As a result the AA has been recommending and assessing establishments for over a century, and each year our professional inspectors anonymously visit and rate thousands of hotels, restaurants, guest accommodations and campsites. We are relied upon for our trustworthy and objective Star, Rosette and Pennant ratings systems, which you will see used in this guide to denote AA-inspected restaurants and campsites.

In 1912 we published our first handwritten routes and our atlas of town plans, and in 1925 our classic touring guide, *The AA Road Book of England and Wales,* appeared. Together, our accurate mapping and in-depth knowledge of places to visit were to set the benchmark for British travel publishing.

Since the 1990s we have dramatically expanded our publishing activities, producing high quality atlases, maps, walking and travel guides for the UK and the rest of the world. In this new series of regional travel guides we are drawing on more than a hundred years of experience to bring you the very best of Britain.